Churches of the
Black Country

Churches of the
Black Country

by

Tim Bridges

Logaston Press

LOGASTON PRESS
Little Logaston Woonton Almeley
Herefordshire HR3 6QH
logastonpress.co.uk

First published by Logaston Press 2008
Copyright © Tim Bridges 2008

ISBN 978 1 906663 04 9

Set in Times by Logaston Press
and printed in Great Britain by
Bell & Bain Ltd., Glasgow

For my parents Harry and Gill Bridges

Contents

Preface and Acknowledgements

This book follows the publication in 2000, and revision in 2005, of *Churches of Worcestershire*, which resulted in suggestions that I should cover the churches of the rest of the Diocese of Worcester. An investigation into this possibility concluded that a more substantial volume might be attempted if the study was expanded to include the churches of the three metropolitan boroughs of Dudley, Sandwell and Walsall, together with the city of Wolverhampton. Therefore, many churches in the Diocese of Lichfield, and a smaller though significant number in the Diocese of Birmingham are also described here. These churches from within the three dioceses and indeed two historic counties, Worcestershire and Staffordshire, have not been previously considered as an entire group in this way, and so compiling the information for this book has involved considerable travel around the region to visit some places previously unfamiliar to me, as well as searching a diverse number of sources. Over the last four years whilst research has been ongoing, I have been lecturing, teaching evening classes and leading guided visits to many of the remarkable churches in the area, building on work I have done throughout the West Midland and Welsh Border region over the past twenty years.

The historic Anglican churches of the Black Country form the core of this book, whilst information on modern church buildings is included where it has been available. I have attempted to include references to the wealth of nineteenth- and twentieth-century Anglican mission chapels and halls, especially where their establishment formed part of the story of planting churches in the developing parts of larger parishes. There are also details of the numerous churches, mainly of similar date, which have since been demolished, largely during the second half of the twentieth century. The book is limited to Anglican churches, but it is testament to the growing interest in churches of all denominations that non-conformist churches and chapels are covered by the three splendid photographic volumes on Black Country chapels produced by Ned Williams since 2004.

As with *Churches of Worcestershire*, this book offers a look at churches from an architectural and historical perspective, reflecting my own knowledge and interest, whilst acknowledging the importance of the spiritual and social role of the church in the community, both historically and today. There is reference to key historical figures, many of whom are commemorated in the churches, but it is the often unpublicised and unknown role of the thousands of worshippers and visitors through the centuries that has shaped the churches and given each its special atmosphere. Visitors to churches are always affected, sometimes deeply, by their atmosphere, and it is noticeable that in the Black Country visitors frequently remark upon the evidence of great care and attention given to the buildings by those who worship in them and look after them, often in difficult circumstances.

The church buildings themselves, and their contents, play a large part in the creation of that atmosphere, though relatively little has been written on them in the past. Much of the information offered here is the result of site visits, and its discovery has been influenced by the research in Sir Nikolaus Pevsner's 1974 edition of Staffordshire and 1968 edition of Worcestershire in the Buildings of England series. However, the Worcestershire section of the Black Country falls outside the scope of the revised Worcestershire edition, and a considerable portion of it is only currently covered by a single general entry as 'Birmingham Outer Western Suburbs' in the 1968 edition. A new volume covering this area of the urban West Midlands is currently under production and eagerly awaited. The Victoria County History volumes for Worcestershire and Staffordshire provide much valuable information, and are supported by numerous local historical books and pamphlets, many of which cover the stories of individual places in some considerable detail. These are listed in the reference section, which is also intended as a source list for anyone wishing to examine the churches in greater detail or pursuing historical family connections. However, the numerous good, but often unattributed, guidebooks and information sheets to be found in churches are not included in this list, though the increase in their availability is a highly encouraging response to the growing wish of local people and visitors to know more about their churches. The internet has also played a valuable part in this development with numerous websites devoted to the history of this area and family history, as well as the diocesan and local authority websites, along with those of regional bodies and national institutions. There is an increasing number of excellent websites offered by churches themselves, many of which contain fascinating historical and architectural information, along with details of services and access arrangements. Indeed such increased awareness is leading to the greater accessibility of churches within the urban area. There is a national trend for improved access to churches, and it is hoped that more of the churches included in this book will, if they are not normally open during the day, be able to make available details of any regular opening times or access arrangements, along with times of services, whilst obviously addressing concerns about security. All these churches can provide welcome quiet spaces, and many have features of interest, all of which is to be treasured by those who use them regularly and anyone visiting for the first time.

I would therefore like to acknowledge the work of all those clergy, churchwardens and congregations in whose care these churches are placed, for all that they do to preserve, maintain and keep them in use. The support, financial and otherwise, of organisations such as English Heritage, grant making trusts, dioceses and local authorities should also be recorded. Some church buildings are now in the care of other denominations or churches, or indeed other organisations, companies or private individuals, and their various roles in looking after the buildings are also significant. However, the maintenance of churches in use is often difficult, and it is the role of the county churches trusts to allocate grants to support churches with their restoration projects wherever possible. I have served as a trustee of the Worcestershire and Dudley Historic Churches Trust since 1996, and am aware of many of the problems of upkeep faced by churches in the area of the Diocese of Worcester. Therefore, I am very pleased that a small part of the proceeds from the sale of this book will contribute to the work of both the Worcestershire and Dudley Historic

Churches Trust and the Staffordshire Historic Churches Trust, who assist with the preservation of churches of all ages within the Black Country.

The production of this book, as with *Churches of Worcestershire*, has only been possible with the great support which I have received from others. I am very grateful to Andy Johnson of Logaston Press for providing the opportunity to write on these churches, and for the huge amount of patience and great skill that both he and Karen Stout have shown in editing and indexing my work. However, as before, any mistakes or omissions in the text are my own responsibility, and I would be grateful to know of them via Logaston Press. My parents, Harry and Gill Bridges, have been unfailing in their encouragement of my interest in churches and have given their wholehearted support to my work on this book. Some of the photographs are taken from their slides, whilst the remainder are from my own collection. My fellow trustees of the Worcestershire and Dudley Historic Churches Trust have been most supportive of this project. I have worked with the former secretary, John Lakeman, on grants towards many churches mentioned in the text, and been grateful for the advice of Annette Leech on visits to churches. The advice of colleagues on the Worcester Diocesan Advisory Committee has been invaluable, and I would particularly like to thank the Secretary, John Dentith, the Chairman, John Bailey, and the Archdeacon of Dudley, Fred Trethewey, for their encouragement. Similarly, colleagues in the Birmingham group of the Victorian Society have been extremely supportive, and I am most grateful to Andy Foster for his generous response to my requests for architectural details. Once again Michael Tavinor has very kindly read the proofs, and I would also like to thank him for making many excellent suggestions and improvements to the text. Helpful assistance has been received and queries have been answered by many people, including Robin and Sue Passant, Christine Buckley, Robert Hughes, Carolyn Morgan-Jones and Roy Peacock. My family and many friends, colleagues and students have been constantly encouraging of my work with churches and the production of this book. It appears with thanks to all and in the hope that more people will be drawn to discover the often remarkable, yet all too frequently overlooked, churches of the Black Country.

Tim Bridges
October 2008

Map of the Black Country showing the location of many of the places mentioned in the text

The History of the Churches of the Black Country

The Black Country

It is difficult to define the Black Country as an area. For the purposes of this book it covers the boroughs of Dudley, Sandwell and Walsall and the city of Wolverhampton. However, some places included in these pages would not regard themselves as typical of the Black Country. A broad definition might be that it is the region of industrial activity based on the mining of coal, quarrying of limestone and working of iron to the west of Birmingham and straddling the hills south from Wolverhampton. The name was first given to the area by Walter White in 1860 in his book *All around the Wrekin* and was used through the rest of the nineteenth century by writers describing the smoke from thousands of furnaces and chimneys in the towns and villages of the area. The coal comes from the thick South Staffordshire seam and its extraction has caused continuous subsidence, while the limestone quarrying has brought dereliction to considerable areas of land. Other industries for which the Black Country became noted include glassmaking around Stourbridge and leatherworking in Walsall, but perhaps the most distinctive feature has been the way in which the separate communities of the area have kept their own identity often by pursuing a particular type of metalworking and product during the post medieval period. Thus, for instance, Willenhall became famous for locks, Wednesfield for traps, Wednesbury for gun barrels, Cradley and the surrounding villages for chains, and Rowley Regis for nails. The development of the blast furnace, and the arrival of the canals and then the railways in the late eighteenth and early nineteenth century, transformed the Black Country, with the population of the urban area increasing from 97,000 to 129,000 between 1801 and 1811, then almost doubling to 205,000 by 1821 and doubling again to 450,000 by 1831. The distinct Black Country accents and dialects have their roots in Anglo-Saxon speech and have survived in the everyday language of this vast population. What had been an isolated area in the Middle Ages with no major river, and much forest on high ground of little agricultural worth, became part of the great 'Workshop of the World' that was the West Midlands of the nineteenth century. The churches of the Black Country reflect this story, with few notable churches from the Middle Ages, though there are great treasures to be discovered, including the parish churches of Halesowen and Wolverhampton. Some significant eighteenth-century churches were erected in the developing towns, before a vast number of churches were built during the nineteenth and twentieth centuries. More recently the area has experienced economic decline with the loss of its mining and much traditional industry accompanied by great social changes, but cushioned by the friendliness and generosity of its people. The consideration of the heritage, including the little known churches, of this unique industrial region as an asset is just beginning. It is not without significance that the Ordnance Survey has this year announced that the name 'The Black Country' will appear for the first time on its maps.

The Early Church in the Black Country to *c.*1066

Both Worcestershire and Staffordshire are rich in Prehistoric and Roman sites, and the evocative remains of the great Roman city of Wroxeter lie some twenty miles to the west of the Black Country. However, physical remains from these periods in the area are scant, and there has been little archaeological evidence discovered to give insights into the devotions or beliefs of the people here before the end of the Roman period. Early sacred sites became absorbed in the Christianisation of Roman Britain, and yet the hilltop settings of the medieval churches at Walsall and Wednesbury would point to the possibility of the continued use of ancient sites for religious purposes. The discovery of pre-Christian burials in the churchyard of another hilltop church, St. Thomas, Dudley seems to give this further credence. Similarly the location of churches close to water sources of which the church of St. Kenelm at Romsley on the Clent Hills, just into Worcestershire, is an excellent example, further suggests that old beliefs were adapted into the new religion. That this church and well grew up to be a centre of pilgrimage associated with Halesowen Abbey in the Middle Ages, based on the legendary story of a Mercian boy king, who was murdered on the order of his sister, shows the development of an ancient site through the church.

The c.twelfth-century figure popularly believed to be that of St. Kenelm carved on a stone built into the exterior south wall of St. Kenelm's church, Romsley, near Clent, Worcestershire

To the west of the Black Country across Shropshire and into Wales, Christian communities continued to flourish from the fourth century. However, from the fifth century pagan Anglo-Saxon culture advanced to the river Severn from south-east England. From the place names ending in '-ley' meaning a clearing, as in Cradley or Coseley, it would seem that Anglo-Saxon settlement of the high woodland areas of the Black Country was thorough, and the use of the name of the god Woden in the place names of Wednesfield and Wednesbury highlights the presence of paganism. The mission to convert the pagan Anglo-Saxon peoples of England was sent in 597 by Pope Gregory to be led by St. Augustine, and spread from the south-east. Yet the continued presence of Christianity to the west is evident from the meetings between Augustine and the British church leaders, which are believed to have taken place in what is now Worcestershire. These meetings were held to resolve differences which had developed over time regarding matters such as the celebration of Easter, issues which were eventually settled by the Synod of Whitby in 664, when the current practices of the church in Rome became universal.

It was Augustine's mission which developed the organisation of the church in Anglo-Saxon England. The main minster or monastery churches were founded at strategic points, usually in existing centres of population, from which the associated ancient estates or geographical hinterland often became extensive parishes. The survival of the element 'minster' in the place name Kidderminster, nearby in Worcestershire, suggests the site of one such church, but it is likely that churches at places such as Halesowen and St. Peter, Wolverhampton were similarly important. Smaller churches were subsequently founded as chapels of ease in other local centres. By 680 the ancient tribal centre of the Hwicce at Worcester became the seat of a diocese in the lower Severn Valley, whilst a monk called Chad, once abbot of Lastingham in Yorkshire, had been chosen by Theodore, Archbishop of Canterbury, to become the first bishop of the Mercians in 669. Over the next three years, until his death in 672, Chad founded a monastery and the cathedral at Lichfield, which was the seat of a diocese extending from Warwickshire to Lancashire. Following his death, Chad was venerated as a saint and his shrine became a significant centre of pilgrimage during the Middle Ages. The dedication of several churches to St. Chad during the nineteenth and twentieth centuries in the northern part of the Black Country is testimony to the lasting influence of the first bishop of Lichfield.

There is no visible evidence of Anglo-Saxon churches in the Black Country, as they have all subsequently been rebuilt. However, the remarkable carved tenth-century pillar in the churchyard of St. Peter, Wolverhampton (see illustration on p.127), which is probably the shaft of an Anglo-Saxon cross, provides an insight into the cultural and artistic wealth of the period, and can be compared with other Anglo-Saxon sculptural fragments such as the cross head at Cropthorne in Worcestershire. The possibility that the cross

2

bases at Bushbury and Penn are of similar date is exciting, as is the story that the latter may have been for a cross set up by Lady Godiva on the estates of Earl Leofric, thus making a connection to one of the most famous characters of Anglo-Saxon Mercia. Examples of Anglo-Saxon architecture can be seen in the region at the churches of Wroxeter and Diddlebury in Shropshire, Wootton Wawen in Warwickshire, and in the priory church and the mid-eleventh century Odda's chapel at Deerhurst in Gloucestershire.

The Norman and Medieval Period, *c.*1066 to *c.*1530

Little physical evidence of pre-Conquest churches survived the years immediately following the Norman Conquest, when there was a huge building and rebuilding campaign. Almost half of Worcestershire's two hundred churches contain some Norman stonework, and there is also much to be seen in nearby Staffordshire and Shropshire. Norman lords such as Roger Montgomery, Earl of Shrewsbury, who held Halesowen, and William FitzAnsculf of Dudley, built castles and rebuilt or constructed new churches to go with them. The Romanesque style reflected the might of the conquering Normans, with round-headed doorways and

The reset Norman chancel arch at Pedmore

windows set in thick walls, which were effective in castle building, and made their churches similarly massive. Little survives *in situ* of the Norman churches in the Black Country, though the doorways, arches and remains of the vault at Halesowen are very impressive, and there is a reset Norman chancel arch at Pedmore. However, there are two fine pieces of Norman sculpture to be seen in the tympana from doorways at both Pedmore and Kingswinford. It is possible that these are associated with the 'Herefordshire School of Sculpture' though only Pedmore has been so attributed. The 'School' was a team of sculptors who carried out work for patrons across the south-west Midlands during the mid-twelfth century. It seems that its origins stem from Oliver de Merlimond who founded a priory at Shobdon in Herefordshire, following a pilgrimage to the shrine of St. James at Santiago de Compostela in Spain. The masons working on Shobdon were greatly influenced by the carvings on churches on the pilgrimage route in southern France and northern Spain, whilst also using elements of designs from Celtic, Anglo-Saxon and Viking work. The carvings at Pedmore and Kingswinford have many parallels to other works by these masons, and form part of a group of significant Norman sculpture in this area, together with pieces at Hagley and Romsley in Worcestershire and Alveley in Shropshire. There are few survivals of features from the interiors of Norman churches, and virtually nothing in the Black Country, but the extraordinary font with pillars at Halesowen is a reflection of the significance of that church in the early Middle Ages.

The medieval Gothic styles developed with the use of the pointed arch, which had its origins in the Middle East, but spread throughout Europe at the time of the Crusades. Some of the earliest examples in the region can be seen in the late twelfth-century west end of the nave of Worcester Cathedral. This was the transition from Norman Romanesque to Early English Gothic. The elegant lancet windows and pointed arches, which were to be replicated in the churches of the early 19th century, were much developed in the architecture of the Cistercian monks, as can still be seen at Abbey Dore in Herefordshire, but were also used in the rebuilding of the east ends of the cathedrals at Lichfield and Worcester in the early thirteenth century.

The south transept and tower at St. Peter, Wolverhampton showing Decorated style windows and the Perpendicular style in the battlements and tower architecture

These greater churches no doubt influenced the architecture of others in the region, and is also likely that the development of the collegiate churches at Tettenhall and St. Peter, Wolverhampton had an effect on the architectural development of medieval churches in the Black Country.

The fourteenth century saw the coming of the more flamboyant Decorated style, which was much influenced by architecture in France and reinforced by continuing strong political and economic links. Elaborate window tracery with Y-shaped divisions enhanced by cusps and ogee curves with trefoils and quatrefoils can be seen in the south transept of St. Peter, Wolverhampton, and a tower with bell-openings, doorways and windows which can be dated by their design can be seen at Aldridge.

During the fifteenth and early sixteenth centuries English architecture developed into the distinctive Perpendicular. A more insular period commenced with the close of the Hundred Years War with France, whilst difficult economic times as a result of the Black Death were compounded by the internal political problems of the Wars of the Roses. The accompanying architectural style is characterised by lower, and later flat, arches and octagonal piers. Lower roof pitches were lined with parapets and battlements and often adorned with pinnacles. Windows were larger than before, with tracery which was made up of an increasing number of straight lines and right angles. The nave with clerestorey and tower of St. Peter, Wolverhampton are fine Perpendicular work, as is the extraordinary eastern part of the nave together with the tower and spire at Halesowen.

The Reformation and after, *c.*1530 to *c.*1800

The Reformation was spread over a century and brought changes towards Protestantism in place of the medieval Catholic church. There were several swings between the two more extreme positions, with a brief return to Catholicism under Mary Tudor, and periods when more Catholic practices were reinstated in church worship under Charles I and Charles II. However, sweeping reforms were made, especially as in the reign of Edward VI and under Oliver Cromwell.

The effect of these changes and reforms was felt in the Black Country area. The Dissolution of the Monasteries between 1536 and 1540 saw the closure of Halesowen Abbey, and Sandwell and Dudley Priories. There are interesting remains of the church at Dudley which can be readily visited, whilst that at Halesowen remains in part but in private ownership, and the church has all but disappeared at Sandwell where the excavated remains of the priory are preserved and interpreted. The Dissolution of the Chantries in 1547 affected the great collegiate churches at Tettenhall and St. Peter, Wolverhampton, where the chancel became ruinous, along with the chapel at Stourbridge. Many other chantries were simply absorbed into the parish churches and little evidence for them survives except for perhaps a piscina as at Pedmore, or screens as at St. Peter, Wolverhampton. Both Worcestershire and Staffordshire maintained a strong if necessarily secretive Catholic tradition during this period. The secret chapels and priest holes at Harvington Hall, and the vigour with which the Giffards of Chillington built the Catholic church, now St. Peter and St. Paul, in Wolverhampton is testimony to this.

There was little new church building during this time. Repair and adaptation of the often increasingly inadequate medieval churches was the normal course, with the removal of the imagery of Christ and the saints and replacement of furnishings to suit the Protestant style. Walls were whitewashed though often painted with text, and plain glass filled the windows. A tall pulpit was often placed centrally in the nave of the church surrounded on all sides by seating, and communion tables with rails replaced the altar and screens in the chancel, which ceased to be divided from the rest of the church. Damage during the Civil War was considerable, not least the destruction of the medieval St. Edmund, Dudley during the siege of Dudley Castle. Repair work was sometimes carried out, such as the rebuilding of the tower at St. John, Tipton.

Where there was new work it was in a more Renaissance style of which the north transept at St. Peter, Wolverhampton is an example. However an increased interest in Classical architecture can be seen in the monuments from this period, including the Leveson and Lane memorials in St. Peter, Wolverhampton. Features and details copied from the buildings of ancient Greece and Rome such as pilasters, pediments cartouches or columns can be seen on seventeenth-century memorials and tablets in St. Bartholomew, Wednesbury and Oldswinford. These are the predecessors of the Classical buildings which were to become popular in this developing area during the eighteenth century.

The Protestant style of worship continued to be used and developed throughout the eighteenth century, and is reflected in the nature of the church buildings. Medieval churches continued to be altered or rebuilt as can be seen at Kingswinford, and there is pictorial evidence for the removal of tracery from windows and the insertion of galleries into the medieval buildings at Rowley Regis and St. Thomas, Dudley. Such changes were usually reversed or further altered during the restoration of surviving medieval buildings during the nineteenth century.

In surrounding rural areas new church building of the eighteenth century was largely confined to the estates of the nobility, as can be seen at nearby Patshull in Staffordshire, rebuilt by James Gibbs in 1743. However in the increasingly urban area a need for new churches was acknowledged. There was much new domestic building in the streets of the major towns, of which Wolverhampton Street, Dudley retains some good examples. Increased industrialisation also brought new structures in factories and commercial buildings. New façades were added to older buildings in Wolverhampton and Wednesbury, and some construction of new churches was undertaken, as at St. Edmund, Dudley. Funds for rebuilding came from private individuals or trusts, of which the work of Dorothy Parkes at Smethwick is perhaps the best instance (see p.89). It was not always without controversy, as the decision to erect a new independent chapel at Stourbridge was to show, and in one case a building which started as one of the many new non-conformist chapels, the Cradley Chapel, was brought into the established church when funding began to fail. These churches followed the architectural form established in the seventeenth century, with Classical symmetry and proportions which were well adapted to the large naves and short chancels required. St. John, Wolverhampton is an excellent

The eighteenth-century church of St. Edmund, Dudley

example of this with its Venetian blind east window, pedimented west front and the series of windows to the sides. Similar details typical of this period including pilasters and urns can be seen at St. Thomas, Wednesfield and St. Thomas, Stourbridge, where the fine church has been compared to buildings designed by James Gibbs. However, the Gothic styles never completely disappeared from churches, not least with the retention of medieval features such as the tower at Kingswinford, and is noticeable in the windows and bell-openings of the brick recasing of the tower at Penn.

St. John, Wolverhampton.
A Georgian church in
a Georgian suburb,
since much redeveloped

The Nineteenth Century and after

There was a steadily increasing tolerance by the Establishment towards other churches and religious groups during the late eighteenth century which led to the emancipation of Roman Catholics in 1829, itself contemporary with a renewed religious fervour within the established church. In the Black Country this was particularly relevant as it was also matched by a huge impetus from nonconformists, who developed new churches and missions in an area which was inadequately covered by the churches of the large and scattered medieval parishes. The Baptists, Methodists and Congregationalists were amongst the principal denominations to minister to the growing populations in the rapidly developing towns and villages, bringing spiritual guidance and sometimes much needed practical help to people who were often living in harsh conditions in great poverty. Lower Gornal is just one example of an area where chapels erected during the nineteenth century surround the parish church, and here there is the added fascination of the story of the first incumbent of St. James' church and the independent chapel (see pp.65-66).

In 1818 £1 million was voted by Parliament to be overseen by Commissioners, and spent on the building of new churches. Other subsequent amounts followed during the early nineteenth century. Several churches were built during this period to house potentially large congregations in competition with nonconformist chapels. These are the Commissioners' churches. Many were cheaply built and proved structurally inadequate, but the large naves held galleries and numerous pews all still focused attention on the central pulpit.

Short chancels and often slender west towers, with side vestibules housing staircases to give access to the galleries, were further characteristic features of this type of church. Some churches were in Classical style such as St. Leonard, Bilston by Francis Goodwin. However, his other church of St. Mary in that town is in the more usual Early English gothic. Goodwin was noted for his churches of this period and the loss of his Christ Church, West Bromwich is most regrettable, though the very similar St. George, Kidderminster, Worcestershire offers an experience of something of its presence in the townscape and the Perpendicular style in which it was built. Lewis Vulliamy also used the Perpendicular style at Wordsley. Gothic styles other than Early English were therefore experimented with in the design of these buildings, including neo-Norman at Brockmoor. However, most are Early English, and include churches by Robert Ebbels at Tipton and Upper Gornal, Isaac Highway at St. Peter, Walsall, and Thomas Smith at Quarry Bank, as well as the group of churches designed by Thomas Lee on the Earl of Dudley's estates at Coseley, Netherton, Lower Gornal and Sedgley. All Saints', Sedgley represents one of the many rebuildings at this time of an earlier church which incorporates the base of the medieval tower. The result is an elegant building in the Perpendicular style which can be compared with Goodwin's splendid treatment of St. Matthew, Walsall. Both this church and the reconstruction of St. Thomas, Dudley by William Brooks also show the innovative use of cast

St. Matthew, Walsall — the east end of the nave
with its clerestorey by Francis Goodwin

iron in their construction, not least in the fine structure of the windows. Iron was also frequently used in piers in the naves of Black Country churches of this date, as well as for supports for the numerous galleries, but it was on the whole not considered suitable for use in church architecture, and more appropriate for buildings associated with industry, commerce and transport.

The Gothic Revival of the nineteenth century was also given some impetus by the studies of a Birmingham architect, Thomas Rickman, who was the first to use the terms Early English, Decorated and Perpendicular. Rickman designed a number of churches in the area including several for the Commissioners in Birmingham, such as the now demolished St. George where he was buried, though his work is not represented in the Black Country. Examples nearby include the churches at Ombersley and Hartlebury in Worcestershire. A more experimental approach to Gothic architecture was coupled with a change of direction within the established church, often towards more Catholic ideas following the Roman Catholic revival in England of the 1820s and 1830s. Under the influence of the Oxford Movement and the Cambridge Camden Society a greater emphasis was placed on ritual within church services. The altar once again became an important focal point at the east end, and larger chancels were required to house robed choirs, whilst the pulpit became less dominant. The eastern extensions of St. James, Wednesbury are particularly reflective of this change. Church buildings of the eighteenth and early nineteenth centuries, particularly those in the Classical style, were seen as undistinguished and unworthy, and too similar to the vast number of non-conformist chapels. A desire to build new churches in more convincing medieval styles, particularly the 'pure' Gothic of fourteenth-century Decorated, was led by the Roman Catholic architect, Augustus Welby Northmore Pugin. He designed Catholic churches in this form for wealthy patrons, of which St. Giles, Cheadle in Staffordshire for the Earl of Shrewsbury, remains as one of the most splendid Gothic Revival churches in the country. Pugin's work was inspirational in the design of new churches, though it is interesting to note the style he used for his Roman Catholic cathedral of St. Chad, Birmingham, which was the first Catholic cathedral to be built since the Reformation. With its use of brick and Baltic style Gothic this was deliberately conceived to be different from the architecture of the many new Anglican churches which had been influenced by his work to date.

These churches were designed to have an altar in a position of significance at the east end of a separate chancel, which had to be proportionally smaller than the nave and divided from it by an arch, and ornamented with carving, painting, tilework and stained glass as funding allowed. Other typical features to be included were porches, aisles, towers or bellcotes, organ chambers and vestries. Transepts were often built to make the churches cruciform in plan but these were often underused spaces. Further Christian symbolism was expressed through the architecture in details such as triple lancets at the east end or the use of three steps to access raised sanctuary floors, both of which were considered to be representational of the Trinity. These elements are very much in evidence in churches of the Black Country designed during the third quarter of the nineteenth century by some celebrated architects. George Edmund Street, whose Law Courts

John Macduff Derick's church at Pensnett

on the Strand in London are famed for their exuberant Decorated style, was architect of St. John, Stourbridge and the destroyed All Saints, Darlaston, whilst his son Arthur Edmund designed the since demolished St. Michael, Smethwick. John Macduff Derick, who had designed St. Saviour, Leeds for one of the key figures of the Oxford Movement, Dr. Edward Pusey, was architect of the magnificent church at Pensnett. However, most of the new church building in the area was perhaps for economic reasons the work of more locally based architects. At Pensnett, the Early English style is dominant on the exterior of the church with its lancet windows arranged singly and in groups. The rose window at the east end is an indicator of the grandeur of the interior, and a reminder that despite the great technological advances of the nineteenth century, architects of Gothic Revival churches sought a pure Gothic style drawn from the development of Early English into Decorated from the thirteenth and fourteenth centuries. The dark stone of the exterior of St. Bartholomew, Wednesbury gives little indication of the richly decorated interior, with wall paintings, alabaster and woodwork at the east end, which is a reminder of the wealth of decoration once to be found in the interiors of a medieval church, but using the materials and manufactured goods of the nineteenth century. The endowment and embellishment of these churches was the result of financial backing by those in local industry, and the stories of many of these churches is inextricably linked to the names of proprietors of local factories, such as Chance in Smethwick and Elwell at Wood Green. Other philanthropists included Members of Parliament and landowners such as Lord Hatherton at St. George, Walsall and the Earl of Dudley at Pensnett. However, in some instances lack of funding meant that buildings were not completed, as is testified by the unbuilt towers at Bearwood and Tettenhall Wood.

There was also a continuing interest at this time in using Italianate Classical architecture in houses, municipal and commercial buildings, of which Julius Alfred Chatwin's Lloyds Bank and Art Gallery in central Wolverhampton are key examples. Sympathetic additions to Classical churches during the nineteenth century were undertaken, such as David Brandon and Thomas Henry Wyatt's chancel at St. Thomas Wednesfield, and John Cotton and William Henry Bidlake's east end at St. Thomas, Stourbridge. Chatwin's seamless extension of the east end of Thomas Archer's Georgian St. Philip's church (now cathedral), Birmingham is a remarkable further example of this approach in the region.

The expansive roof structure by James Cranston at Rushall has links to his interesting secular buildings such as the spa and market at Tenbury Wells in Worcestershire, which gained their unusual form as a result of Cranston's experience as a greenhouse architect. Some Protestant churches such as Old Hill have large roof structures to cover the greatest possible accommodation, of which the splendid St. John, Sparkhill in Birmingham is a further example. These provide a contrast to the exotic St. Luke, Wolverhampton by Leamington architect George Thomas Robinson, which shows in its use of strong Gothic with polychrome brick- and stonework a link to William Butterfield, a follower of the Oxford Movement who enjoyed experimenting with architectural styles alongside the traditional, and whose most noted work of this type in central England is Keble College, Oxford, begun in 1867. A further contrast can be drawn to the simple mission churches founded throughout the region as the nineteenth century progressed; most were temporary structures in wood or iron and were replaced as soon as funds allowed with more substantial buildings in brick or stone. The churches of the growing outer areas of West Bromwich or Walsall have many examples of churches with this kind of story, but few mission churches survive in use today. The church at The Straits and the Pond Street Mission from St. Luke, Wolverhampton are notable exceptions, whilst the extraordinary story of the rebuilding of St. John, Tipton should also be noted in this context (see pp.100-101).

Other more nationally famous architects were involved in the restoration, alteration or rebuilding of older churches: Anthony Salvin at Aldridge, Ewan Christian in the chancels at St. Matthew, Walsall and St. Peter, Wolverhampton, Henry Curzon and John Oldrid Scott at Halesowen, Basil Champneys at St. Bartholomew, Wednesbury and Edward Paley at Penn. Penn also has work by the local architect Edward Banks, who in addition undertook the substantial restoration at Bushbury. Other local architects were also used for major work on older churches such as the rebuilding of St. Giles, Willenhall by William Darby Griffin and Pedmore by Worcester architect Frederick Preedy. Preedy showed a genuine interest in retaining original features including the Norman doorway and chancel arch, both of which were reset in the enlarged structure. Not only was the medieval church here too small for the growing community, but its poor state by the mid nineteenth century is a reminder that only minimal repair works had been undertaken to most of these buildings since the sixteenth century, though most had seen several modifications to meet changing worship needs.

There is a considerable list of architects, based in and around the West Midlands, who were commissioned to produce designs for the huge number of churches to be constructed in the Black Country during the later nineteenth century. Three Wolverhampton practices were dominant. The churches by George Bidlake at Wollaston and St. Jude, Wolverhampton are important survivals, particularly since the loss of his church at Bradley. Edward Banks designed three churches in his home town as well as being responsible for the restoration of two others. Thomas Henry Fleming's buildings at St. Chad, Coseley and the nearby St. Mary, Hurst Hill are more elaborate buildings than his St. Barnabas, Wolverhampton. Fleming also enlarged the church at Pelsall and added the tower and spire to St. Jude, Wolverhampton. Although Birmingham architect Julius Alfred Chatwin was prolific in that city, his ecclesiastical work can only be seen in the Black Country at Bearwood and in his chancel at Oldswinford, though one of his finest church buildings, St. Augustine, Edgbaston and one of his most extraordinary, St. James, Handsworth are only a short distance across the boundary. Blackheath is the sole work in the area of Worcester diocesan architect William Jeffrey Hopkins, who was responsible for so much church building and restoration within Worcestershire. Similarly work by Thomas Johnson of Lichfield can be seen at Greets Green and Holy Trinity, Smethwick. Although St. John, Wednesbury has gone, there is still the Commissioners' type Holy Trinity, West Bromwich by Samuel Whitfield Daukes; he and Davies and Middleton represent Gloucestershire architects to be used here. Davies and Middleton's St. Luke, Dudley and St. Michael, Tividale have also been demolished, but their execution of St. Matthew, Tipton and their remodelling of All Saints, Bloxwich have created fine church buildings. George Thomas Robinson, who worked across the Midland region produced the simple yet most attractive church at Brownhills, as well as the powerful St. Luke, Wolverhampton.

Heavy restoration of medieval churches often resulted, as at Bushbury or All Saints, West Bromwich, in rebuilding in the fashionable Early English and Decorated styles of the Gothic Revival. However, there was a change of approach towards the close of the nineteenth century. Scraped stone interiors were particularly fought against, not just because of the gloomy result of exposing dark stone which is a particular problem in many Staffordshire churches, but also with the recognition that the removal of frequently unstable plaster to expose features of antiquarian interest, such as blocked doorways and windows, also involved the destruction of the remains of older wall paintings, often without record. William Morris founded the Society

Lavender and Twentyman's twentieth-century
church of St. Gabriel, Fullbrook.
Top: interior looking east
Bottom: exterior showing the chancel and belfry

for the Preservation of Ancient Buildings in 1877 as a reaction to the heavy restoration of Tewkesbury Abbey in Gloucestershire, and the growing Arts and Crafts movement towards the end of the century changed the emphasis on church restoration, advocating attempts to preserve more historic features and the use of traditional materials and craftsmanship. There is little evidence of this in the restoration of medieval Black Country churches, perhaps because most major restoration work had been recently completed. However, the use of the Perpendicular style in spacious buildings with plentiful natural light was favoured by many church architects from the closing years of the nineteenth century. George Frederick Bodley was instrumental in this change, as can be seen in his church at Hoar Cross near Lichfield, Staffordshire. Tettenhall Wood is the location of Wightwick Manor, the fine Arts and Crafts house by Edward Ould which is regarded by many as an icon of the movement because of its associations with the work of William Morris and Edward Burne-Jones. There are no major churches by significant architects of the early twentieth century, such as John Dando Sedding of London or William Henry Bidlake of Birmingham, although there are many fittings and much stained glass from the period. However, the work of Frederick Beck — largely in Wolverhampton — Wood and Kendrick's churches in West Bromwich and those by the two John Cutts at Hasbury and St. Andrew, Walsall are worth mentioning as examples influenced by Arts and Crafts principles. The rebuilding of Rowley Regis in 1920 by Arthur Stansfield Dixon and William Holland Hobbis is notable for their pursuit of the style of the early churches of southern Europe. This is also manifest twenty years later at St. Francis, West Bromwich by William Alexander Harvey and Herbert Wicks, and St. Hilda, Warley Woods by Edwin Francis Reynolds. Dudley Wood has the attractive church of 1931 by Charles Nicholson, who had direct links to the Arts and Crafts movement. The rebuilding of the great medieval church at Tettenhall by Bernard Miller, necessitated by the disastrous fire of 1950, has resulted in a remarkable building which seems in many ways to extend the Arts and Crafts movement into the latter part of the twentieth century. Second World War damage was relatively slight for a major industrial area, but the destruction of George Edmund Street's All Saints, Darlaston was a sad loss.

The churches of Lavender and Twentyman around Wolverhampton have roots in the Arts and Crafts movement, as is demonstrated at St. Martin, Ettingshall, built during the Second World War era. Their later twentieth-century buildings show more modern styles of architecture with larger windows and flat roofs such as at St. Gabriel, Fullbrook. Their church of Emmanuel, Bentley of 1956 and Richard Twentyman's rebuilding of St. Andrew, Wolverhampton from 1965 also embrace a recognition of the growing need in churches for community facilities as the range of activities undertaken has expanded. This and innovative styles of worship have led to churches and halls, with convenience and flexibility as major priorities, being constructed on the later twentieth-century housing estates. Hawbush, Norton, Pendeford, Pheasey, St. Alban, Wednesfield and St. Martin, Walsall are all good examples of this development. Other significant later twentieth-century church architecture includes Lapal by Peter Falconer. There has also been a desire to replace inadequate or unsafe church buildings from the nineteenth century, and the new buildings at Clayhanger, Pleck and Bescot, Shelfield, as well as St. James, West Bromwich and St. Stephen, Willenhall have doubtless improved facilities for their congregations and the local communities. Many have incorporated features or key fittings from the previous buildings, for which there was often great affection. Meanwhile there has been significant adaptation and reordering of older buildings, including the extensions at Penn, Pelsall and Walsall Wood, the internal reorganisation at Brierley Hill or St. John, Wolverhampton, and the more radical redevelopment of the interiors of Oldbury, St. Paul, Walsall and St. Philip, Penn Fields, all of which have ensured the continuing viability, better accessibility and wider use of these fine churches. Such improvements are often accompanied by necessary restoration as at Oldswinford, St. Thomas, Dudley or St. Peter, Wolverhampton, and maintenance of historic fabric continues to be a problem in many places. Demographics have also changed with some areas becoming depopulated with the clearance of older, often inadequate housing near the town centres, or others accommodating communities of other faiths. Some churches have been closed for worship during the twentieth century; some have continued in use by other denominations or churches, including St. Barnabas, Wolverhampton and St. Mary, Walsall; whilst several have been adapted for new uses such as St. Alban, Smethwick and St. George, Wolverhampton. Very many more have been demolished with some significant losses, particularly Christ Church, West Bromwich, St. John, Wednesbury and St. Michael, Smethwick. Others have an uncertain future such as St. John, Dudley and St. Michael, Langley, where the charming church of Holy Trinity has already disappeared.

However, the churches of the Black Country of all dates and styles are a source of great pride in the local communities which they serve. Many need huge amounts of money to cope with complicated maintenance and restoration work, and are undertaking great fundraising efforts to achieve this. Whilst there is financial support from organisations such as English Heritage and the two historic churches trusts with a remit in the region, the care of the buildings together with the life of the church

St. Alban, Wednesfield,
designed by Norman Cachmaille-Day in 1965

community is the result of the work of the congregations. Some churches have a very special atmosphere, and all have something of interest such as the association of St. Francis, Dudley with the footballer Duncan Edwards. With increasing awareness of the history and architecture of churches coupled with huge interest, in local and family history more churches are open regularly, or at least occasionally, for visitors and for those wanting to find a quiet space in an increasingly busy world. All the churches in the Black Country, dating to the various periods between Anglo-Saxon times and the present day, are part of the unique heritage of this region and have an important role in their community and beyond.

Church Decoration, Fittings and Setting

Furnishings and Fittings

With so many alterations in the post-medieval period it is difficult to gain an impression of the internal appearance of the medieval churches of the Black Country before the Reformation. Mass would have been celebrated in churches lit by candles, surrounded by colourful wall paintings and stained glass windows. The few surviving medieval fittings within the area include some of high quality, but to describe a typical interior of the Middle Ages requires an overview drawn from many different examples in and around the region.

The font was usually at the west end of the nave, where many can still be seen today. There are several examples of medieval fonts which being of stone have withstood the test of time rather better than wooden fittings. The best Norman font in the Black Country, and indeed one of the most unusual in the Midlands, is at Halesowen. Whilst there are many other Norman examples to be seen in the surrounding counties such as at Broome or Chaddesley Corbett in Worcestershire, the only other example in the Black Country is that preserved from Tettenhall in the modern church at Pendeford. Later medieval fonts followed the architectural style of the day and the fine Perpendicular font at Penn has carved traceried panels. Many of the surviving medieval naves are filled with pews, but early congregations stood or used stone seats around the wall of the church, none of which have survived here. No late medieval pews survive but the fine fifteenth-century stone pulpit in St. Peter, Wolverhampton (see illustration alongside and on p.129) is a reminder of the development of preaching in churches following the coming of the friars from the thirteenth century. Another important survival is the wooden lectern at St. Bartholomew, Wednesbury in the form of a locally significant fighting cock rather than the more usual wooden or brass eagle, emblem of St. John the Evangelist.

The nave and chancel were divided by a rood screen which supported a beam surmounted by the rood or crucifix. No medieval screens survive in this position in the Black Country, but there was also often a rood loft for singers, to which access was gained by a staircase, a good example of which can be seen on the north aisle at Halesowen. Other screens known as parclose screens separated the chantry chapels from the main body of the church, and two fine parclose screens can be seen at St. Peter, Wolverhampton.

The chancel beyond the screen was the sacred space, being separated from the frequently secular activity of the nave and preserved as a sanctuary. Mass was celebrated here by the priest at a stone altar, above which was likely to be a reredos, sometimes of stone. The sacred vessels were kept in aumbries or cupboards to the side, and the chalice and paten washed in the piscina. Medieval piscinae can be seen

The lion carved on the staircase of the stone pulpit at St. Peter, Wolverhampton

at Pedmore and St. Matthew, Walsall. The priest and deacons would be seated on the sedilia, as can be seen at Bushbury, but in churches served by a number of clerics there were stalls, of which those at St. Peter, Wolverhampton and at St. Matthew, Walsall with carved misericords, are remarkable survivals. The stalls at St. Peter, Wolverhampton were brought from Lilleshall Abbey in Shropshire at the Reformation, and are a reminder of the fine furnishings in medieval monastic houses, now mostly lost. At Bushbury, a tomb recess on the north side of the chancel would have served as an Easter Sepulchre, where the sacrament was kept from Maundy Thursday to Easter Day. Another example is at Tenbury Wells in Worcestershire.

The liturgical changes which came with the Reformation period directly affected the way in which church buildings were furnished. Few churches retain the more extreme Protestant arrangements made during the Commonwealth, with a central communion table surrounded by seating or rails, though such a layout can still be seen at Deerhurst and Hailes in Gloucestershire. Several seventeenth-century communion tables survive, along with pulpits of which perhaps the finest example is the panelled pulpit at St. Bartholomew, Wednesbury, though this has been reduced from a dominant three decker with desks for the clerk and reader. Sermons lasting an hour were preached from here, and in Worcestershire a wrought iron hourglass stand survives at Oddingley. The pews were fitted with doors to keep out draughts, and the resulting box pews could be rented, with free seating towards the rear of the church. No seventeenth-century box pews survive in the Black Country, though the woodwork from the Pursehouse pew is preserved in All Saints, Sedgley. During revivals of more Catholic practice under Charles I and Charles II some chancels were once again screened from the nave, and communion tables returned to the east end and surrounded by rails. Many medieval furnishings were adapted for continued use, of which perhaps covers on fonts are the most frequent survival.

The Perpendicular font at St. Matthew, Walsall is carved with angels holding coats of arms. It has a lead lining dated 1712

The north aisle at Halesowen showing the projecting casing for the spiral staircase that gave access to the top of the rood screen

These developments in furnishing continued through the eighteenth century, and the fine Classical churches of this period in the Black Country retain a number of fittings of this date. No complete interior has survived nineteenth- or twentieth-century modification, but a visit to St. Swithin, Worcester gives a clear impression of the typical layout with its numerous box pews and splendid three decker pulpit. Galleries were introduced and fine organs installed, some of which remain including those at St. John, Wolverhampton and St. Thomas, Stourbridge.

Box pews, galleries and large pulpits also filled the naves of the Commissioners' type churches of the early nineteenth century, of which the box pews at Netherton and Oldswinford are splendid survivals. The short chancels of many Black Country churches from the eighteenth and early nineteenth centuries have since been extended, but the prayer and commandment boards which would have been hung on the walls are frequently still to be found, and the remarkable cast iron panels at St. Thomas, Dudley, along with the many examples of iron piers to support galleries, as at St. Leonard, Bilston, reflect the importance of the iron industry in the area.

By the mid nineteenth century, such interiors became more unfashionable with the Gothic Revival and ecclesiological movements, though the Protestant tradition survived and developed in churches like Old Hill and St. Luke, Wolverhampton, where the furnishings continued to reflect the worship style. High Church Anglicanism, however, saw a return to more medieval style furnishing and this was used by many patrons, incumbents and architects in new church buildings of the second half of the nineteenth century. In extreme this could be very lavish, but was usually manifest in the wooden pews, screens, choir stalls, organs and reredoses to be found in the interiors of churches by William Darby Griffin and George Bidlake. The quality of detail in the fittings often shows how the Victorian ability to produce manufactured goods such as floor tiles or ironwork could be linked to the Gothic Revival. In the restoration of medieval buildings such as Penn, Halesowen and St. Bartholomew, Wednesbury, these furnishings frequently recreated something of the medieval setting, and incorporated surviving medieval pieces, such as the pulpit at St. Peter, Wolverhampton, though when introduced to eighteenth-century Classical churches there was indeed a radical change.

The Arts and Crafts movement at the end of the nineteenth century brought a revival of traditional materials and workmanship. Wood and metalwork, often of very high quality, can be found in many churches in the Black Country. The font cover by Ninian Comper at Kingswinford is indicative of his style, and the interior at St. Mary, Wellingborough in Northamptonshire shows him at his most ornate. The rebuilding of Tettenhall by Bernard Miller has seen the creation of a complete 1950s interior with a remarkable font.

In the later twentieth century, reordering schemes to give greater flexibility, creating meeting rooms and providing kitchen and toilet facilities, have given opportunities to create new spaces with appropriate fittings and furnishings, as at Netherton and Oldswinford. The Lye and Aldridge have seen sweeping changes to the interiors of their churches, as has Pensnett, where many Victorian fittings have also been retained.

Glass, Wall Painting and Tiles
There are few fragments of medieval glass in Black Country churches, though the pieces at Bushbury are worthy of note. Medieval glass generally survives in a fragmentary state, and as here the surviving pieces are often collected

The pulpit at St. Gabriel's, Fullbrook.
An example of mid twentieth-century style

together from around the building. Some of the best medieval glass in the Midlands can be seen in the fifteenth-century windows of Great Malvern Priory in Worcestershire, where figures of saints and scenes from the Old Testament and the Life of Christ in rich colours are shown beneath canopies interpreting in glass the architectural style of the period. Such scenes were all created to embellish the buildings and illustrate the teachings of the Church, and need to be considered in context with contemporary sculpture, wall painting and manuscript illustration.

However, little glass survives in the Black Country from before the nineteenth century, though the panels of seventeenth-century Flemish glass at St. Peter, Wolverhampton give an indication of the painted scenes which were sometimes to be found in churches during the time of Archbishop Laud and after the Commonwealth, during which time stained glass was much condemned and early glass often removed. Clear glazing was generally fashionable from the sixteenth to the early nineteenth centuries, though it was sometimes ornamented with geometric and heraldic designs.

Early nineteenth-century glass is also rare. The east window of St. Thomas, Dudley of 1821 showing the Ascension by Joseph Blackler of Stourbridge is a fine exception. It is similar in style to the painted scenes of the eighteenth century, such as can be seen at Great Witley in Worcestershire in the fine windows painted in 1719 by Joshua Price of York, originally in the Duke of Chandos' chapel at Stanmore in Middlesex. However, the Gothic Revival from the mid nineteenth century brought a renewed interest in medieval glass and the techniques of production. Many firms began to produce glass considered to be appropriate for medieval settings. A local example is Hardmans of Birmingham, commissioned by Pugin to realise his design. Other related firms include Powell of Whitefriars in London or Chance of Smethwick, the latter building on the long history of glass manufacture in this area centred on Stourbridge from the seventeenth century. Artists and companies including Clayton and Bell, Michael O'Connor and William Wailes became prominent and their work is represented in the region. Glass designers and makers were making increasingly detailed studies of medieval glass and reproducing elements of its artwork and colour. The glass of Charles Eamer Kempe and his successor, Walter Tower, draws heavily on the glass of the early fifteenth century, and the richness can be experienced in the set of fifteen windows at St. Bartholomew, Wednesbury. Much glass is unattributed and there are many opportunities for research into the designers of this great legacy of nineteenth- and twentieth-century stained glass windows in the Black Country.

The style of stained glass windows changed markedly with the work of William Morris towards the end of the nineteenth century, with clear, bold designs and areas of colour separated by heavy black leadlines. Morris' glass production was a significant part of the pre-Raphaelites and the Arts and Crafts movement, which also brought distinctive work in other media, notably furnishings, paintings, tiles and textiles. Significant collections can be seen at Birmingham Museum and Art Gallery, but the window designs of Edward Burne-Jones are exceptional and some of the best in the Midlands can be seen in the set of four in Birmingham Cathedral. The firm continued production after the death of both Morris and Burne-Jones and the Grazebrook window at Oldswinford is from this period. The influence of the Arts and Crafts movement extended well into the twentieth century, and the glass by Benjamin Warren and Henry Payne of Birmingham, the Camm family and Christopher Whall is of very high quality. Warren's windows at Rowley Regis are most attractive. There is fine glass by the Camm family at Oldbury and St. Michael, Langley. The windows by members of the Bromsgrove Guild, notably Archibald Davies, are becoming increasingly highly regarded, including the glass at Tettenhall Wood and St. Peter, Wolverhampton. Distinctive fifteenth-century style glass by Ninian Comper can be found at Kingswinford and Lower Gornal. Later twentieth-century work is represented by the fine glass by Alan Younger and Rosemary Rutherford at All Saints, Sedgley, and the John Piper window of 1966 at St. Andrew, Wolverhampton deserves to be much better known.

The decoration of walls is linked to the glass. There is little medieval wall painting which survives in Black Country churches, just traces on the pulpit at St. Peter, Wolverhampton. However, nearby can be seen painted medieval scenes which complement glass, the figure of the Virgin and Child at Belbroughton in Worcestershire, and the earlier remarkable battle scene on the nave wall at Claverley in Shropshire. There may be other fragments yet to be discovered on the medieval fabric in the Black Country, but much will have been lost not only in the rebuilding of medieval churches but also in the restoration and scraping of plaster from the walls of those that survive. However, it is worth noting the fine Norman sculpture which can be seen on the tympana at Kingswinford and Pedmore which, with the representations of St. Michael and Christ in Majesty respectively, should be read in the context of the painted decoration which it would have complemented, and the pieces would have no doubt been painted themselves. Following the Reformation, texts and the royal arms were painted on the walls. The royal arms served as a reminder of the position of the monarch as head of the church, and from the eighteenth century tended to be of carved wood or painted on canvas. An example from this period can be seen at Halesowen. However, most church interiors in the Black Country between the sixteenth and nineteenth centuries would have been whitewashed and quite plain.

The nineteenth-century Gothic Revival saw pictorial decoration on the walls in a manner similar to that before the Reformation. The paintings on the chancel walls of St. Peter, Wolverhampton have all but disappeared, but the murals by Reginald Frampton of 1905-6 at Rushall are a good indication of what was desired. For comparison the wall painting at Newland, Worcestershire by Clayton and Bell is worth seeking out. Some nineteenth-century carving, as can be found on several reredoses in the churches of the Black Country, should also be noted.

Although Worcestershire was known as a centre for tile manufacture in the Middle Ages, few examples have survived in the Black Country, though there is a significant group from Halesowen Abbey now in Worcester. However, the production of medieval style tiles was popular in the nineteenth century by firms such as Minton in Stoke-on-Trent and Maw at Ironbridge, and there are many examples of nineteenth-century tiles as at Pedmore and the mosaic pavement at St. Bartholomew, Wednesbury.

Memorials

All but the more recent churches in the Black Country contain a collection of memorials to people associated with that church, and provide a wealth of information about the individuals and families of the parish for family and social historians. Most of the larger memorials to be found in churches relate to wealthy landowners or industrialists, but a look in the often very expansive churchyards which are a feature of so many Black Country churches can reveal extraordinary stories of local people. Typical examples include the graveyards at Wordsley, Cradley, Brockmoor and St. John, Dudley, the latter with the grave of the 'Tipton Slasher'.

The earliest memorials in churches were carved inscriptions or stone coffin lids which could be seen on the church floor. Simple relief designs such as a cross as at Bushbury might indicate the burial of a noted cleric or layman, and examples have often been reset away from their original position. From the thirteenth century, memorials to the wealthy often consisted of an effigy in relief set on a tomb chest, of which the figures of the knight at St. Matthew, Walsall and the priest at Halesowen are good examples. Later medieval memorials have much architectural detail as can be seen at Aldridge. Some were associated with the foundation of chantry chapels, where prayers were said for the souls of the dead, and which became increasingly elaborate until the time of their suppression in 1547. Churches such as St. Bartholomew, Wednesbury and St. Peter, Wolverhampton had several such chapels within their aisles and transepts. Brasses and incised slabs were also less expensive ways to commemorate the deceased and were popular with medieval merchants and manufacturers, but none survive in the Black Country. Meanwhile, ordinary people would

The Leveson memorial by Hubert Le Sueur at St. Peter, Wolverhampton

have been buried in the nave of the church or surrounding churchyard in graves with a simple marker at most. Once the spaces were filled, particularly inside the church, the bones were collected and placed in ossuaries. Could it be that the crypts at St. Matthew, Walsall are in some way linked to this practice?

From the sixteenth century there was an increased desire for elaborate memorials. With the changes of the Reformation there were less opportunities for embellishment of churches, particularly with the dissolution of the chantries, and so highly decorated Renaissance style monuments became popular, not least with members of recusant Catholic families. The Leveson and Lane memorials, attributed to mason Robert Royley, in St. Peter, Wolverhampton are good examples from the start of this trend. Such Classical memorials from the seventeenth century have a wealth of heraldic and costume detail of the period, and the Parkes' memorials at St. Bartholomew, Wednesbury are good examples. Others were commemorated by brass plates with inscriptions, of which those at Halesowen are typical. More of a rarity is the surviving bronze figure and cherubs to Vice-Admiral Sir Richard Leveson by Charles I's court sculptor, Hubert Le Sueur, of about 1635 at St. Peter, Wolverhampton.

By the end of the seventeenth century there were numerous wall-mounted monuments and tablets erected in preference to tomb chests, as can be seen at Oldswinford. Many larger eighteenth-century memorials are upright in black and white marble and Classical in design, but tablets, some carved with urns or foliage, remained popular with wealthy town families. Sculptors are sometimes recorded on these memorials or known from documentary evidence, including work by John Flaxman at Penn and Peter Hollins at St. Edmund, Dudley. There are also fine seventeenth- and eighteenth-century headstones in the churchyards at Kingswinford and Tettenhall.

Tablets were often more simply designed, but also more numerous by the nineteenth century, and examples can be seen throughout the Black Country, including those at St. Giles, Willenhall. Some are inspired by the Gothic Revival in their detail and many reflect the demonstrative mourning which followed the death of Prince Albert. There are also some ceramic plaques and cast iron plates as memorials at St. Leonard and St. Mary, Bilston. The harsh conditions of living in the Black Country at this time are evidenced by the memorials to those who lost their lives in mining disasters such as at Pelsall, or to disease, as in the cholera burials at Netherton. The grave of the Roman Catholic priest at Bushbury is a poignant link to the recusancy of Roman Catholics between the Reformation and emancipation in the nineteenth century.

During the 20th century, the placing of memorials inside churches has become more limited. Smaller plaques in wood, stone or metal often record a memorial donation to the church, and so are linked to stained glass windows or pieces of furniture. However, the many deaths in the First World War led to a number of fine individual commemorations, often in stained glass, while many community memorials were erected either as plaques or often in the form of a cross or lychgate in the churchyard as at Christ Church, Coseley or St. John, Dudley respectively. Many more twentieth-century memorials are in churchyards or cemeteries which show a huge variety of materials, styles and inscriptions indicative of changing fashion through the period. Although some graveyards have been cleared for ease of maintenance with a resulting loss of information about those buried there, there is an increasing interest in preserving the spaces as 'green lungs' with improved management of their vegetation and wildlife, as well as the preservation of the memorials themselves and their part in Black Country heritage.

Setting and Context

The roles of the churches of the Black Country in the towns and villages which surround them has given rise to numerous features around them, which often remain as evidence of past development and change.

Many rural churches were close to the residence of the lord of the manor, and the location of the fine manorial sites at West Bromwich, and particularly Rushall, are typical of this, with the village close by. The dominance of the castle over town and churches at Dudley is also significant. Many public events were held in and around medieval churches alongside services. Town churches such as St. Peter, Wolverhampton would have hosted pageants and plays, whilst processions would have formed an important part of the ritual at festivals such as Corpus Christi. The processional route under the chancel at St. Matthew, Walsall is a rare surviving reminder of the colour of medieval life. The chancel, screened off from the body of the church was the responsibility of the patron, who also appointed the priest. Patrons were sometimes the lord of the manor, but could also be the bishop or a monastery. Chantry chapels, also screened off from the rest of the church, were provided with priests by endowments from individuals or guilds as at St. Matthew, Walsall. There is little evidence in the Black Country, however, for the lifestyle of medieval priests, as there are no surviving examples of priests' houses, vestments or plate. The collections of Worcester and Lichfield Cathedral libraries give just a tantalising glimpse of the wealth of manuscripts and a reminder of the treasures which complemented the architecture and decoration of churches such as Halesowen or St. Peter, Wolverhampton. A good example of a late medieval timber-framed vicarage can be seen by the lychgate at Claverley in Shropshire.

The medieval churchyard offered an open space where preaching could be conducted. This practice began in the Anglo-Saxon period and the survival of the fine carved pillar at Wolverhampton, and the bases at Bushbury and Penn are rare links to the life of the pre-Conquest church. Medieval crosses are more frequent survivals, though most survive as bases and without their heads. Some have been restored as at Penn, but bases remain at Rushall and Kingswinford, which also retains its shaft, whilst the head of a cross is preserved inside the church at Halesowen.

After the Reformation, the residence of the incumbent was often a fine building in the vicinity of the church, of which the Georgian rectory still in use at Oldswinford is a good example. Provision of a clergy house was often subject to separate endowment as at St. Michael, Walsall in the early twentieth century. Churches were frequently associated with the establishment of schools, and the construction of church, school and vicarage to George Bidlake's designs for William Orme Foster at Wollaston in the nineteenth century results from this concept. Such schools were significant in the urban area before the coming of the board schools from the mid nineteenth century. The patronage of industrialists in the Black Country is manifest in the provision of churches for local workers as in the foundation of churches by members of the Mitchell and Chance families in Smethwick. Charitable works since the Reformation have also left evidence in and around churches, such as the seventeenth-century bread dole shelves at Aldridge, and the charity bequest boards at Penn. The development of many twentieth-century churches to include or make use of parish halls and be closely linked to schools is an identifiable progression, and a reminder that the stories of all these churches are inextricably linked to the surrounding communities.

ALDRIDGE   ST. MARY THE VIRGIN, THE GREEN

Aldridge lies to the north of Walsall and was much redeveloped during the late twentieth century. It was a significant centre of coal mining until the 1930s, whilst limestone was quarried until the nineteenth century, and brick and tile making were also undertaken in the area. The Green at the north-east corner of the town still has something of the feeling of a small Staffordshire village, and is the ancient centre of the settlement. This was a royal manor from Anglo-Saxon times, and after the Norman Conquest was within the royal forest of Cannock Chase. The Georgian Manor House is in High Street and the garden of the fine seventeenth- and eighteenth-century Moot House adjoins the churchyard.

The red sandstone church is largely on footings of local limestone, and has a fine fourteenth-century battlemented west tower. Most of the church was rebuilt in the nineteenth century, but the core of the nave and chancel are medieval work and suggest a thirteenth-century building with a short nave and long chancel.

The south aisle was rebuilt in 1841, and the church was further restored with the north aisle and chancel rebuilt by Anthony Salvin in 1852-3. A south vestry was added in 1975 and there are plans to extend the church with a large hall to

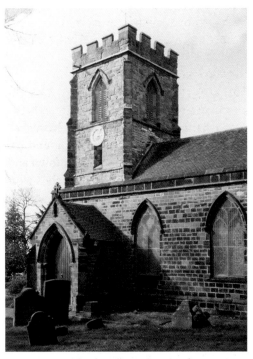

Aldridge from the south

the south-east. The church itself has a uniform Decorated style appearance to the exterior. Pure fourteenth-century Decorated work can be seen in the fine crocketed hood mould to the west doorway and flowing tracery to the west window of the tower. The other exterior windows from the Victorian restorations are fourteenth-century Decorated in style.

The west doorway at Aldridge

Inside, the nave arcades have Perpendicular style arches on octagonal piers, which were much reconstructed during the nineteenth century. The north arcade is one bay longer than the south and extends into the chancel, whilst the eastern two pillars of the south arcade are of plastered brick construction from 1841. There is a fine Decorated arch to the tower, and a Decorated piscina in the chancel. The roof structures reflect the lack of a structural division between the nave and chancel, where in the Middle Ages there would have been a substantial timber rood screen. There is seventeenth-century woodwork in the pulpit, and at the west end of the south aisle is a bread dole cupboard inscribed 'TP 1694'. The nineteenth-century pews were removed from the nave in 1991, and in 1995 the choir stalls were taken out of the chancel, giving an open flexible space to the interior. The Victorian wooden reredos remains at the east end. The font is a memorial to the Allport family of 1853. Amongst the many nineteenth-century stained glass windows, one in the south aisle is of 1865 by Powell of Whitefriars, London and shows Christ with St. Peter.

A fourteenth-century effigy of a priest, possibly Roger de Elyngton who is recorded as founding a chantry chapel in the church, is set in a recess of similar date in the chancel. A further worn medieval effigy of a knight is set on a later stone base in the south aisle. He is Robert de Stapleton, who was lord of the local manor at the end of the thirteenth century. There are several eighteenth-century memorial tablets now in the north aisle.

AMBLECOTE   HOLY TRINITY, VICARAGE ROAD

It is now virtually impossible to distinguish between Amblecote and Stourbridge; indeed the urban district of Amblecote was merged with Stourbridge borough in 1965. However, the ancient settlement of Amblecote lies to the north of the River Stour and is one of the historic areas of glassmaking. The Holloway End glass-works on High Street was in production from the seventeenth century until the 1950s. To the north, cottages and factory buildings are scattered along the 'Crystal Mile', named after the cut lead crystal which became a speciality from the nineteenth century. Coal was also mined here until the twentieth century. Corbett Hospital, close to the church in Vicarage Road, is built around a Georgian House, 'The Hill', and named after its former owner, John Corbett, who became famous as the 'Salt King of Droitwich'.

Holy Trinity church is only a quarter of a mile from the town centre of Stourbridge, yet it stands in a spacious graveyard with an almost rural atmosphere. The building is in unusual yellow brick made from fireclay, which was also mined here, and the bricks used for furnace lining in the glassworks. The church was completed in 1844 to designs by Samuel Heming, and consists of a west tower with large nave and short chancel. It is a Commissioners' type church in the Early English style with long lancet windows. The furnishings largely date from the 1920s after High Church style worship was introduced here, thus changing the interior from its original more Protestant layout.

The church is noted for its stained glass. The earliest, in the east window with Biblical scenes, is probably the work of Michael O'Connor and commemorates the death in 1853 of James Foster, Stourbridge ironmaster and a great benefactor to this church. Foster's firm manufactured several early steam locomotives, including the *Stourbridge Lion*, the first locomotive to run on rails in North America. The iron railings to the churchyard were also made at his foundry.

During the twentieth century the church was embellished with further stained glass, particularly in the late 1940s. The Hambrey window shows St. George, the Turner window is of the Trinity, the Baker window shows Christ with children from all nations, whilst the window commemorating the Scouts is by William Morris of

Amblecote from the south-east

Westminster. In 1965 John Hardman and Co. installed the Egan window which shows St. Francis of Assisi, whilst the Guest and Bomber memorial windows are by Claude Price, who trained at Birmingham School of Art. In 1990 the small Lanchbury memorial window with crowns of thorns and roses was produced by local artist Keith Brettle, who has since installed further fine windows at Stone and Franche in Worcestershire.

There is a fine group of Victorian memorial tablets as well as a Crucifix memorial to twelve former choristers from the church who died during the First World War. The lychgate was erected in 1921 also as a war memorial. The churchyard contains many memorials with associations to the glass industry such as that to William Fritsche, a noted copper wheel engraver. Beside the church and surrounded by iron railings is the grave of John Hall who supplied the bricks for the church.

BEARWOOD   ST. MARY, BEARWOOD ROAD

Bearwood is in the south-eastern part of Smethwick, immediately adjacent to the boundary with the City of Birmingham. The main street, Bearwood Road, is a busy local centre which leads north from the Hagley Road, passed by many *en route* to the city centre. West of the centre Lightwoods Park spreads out from Lightwoods Hall, once home of the Adkins family, now headquarters of Hardmans where contemporary designs for glass are worked on. This continues the tradition of the company founded by John Hardman which produced glass and artefacts for churches to the designs of Pugin.

The church stands on the west side of Bearwood Road at the corner of St. Mary's Road. The parish was established in 1892 from that of Smethwick Old Church, which was part of the ancient parish of Harborne, although St. Mary's had been built as a chapel of ease in 1887. The architect was Julius Alfred Chatwin of Birmingham, and St. Mary represents one of his few works in the Black Country, contrasting with his prolific output in Birmingham. Chatwin's churches include St. Martin-in-the-Bull Ring and the neighbouring church of St. Augustine, Edgbaston is considered one of his finest works. By comparison, St. Mary's church is a smaller red brick building with stone dressings and comprises a chancel at the east end of a long nave with porches. The planned south tower was never constructed, and today there is a small bellcote over the base which houses the south vestry and organ chamber, whilst the north vestry was added in 1939. The baptistery at the west end is a typical feature of many of Chatwin's church designs; this is rectangular, but can be compared in concept to the polygonal baptisteries of Chatwin's churches at St. James, Handsworth or St. Mary and St. Ambrose, Edgbaston. To the west the halls were erected in 1897 and modernised and extended in 1994.

Inside there are brick and stone dressings to the nave with Early English style arcades, whilst the chancel is plastered and contains wood panelling. The fine pulpit is of traceried sandstone. The organ of 1952 replaced one dating from the nineteenth-century. There is stained glass by John Hardman as well as by the Camm family of Smethwick. The glass in the three light east window is by Charles Eamer Kempe of 1904.

Bearwood from the south

BEARWOOD   ST. DUNSTAN, MARLBOROUGH ROAD

This small mission church from St. Mary's church was erected in 1911, but closed in the late 1920s before being sold in 1936.

BENTLEY   EMMANUEL, QUEEN ELIZABETH AVENUE

Bentley was a small hamlet of Anglo-Saxon origin but today it comprises some large housing estates just to the west of the M6 near junction 10. During the seventeenth century Bentley Hall was home to the Lane family, whose name is still commemorated in the Lane Arms public house. In 1651 Jane Lane accompanied King Charles II, disguised as her groom, as he escaped to France via Boscobel and Bentley after the Battle of Worcester. Emmanuel church stands by the site of Bentley

Bentley from the south

Hall, which was demolished in 1929 after it had largely collapsed as a result of mining subsidence. The hall is commemorated by the cairn in a fenced enclosure next to the church.

The present parish was created in 1954 out of St. Giles, Willenhall, and the church was funded and erected by the family of Alfred Owen, head of the car and aircraft component manufacturers Rubery Owen. It was completed in 1956 to designs by the Wolverhampton firm of Lavender, Twentyman and Percy. Standing on a hill, the church is an imposing building of red brick with green copper low pitched roofs. It has a tall, plain square west tower with eight rectangular bell openings to each face. To the south the church hall of contemporary design projects at a right angle to the body of the church. The church is built to a traditional plan, but in an angular style reflective of the era of the Festival of Britain; the nave even has a clerestorey of tiny square windows on the south side which gives a traditional feel, whilst the long thin windows to the north aisle and chancel are more contemporary. The spacious, light interior is open to the roof and retains many of its original features and fittings, of which the organ in a chamber beside the chancel is of note.

BILSTON   ST. LEONARD, CHURCH STREET

The market town of Bilston expanded from the late eighteenth century with the development of iron smelting and manufacture by John 'iron-mad' Wilkinson, but became famous for the production of enamel and Japanned wares in the late nineteenth century. Today the centre retains several early buildings, including the timber-framed Greyhound Inn in High Street, and those grouped around the parish church.

Of Anglo-Saxon origin, the church was originally a chapelry of St. Peter, Wolverhampton, and a chantry of St. Leonard was recorded by 1458. A new church was built in 1733 incorporating the base of the medieval tower, and parts of this were further reused in the construction of the present church.

This is of 1825-6, when the church was rebuilt in brick by Francis Goodwin to a Classical design at a cost of over £8,000. Goodwin designed several churches for the Church Commission in the early nineteenth century, but St. Leonard's church is unusual as the majority are in the Gothic style.

The influence of Sir John Soane's church of St. John, Smith Square, in Westminster, can be seen in the exterior of this large box-shaped building, with its long round-headed windows and tower, square in plan but with canted corners rising from a square base above the west doorway. The tower has prominent clock faces, is roofed with a low dome and surmounted by a gilded wrought iron weather vane. The west doorway is sheltered by a porch with rustication, pilasters and an entablature. To the sides of the iron gates are iron pillars, perhaps meant to carry lamps, which are inscribed with Goodwin's name and the date of completion. At the east end the nave walls are canted and there is a short chancel.

Apart from rendering the exterior (which is strikingly painted white), the restoration completed in 1883 by Ewan Christian seems to have been confined largely to renewal and refurnishing of the interior, including the removal of the box pews. The interior is thus a wide and airy space, decorated in pink and white. The original galleries, with their slender piers above and below, remain to the west, north and south sides, and there is a fine vaulted plaster ceiling. The west gallery houses the organ of 1826 in a Classical style

Bilston, St. Leonard — the west front

Bilston, St. Leonard — the east end

23

case, whilst the area beneath was partitioned in 1982 to form a meeting space. Either side of the apse, which has a delightful coved ceiling, are Ionic columns which were flanked by twin pulpits until 1883. The lectern dates from 1877, when choir stalls were also set out at the east end of the nave, though these have since been removed. The font of 1673 has a fluted bowl. The stained glass of the east window shows the Crucifixion and was installed following the destruction of the previous window in a gas explosion in 1907.

Among the numerous monuments are tablets to Sarah Riley, who died in 1835, by William Weale, showing her portrait on a medallion, being carried to heaven by an angel, and Sarah Willim, who died in 1834, represented by a figure standing next to an altar. Mary Pearce, who died in 1836, is recorded as being descended from three children of Edward I. There are unusual ceramic tile tablets to Henry Nokes, Solon, Newton, Joseph and Obadiah Johnson, who died between 1863 and 1870, all aged under thirty. A further tablet commemorates over seven hundred victims of the cholera outbreak of 1832.

Outside in the churchyard are many fine nineteenth-century memorials, including some fine chest tombs, such as that to Job and Daniel Smith, and some unusual cast iron plates with initials as memorials. Goodwin also designed the elegant Georgian parsonage at the north-east corner of the church.

BILSTON   ST. LUKE, MARKET STREET

Built in 1852 by Thomas Johnson and Sons of Lichfield to serve an area of St. Leonard's parish, the church, built in the Early English style with lancet windows, had an aisled nave with west gallery, chancel, vestry and organ chamber. It was closed in 1969 and demolished in 1973.

BILSTON   ST. MARY, OXFORD STREET

The church was completed in 1829 to the design of Francis Goodwin. It is in complete contrast to St. Leonard's (see above) being an example of Goodwin's more usual Gothic architecture. The style is Early English with a large nave, at the east end of which is unusually placed an octagonal tower. This is crowned

Bilston, St. Mary from the south-east

with a parapet and pinnacles, and supported by low flying buttresses. The tower has lancet bell openings whilst the windows of the body of the church have cusped Y-shaped iron tracery. Buttresses are placed between the windows, and the entrances at the west and east ends. The corners are canted so the plan reflects that of an octagonal Wesleyan chapel of the eighteenth century. There are blind lancets on the short east and west walls, and the western apse.

The nave has three galleries supported by iron columns. The interior was restored in 1866 and 1890, and refurbished in 1919 when a Lady Chapel was established. Among several nineteenth-century memorial tablets is one to Joseph Meek who drowned in 1845 aged eight in the cistern of the adjacent school.

The churchyard is bounded from the road by fine iron railings and gates, probably locally produced and contemporary with the church. They also surround a granite drinking fountain of 1866, a memorial to Joseph Percival. As at St. Leonard's church, several unusual inscribed cast iron plates serve as memorials in the graveyard to the north of the church. Here, too, a simple slate recalls the death of Thomas Briggs, one of seven miners killed in a colliery explosion at West Bromwich in 1844. The inscription on the stone with its poetic *memento mori* erected by the St. Mary's Miners Guild recalls the dangers of life in the mines, the short life expectancy of the area, as well as the charity to be found here. A fine scrolled chest tomb by Cope commemorates Elizabeth Cooper who died in the cholera epidemic of 1849.

The poet Sir Henry Newbolt was born in Bilston in 1862 whilst his father was incumbent of this church. There is a commemorative plaque on the Vicarage. Newbolt is noted for his patriotic sea songs and verses, such as 'Drake's Drum'.

BLACKHEATH   ST. PAUL, LONG LANE

The town centre of this former mining community close to Rowley Regis has a mixture of late nineteenth- and twentieth-century buildings. It is dominated by the spire of the nineteenth-century former Methodist church, rather than by the towerless parish church. The latter is a large red brick building designed by the Worcester architect William Jeffrey Hopkins. Consecrated in 1869 it stands in a vast graveyard. It has an aisled nave with chancel, north and south transepts and north porch. The Early English style predominates with lancet windows. A single gable at the east end of each side of the clerestorey allows for a Decorated style window to throw more light into the nave by the pulpit and former screen. The planned tall west tower and spire were never built. Subsidence affected the church before it could be completed, and the small belfry which was erected instead has since been removed. The west porch and window in the arch intended for the tower date from 1934 and give a plain finish to the west wall of the church. This was made the main entrance in 1962 and the north porch was converted to a room.

The interior is brick faced with stone dressings to the nave arcades, which have pointed arches and circular brick piers with Early English style capitals. There is an octagonal font with carved panels. The altar has carved details and gilded decoration, whilst the Gothic reredos with statues of St. Peter and St. Paul is in memory of the first incumbent, F.R. Keatch. The white stone lectern is a pulpit from a church near Worcester. The organ was installed in 1875. The wrought iron screen was removed in 1971, whilst the stalls, pulpit and altar rails date from the early 1960s. Further reordering was undertaken in 2005. There is good stained glass in the south aisle windows, while the east window showing the Crucifixion commemorates the coronation of King Edward VII and Queen Alexandra in 1902.

BLAKENALL HEATH   CHRIST CHURCH, BLAKENALL LANE

There is a village-like centre to this suburb which grew up in the late nineteenth century to the south-east of Bloxwich, but today it is comprised mainly of large areas of local authority housing.

Christ Church was completed in 1870 to the design of Thomas Naden of Birmingham and has an aisled nave with clerestorey and porch. To the east the chancel has short transepts which serve as a vestry and organ chamber. The north-west tower was not finished until 1882 with battlements and pinnacles replacing Naden's intended broach spire. It is a limestone building mainly in the Early English style, of which the geometric tracery to the west window, the mouldings to the west doorway, quatrefoil windows and lancet bell openings are all characteristic. The west window tracery is reflected in that of the transepts and east window. Much restoration work was undertaken in 1998 and 2002. The Victorian vicarage was rebuilt in 1968.

The church has a spacious white-washed interior. The nave arcades have pointed arches on round columns with carved foliage to the capitals, and the similar style of the moulded chancel arch with its corbels continues the thirteenth-century style inside. There are fine king post roofs supported by carved corbels in the nave and chancel. The font is octagonal and fine Victorian tiles can be found throughout. There are Victorian choir stalls in the chancel by the high altar and reredos, which has panels painted by E. Warre in 1887. This was brought here from Edington Priory in Wiltshire in 1941 as a memorial to Amelia Wardle, mother of the then incumbent. The nave altar was installed during late twentieth-

Blakenall Heath, Christ Church from the south-west

century reordering. The light coloured stained glass in the east window shows the Crucifixion. The Lady Chapel in the south transept has glass in the south window showing Christ and the Apostles, above the war memorials. The north transept window shows Christ in Majesty. In the south aisle, the Wood memorial window of 2001 depicts Christ with children and the Wilkes memorial window shows the Virgin and Child with symbols of the life of Christ.

BLAKENALL HEATH   ST. AIDAN, HAWBUSH ROAD, FOREST ESTATE

The church and its associated centre were opened in 1964. They are of plain brick construction with sweeping roofs. Inside there is a traditional arrangement with the sanctuary area divided from the congregation by a semi-circular arch.

BLAKENALL HEATH   ST. CATHERINE & ST. CHAD, BEECHDALE ESTATE

The Roman Catholic church of St. Catherine was refurbished in 1995 to make it more suitable for a joint congregation following the amalgamation with the former mission church of St. Chad. This had been opened in 1958 in a separate building, but its congregation had worshipped at St. Catherine's from 1970. It is an octagonal building with low gables and full length windows to each face apart from the main entrance, which has a porch facing the road. There is a hall to the rear. The central fleche to the roof makes the building something of a local landmark.

BLAKENALL HEATH   ST. JOHN, LEAMORE

A mission church of Christ Church was opened in 1883 and rebuilt in 1931. However, it was demolished in 1967.

BLAKENALL HEATH

ST. MARY, COAL POOL

This was another mission church of Christ Church which was opened in 1892 in the southern part of this suburb. However, it was closed in 1965 and demolished five years later.

BLOXWICH

ALL SAINTS, ELMORE GREEN ROAD

Bloxwich lies to the north of Walsall, and is a settlement of Anglo-Saxon origin. The centre surrounding the parish church on the green still retains the feel of a large village or small town. Coalmining in the area led to much industrial growth from the early nineteenth century with awls, nails, needles and saddle slades being the principal products. Opposite the church stands Bloxwich Hall of 1830, which has recently been restored as offices, whilst parts of the Old Vicarage date back to the seventeenth century.

The medieval chapel of ease to Walsall parish church was originally dedicated to St. Thomas of Canterbury. It appears to have been founded in the

Bloxwich, All Saints from the south

fifteenth century, but Bloxwich did not become a separate parish until 1842. The medieval church was first rebuilt as a simple brick building in 1702. The present red sandstone church comprises a tall aisled nave with clerestorey and south porch, chancel with vestry, and west tower with a pyramidal roof set behind large parapets with gabled clockfaces. The tower is of the Early English style with lancet bell openings and is flanked to either side at the base by western extensions of the side aisles. The windows of the aisles reflect the Classical style layout of the windows of the eighteenth-century church, as the core of the nave and aisles date to a Georgian rebuilding of 1791-4 by Samuel Whitehouse. There are lancets at the lower level with Decorated style tracery to the upper, and then triple lancets above to the clerestorey of the nave. The chancel has lancet side windows with plate tracery to the east window. A short apsidal chancel had been added in 1833, but this was rebuilt when the church was reworked in the Gothic style by Davies and Middleton in 1875-7. The tower and porches were also added at this time.

Inside there is much exposed brickwork. Indeed the nave arcades have pointed arches in brick, supported by round red sandstone piers with carved foliage to the capitals. The north and south galleries survive with blind arcading to the fronts, supported by thin iron columns as can also be found at St. James' and St. John's churches in Dudley. There is a fine timber roof. The large brick chancel arch was filled with a wrought iron screen, until this was removed in the 1950s. The piscina, sedilia and font have carved details, whilst the pulpit is painted. Some windows contain nineteenth-century stained glass. The war memorial includes the name of the aspiring Bloxwich poet Harold Parry, killed in Belgium aged twenty-one in 1917.

To the south-east of the porch is the elegant sandstone churchyard cross of about 1700, with a tall shaft and ball finial. The lychgate was erected in 1936.

BLOXWICH · HOLY ASCENSION, LOWER FARM ESTATE

Holy Ascension was built in 1968 as a church and community hall in a plain modern style to serve this large development of local authority housing.

BLOXWICH · ST. JAMES, OLD LANE

This small brick mission church was erected in 1904. It is typical of such churches of the period with a plain exterior and lancet windows and presents a double porch to the street.

BLOXWICH · ST. PAUL, LITTLE BLOXWICH

A mission church from Christ Church, Blakenall Heath was erected here in 1876 but had closed by 1970.

BLOXWICH · ST. THOMAS, CRESSWELL CRESCENT, MOSSLEY

St. Thomas' church and hall was built in 1959 to serve the developing housing estates of the Mossley area to the west of Bloxwich station. It is a compact institute-type building of red brick, which has an attractive round-headed arch to the main entrance porch in the centre of the main frontage. Inside, the brick-faced hall opens into a three-sided sanctuary area with an attractive window in the shape of a cross behind the altar. The church replaces the mission church of St. John in Sneyd Lane, which had been erected in 1886.

BRADLEY · ST. MARTIN, KING STREET

South of Bilston town centre, Bradley was a medieval settlement which became increasingly industrialised following the establishment of John 'iron-mad' Wilkinson's ironworks here in 1758. The site of the factory became that of the John Wilkinson School, whilst around an arm of the canal are the sites of several other iron and steelworks. These, along with numerous coal pits, were the reason for the industrial development of both Bradley and Bilston.

There was a generous bequest from William Baldwin, of the prominent family of ironmasters, to fund the building of schools and a church in Bradley, and St. Martin's was designed by George Bidlake of Wolverhampton. The church was completed in 1868 and had a number of similar features to his church at Wollaston. It had a tall south-east tower supporting an impressive broach spire. The aisled nave and chancel with polygonal apse were in the Decorated style with elaborate tracery to the windows, particularly that at the west. The clerestorey was a series of attractive quatrefoils. The fine stained glass in the east window was by William Gardner of St. Helens in Lancashire. The church was closed and demolished in the 1970s, and the school buildings erected by Christopher Thomas in 1866 are now used for worship.

BRIERLEY HILL · ST. MICHAEL, CHURCH STREET

The name Brierley Hill aptly describes the setting of this town high up on the ridge to the south of Dudley with views towards Shropshire to the west, while 'Brierley' refers to the brambles on what was a wild area of common land. This part of the Dudley estates developed from the seventeenth century as a squatter settlement of ironworkers, and more extensively in the nineteenth century following the creation of the turnpike road, then the canals, and the opening of the railway. Major industries included the production of glassware at the famous Royal Brierley Crystal, (the buildings of which are being converted to residential use in North Street), along with butchery, bacon and pies at Marsh and Baxter, the site of which is now occupied by the shopping centre. The recent large development of Merry Hill just to the east of the town on the site of the vast Round Oak steelworks led to the decline of the town centre, along with others in this part of the Black Country. However, there is a good survival rate of Victorian buildings in and around the High Street, and the conservation and sensitive development of these is being actively encouraged.

Brierley Hill, St. Michael from the south-west

St. Michael stands on the crest of the hill to the west of the town centre. Its dominant position was challenged by the construction of a group of tower blocks in the 1960s on the opposite side of Church Street. However, the large red brick church still has a powerful presence standing alone in a large graveyard. A separate parish of Brierley Hill was created in 1865, but the church had been consecrated in 1765 as a chapel of ease in the parish of Kingswinford. The building could seat two hundred and fifty people and had a plain Georgian nave with a west gallery, short chancel and west tower, which survive as the core of the present building. By 1823 the side transepts had been added, and then in 1837 it was further extended to the east to provide a larger chancel. The base of the tower was altered to form a porch in 1885 as a memorial to Walter Marsh of Marsh and Baxter, and the tower recased and much rebuilt to its present form in 1900. The tower is substantial with Classical details to the openings and surmounted by a parapet with large pinnacles. The resultant building is massive and almost square in plan as a result of the various extensions. It has large pediments with dentil decoration to the side transepts. The windows on two tiers to the sides of the church are rectangular, almost domestic in appearance, whilst those to the tower and east end are round headed.

The interior is a delightful surprise. Whitewashed walls with Classical columns and galleries give the impression of a colonial or American Georgian church. Many changes were made to the Georgian interior in the nineteenth and twentieth centuries. These include the recent reordering in which some of the spaces under the galleries in the side aisle have been screened off with glass partitions. However, the overall effect is one of sympathetic and cumulative development. The box pews survived until 1900. Some of the earlier flooring and panelling on the south side were moved from the north aisle in 1935. The font is of 1900, and the lectern was given by the Marsh family in the same year. In 1994 the pulpit was moved and reduced in height. It was originally a three decker. The reredos and communion rails were installed in 1934. The organ of 1954 was destroyed in an arson attack in 2001. The bells were recast in 1899.

There is some fine stained glass. The east window shows the Crucifixion, Good Samaritan and Prodigal Son, whilst the coats of arms below show the elephant and castle as well as a raven. The window is a memorial to John and Hannah Corbett who are buried in the churchyard. They were the parents of John Corbett,

Brierley Hill, St. Michael — the interior looking east with, above, a detail of the east window

the Droitwich salt magnate and philanthropist, whose emblem, a raven, is commemorated in the Raven Hotel in that town. The Stone memorial window at the west end shows the Light of the World, whilst the Good Shepherd window is a memorial to Sarah Stone, wife of rector Josiah Stone. The Resurrection window at the east end of the south side is a memorial to the Weaver family. The window depicting 'Suffer little children' is a memorial to mining charter master John Gordon of 1913, whilst that in the middle on the south side is a memorial to those killed in the First World War. Some of this glass was moved to the south side from the north during the 1994 alterations.

There are many memorial tablets in the church, of which the earliest is in the chancel. It commemorates John Pidcock who died in 1791, and his wife Mary who is described as the heiress to Robert Honeybourne, a glassmaker. The incumbents of this church in the eighteenth century included a minor poet called Thomas Moss.

The font in the churchyard is from the former mission church at Delph. Nearby are several grave memorials of people connected with the glass industry here, such as the Stevens family on the south side. A memorial now lost recorded the hazards of industry in the nineteenth century; Cornelius and David Turner, John Thompson and Thomas Dimmock were all killed in a mining accident in 1815. Next to the gateway of 1765 on the south side is a memorial to the 'Brierley Hill Giant', George Lovett, who died in 1932 weighing forty-eight stone.

BRIERLEY HILL   GOOD SHEPHERD, DELPH

A small mission church was built in 1886 to serve what had been a small squatter settlement at Delph. It stood on Delph Road close to the flight of nine locks on the Stourbridge Canal, south of St. Michael's church. Plans to replace the church were postponed by the First and Second World Wars, and the building was demolished in 1952 after it had become unsafe through mining subsidence. It was a small brick church with the appearance of a school, and had a small spirelet. The font can be found in the churchyard of St. Michael's.

BRIERLEY HILL   HARTS HILL MISSION CHURCH

A former dissenting chapel near the site of Brierley Hill Ironworks was purchased as a mission to the northern end of the parish in 1838. From 1930 it became a chapel to St. Augustine, Holly Hall, Dudley. The small brick building was a Classical style non-conformist chapel with symmetrical frontage and bellcote over a pediment. It was demolished as unsafe in the late 1930s.

BROCKMOOR   ST. JOHN, HIGH STREET

This mixed residential and industrial area grew up on the high ground to the north-west of Brierley Hill in the nineteenth century. The locks and pools of Cockley Wharf form a pretty interlude to the buildings on Leys Road to the west of the church. The story of Brockmoor is closely interwoven with the industrial development of Brierley Hill, and it was the birthplace in 1863 of glassmaker Frederick Carder, who emigrated to found the Steuben glassworks in New York.

St. John is a Commissioners' type church built to designs by Thomas Smith in 1844-5. It is of purple brick with yellow brick dressings, and is in an unusual neo-Norman style with carved decoration and long round-headed windows. The wide nave has a bellcote above the doorway at the west end. There are north and south transepts and a short chancel with triple lights to the east window, stepped in the manner of the Early English style.

Brockmoor in its large churchyard

The spacious interior was much reordered in the late 1990s. However, there is an octagonal Victorian font resting on marble shafts with carved foliage capitals, and good late nineteenth-century stained glass in the east windows.

The church stands in the midst of a very large Black Country type churchyard with numerous memorials of the nineteenth and twentieth centuries. The main entrance is through a lychgate in the same neo-Norman style as the church.

BROWNHILLS   ST. JAMES, CHURCH ROAD

The name Brownhills has only been used since the eighteenth century. It is now a substantial mining town to the north of Walsall towards Cannock Chase. The site of the town was the commons of Ogley Hay, part of the parish of Norton Canes, which became developed as the need for coal encouraged mining of the deeper seams of the Cannock coalfield which lay here, and in 1838 a new parish was created. Further rapid growth took place after the South Staffordshire Railway was opened in 1850, and in 1877 Brownhills became an urban district. Mining declined in the twentieth century but is celebrated by the giant statue of a miner known as the 'Brownhills Colossus' by John McKenna, which was erected at the north end of High Street in 2006.

The church was built in 1851, and the parish is still known as Brownhills with Ogley Hay. It lies to the north-east of the High Street in a churchyard with mature trees that forms a square in the residential streets. It is of brown sandstone and has a wide nave with transepts, chancel with organ chamber, and a slender tower built into the west end of the nave with a small spire rising from gables above the belfry. The doorways and windows including several lancets are of the Early English and Decorated styles. The architect was George Thomas Robinson who also designed St. Luke, Wolverhampton and cost over £3,000. Robinson's west porch now leads to a meeting room, added in 1990.

Brownhills from the south-east

The interior is white with stone dressings. Many of the fittings date from the later nineteenth century. The fine Early English style chancel arch is filled by a contemporary screen with plate tracery details. There is good early twentieth-century stained glass in the west window.

BUSHBURY   ST. MARY

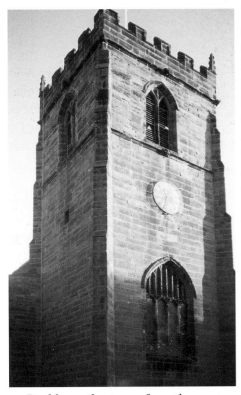

Bushbury, the tower from the west

The medieval church at Bushbury stands on the edge of the urban area of Wolverhampton, next to the Georgian Bushbury Hall and with green space to the north. It is not far from the well-known Moseley Old Hall, a timber-framed house, now encased in blue brick. Here King Charles II stayed with the Whitgreave family as he fled to France after the Battle of Worcester in 1651, disguised as a servant. From here he went to Bentley near Walsall. Another large house, Fallings Park, gives its name to the district to the south which links it to Wolverhampton, and was laid out as a garden suburb in 1907. Today, however, it is later twentieth-century housing which predominates at Bushbury.

The Anglo-Saxon origins of the church site are evident in the survival of the circular base of a tenth- or eleventh-century cross to the south of the church, similar to that at Penn. Could this base have carried a shaft like that at St. Peter, Wolverhampton? The fine red sandstone church was heavily restored in the mid nineteenth century by Edward Banks, but much remains from the fourteenth century in the fabric. There is a good example of a fifteenth-century Staffordshire type Perpendicular tower at the west end with battlements, pinnacles, bell openings and large west window. The height of the taller chancel at the east end is accentuated by the sloping site. It is a fine Decorated structure with impressive side windows and a nineteenth-century east window. The nave has aisles, that to the south having a separate roof structure, with Decorated east and west windows, as well as nineteenth-century windows to the south wall. The south aisle is continued to the south-east of the chancel by a side chapel. There is a nineteenth-century gabled porch. The north aisle has mainly nineteenth-century windows, but at the east end is the reconstructed north chapel in which is reset a simple and apparently Norman doorway with round arch and tympanum.

The many medieval features to the wide interior include a fifteenth-century hammerbeam roof to the chancel. The sedilia and piscina on the south side in the chancel are fourteenth-century Decorated, as is probably the Easter Sepulchre on the north. The nave arcades

Bushbury, seen across the churchyard

33

appear Perpendicular with octagonal piers and carry a nineteenth-century roof. At the west end the fine tower arch is also Perpendicular. Banks' arches with ogees lead to the vestry and organ loft. The font is Norman but was retooled in the sixteenth century with carved leaves and a figure, possibly Christ with his hand raised in blessing. Most furnishings date to Banks' restoration, when the box pews and galleries filling the north and south aisles were replaced. The reredos with creed and commandment boards is early nineteenth century. The richly carved stone pulpit and lectern were given in 1878 by John Moreton. There are some fragments of fourteenth-century stained glass, with the figure of a priest and a Virgin with Child in the chancel, as well as Christ in Majesty in the south aisle. The nineteenth-century glass includes the east window designed by Charles Winton, as well as work by Powell and Ward and Hughes.

Bushbury, Saxon cross base

The Easter Sepulchre houses a worn fourteenth-century effigy of a priest, possibly Hugh de Byshbury, and there are a number of seventeenth-century incised slabs at the east end of the church. There are several seventeenth- and eighteenth-century wall tablets to local families including the Goughs, and a brass plate to Thomas Leacroft. Among the memorials to the Whitgreave family of Moseley Old Hall is a tablet to Thomas Whitgreave who assisted with the escape of King Charles II. The south-east chapel, also known as the Hordern Chapel, contains memorials to members of that family. One of the six bells dates from 1593, whilst the plate includes a fourteenth-century paten. A church service of 1825 that is described by George Borrow in *Romany Rye* has long been believed to have been held at this church, but recent research suggests that the description is more likely to be of Madeley in north Staffordshire.

To the west of the porch is a grave memorial slab of about 1400, with a carved cross and shield. There are several good seventeenth-, eighteenth- and early nineteenth-century gravestones around the south side of the church, including a good survival of some small rectangular headstones of about 1800, some of which are just carved with initials. These are an uncommon survival of more ordinary memorials of that date, as most have since been forgotten and lost. To the south of the church is the headstone to John Carter, a Roman Catholic priest who died in 1803, with a carved Calvary cross above a long inscription. This is a testament to the toleration extended to Catholics in this area, of which the most significant evidence is the church of St. Peter and St. Paul at Giffard House, Wolverhampton, which dates to 1727, long before Roman Catholic emancipation.

Bushbury, medieval tomb slab

CLAYHANGER   HOLY TRINITY, CHURCH STREET

This coalmining village with a large brickworks developed in the nineteenth century on an area of fields to the south-west of Brownhills.

A mission church from Walsall Wood was founded here in 1879. The church, designed by D. Shenton Hill of Birmingham, was a rendered brick building with a bellcote, which was demolished in the 1970s. Since 2000 the congregation has met in the modern school and church building on the site.

COSELEY   CHRIST CHURCH, CHURCH ROAD

Coseley today is at the north-eastern tip of the diocese of Worcester, yet this is the heart of the Black Country. It was a small village until the nineteenth century, when there were more than fifty coal pits in the parish. As well as being one of the centres for nailmaking, significant ironworks, such as Cannon were also located here. Until 1830 there was no church in Coseley other than non-conformist chapels, and the village was in the parish of Sedgley.

Christ Church stands at the heart of the older settlement and is one of the group of churches built by public subscription and through the Commissioners on land given by the Earl of Dudley. The architect was Thomas Lee, and building was completed in 1830. It is faced in brown sandstone which has weathered to black, and in design is typical of the Commissioners' type churches. The slender west tower has pairs of long lancet bell openings to each face and is crowned with a parapet and four large pinnacles to the corners with four smaller ones to the centre of each face. The large, wide nave and short chancel have a low pitched roof, also with parapets and pinnacles. The windows are long Early English style lancets to the sides, with a large Decorated style window at the east end. The church is very similar in appearance to St. Andrew, Netherton.

The church was restored in 1866 when new chancel furnishings were introduced. The Lady Chapel is the work of Birmingham architect, A.T. Butler, undertaken in 1910. Many of the later nineteenth-century furnishings, including the screen, were installed during the incumbency from 1883 to 1912 of William Spencer, who used his private means to further embellish the church and even installed a short-lived wind turbine system to generate electricity to provide light. The stained glass including that in the east window also dates from this period. There is a memorial to Thomas Barrett, a private in the South Staffordshire Regiment who was awarded the Victoria Cross after his death in 1917, which occurred when helping to prevent a German advance near Ypres. Several floor tiles are also inscribed with the names of former choristers including those who were killed in the First World War.

Coseley, Christ Church from the south

Coseley, some of the tombs in Christ Church graveyard

The Victorian bells were recast in 1936. The large graveyard with mature trees contains a number of significant nineteenth- and twentieth-century grave memorials, including the impressive war memorial of 1920 at the east end of the church.

COSELEY ST. CHAD, OAK STREET

This church, serving the western part of Coseley, is located on the edge of Swan Village by the Silver Jubilee Park and in a prominent location by the Wolverhampton New Road. Nearby in Oak Street stands the tower of a windmill now in residential use. Whilst the Earl of Dudley gave the land for the site, the cost of building the new church, which was almost completed by 1883 for just under £4,000, was mostly funded by the parish of St. Mary Abbots at Kensington, London. This was the previous parish of William Dalrymple Maclagan, Bishop of Lichfield who was instrumental in the establishment of this church, which replaced a small mission chapel in a poor industrial area around Claycroft mine.

This large red brick building has an aisled nave and chancel and was designed by Thomas Henry Fleeming. Until 1967 there was a bell turret with small spire over the east end of the nave. There is a narthex at the west end, whilst to the south of the chancel are vestries and a hall. The style is plain Romanesque with rounded heads to the windows though the east window has Decorated style tracery. The glass in the east window is a Second World War memorial, and there is good late nineteenth- and early twentieth-century glass in several side windows.

COSELEY ST. AIDAN, DAISY BANK

A mission church from Christ Church was founded at Daisy Bank in the 1880s, but subsequently closed.

COSELEY ST. OSWALD, LADYMOOR

This simple Tudor style mission hall building was erected in the 1880s close to Ettingshall, and closed in the late twentieth century.

COSELEY ST. CUTHBERT, WALLBROOK

Wallbrook lies to the east of the railway close to Tipton. This mission church of 1896 from Christ Church was closed in 2004.

CRADLEY

ST. PETER, COLLEY LANE

The medieval settlement of Cradley lay on the southern slopes of the steep-sided valley of the River Stour at the north end of the large parish of Halesowen. Here it is believed that Dud Dudley, illegitimate son of the Earl of Dudley, conducted experiments using coal rather than the dwindling supplies of wood to smelt iron in the mid seventeenth century. Together with Cradley Heath, Cradley developed as a key location for the manufacture of chains. Both chain- and nailmaking thrived here up until the early twentieth century. In lasting tribute to these industries, Jones and Lloyd's chainmakers' workshop was relocated

Cradley, St. Peter from the south-west

from Cradley to Avoncroft Museum of Buildings near Bromsgrove in 1970. The Attwood family were one of the principal landowners and ironmasters, and Thomas Attwood became member of Parliament for Birmingham and supporter of the Reform Act of 1832. Their large Georgian Gothic house, Corngreaves Hall, stands derelict awaiting renovation. William Caslon, one of the first typeset makers in England, was born in Cradley in 1693 and trained as a gunmaker. Caslon type became almost as well known as Baskerville. Cradley is also reputed to be where Staffordshire Bull Terrier dogs were first bred for bull-baiting in the early twentieth century.

Cradley, St. Peter from the north-east showing the former Countess Huntingdon chapel, now the nave

Non-conformity was strong in the eighteenth and nineteenth centuries in this remote part of Halesowen. Nearby in Park Lane is a remarkable survival of a Unitarian chapel with its tower and short spire that retains much of an earlier structure of 1796. There are also two Victorian ragged school chapels still in use at High Town and Two Gates. Closer to St. Peter's church, large Methodist and Baptist churches stood on the steep bank of Colley Lane. Their sites are still identifiable as the graveyard of the Methodist church, with mature trees and some fragments of the steps to the entrance of the Baptist church, remains by a car park. The present Baptist church is in the former school building opposite the gateway to St. Peter's churchyard in Church Road.

The early history of St. Peter's is as a non-conformist church. It began as an independent congregational society and its origins are similar to those of St. Thomas, Stourbridge. Here, Thomas Best of Stourbridge became a member of the Countess of Huntingdon's Connexion and was ordained minister in 1784 when he came to Cradley. In 1786 he purchased a Wesleyan chapel in Butchers Lane. Some four years later he demolished this and reused the materials in the construction of this building, the 'Cradley Chapel', which opened in 1791 together with a school for thirty girls and thirty boys. The architect of the chapel was Mark Jones, whose death in 1833 is commemorated by a memorial which can be seen by the entrance to the churchyard. This building with box pews and galleries forms the nave of the present church, with canted corners at the east end.

When the independent society ran into financial difficulties, Best thought that Parliament would come to the rescue if it became part of the established church. To the surprise and dismay of the congregation Best became a Church of England minister in 1798, and was made perpetual curate of Cradley in the gift of Lord Lyttleton, the patron of Halesowen. Those not wishing to support the change left to worship elsewhere, but following Best's death in 1821 the church continued to grow, and a separate parish was created in 1841. However, it did not receive its dedication to St. Peter until 1898. The church was restored in 1874-5 when the tower was added at the east end, designed by Bromsgrove architect John Cotton and built by the local firm Nelson and Bloomer. The tower forms a contrast to the body of the church with its lancet bell openings and Gothic Revival detailing. It was originally crowned above the existing traceried parapet by a short spire with gables, sometimes known as the 'pepperpot'. However, in 1933 considerable alterations were made to the church partly as a result of mining subsidence, and the 'pepperpot' was removed as the top of the tower was leaning an alarming sixteen inches out of true. At the same time new side entrances were made to the church and the present chancel with its three-sided apse was erected at the west end. It has round-headed windows in groups of three. The result is that this extraordinary church is orientated east to west, yet the chancel is at the opposite end to that expected.

The interior has been substantially altered since the eighteenth century. There are still galleries, but new nave furnishings were provided by the Hingley family in the late nineteenth century to replace the box pews. The Gray and Davison organ was given in 1874 by Mrs. James Wood Aston, who also acquired the peal of eight bells from the Vienna Exhibition of the previous year. Stained glass includes a memorial window to Ann Hingley, who died in 1871, erected by Noah Hingley, whose family had one of the most important chain manufacturing companies in the area. The window was relocated in the 1933 refurbishment to above the entrance to the vestry. A number of interesting memorial tablets include those to the founder Thomas Best and incumbent James Hesselgrove Thompson, who oversaw the 1874-5 restoration.

The graveyard covers twenty-four acres across the hillside, having been expanded four times since the eighteenth century.

CRADLEY   ST. KATHERINE, BEECHER STREET

This was the daughter church to St. Peter erected in 1909 to serve the southern end of the parish. J.T. Meredith of Kidderminster was the architect of this Early English style brick building, the east end of which was never completed. The church closed in the 1990s.

CRADLEY   GOOD SHEPHERD, LYDE GREEN

A small, typical timber mission church with hall, clad in corrugated iron, was erected here in 1909. It had a short spire to the bellcote at the west end, whilst the interior was furnished in the Gothic style. The church was destroyed by fire in 1958 and not rebuilt.

CRADLEY HEATH   ST. LUKE, UPPER HIGH STREET, REDDALL HILL

To the north of Cradley and the River Stour, Cradley Heath was in the ancient parish of Rowley Regis and developed as another centre for chainmaking in the nineteenth century. Much of the character of Cradley Heath has been lost in very recent times. The north side of the High Street has been largely demolished to make way for a supermarket, whilst significant ecclesiastical losses include the large Baptist chapel at Five Ways, the western crossroads, and the fine Arts and Crafts Methodist Church in Graingers Lane, though some of the stained glass windows by Henry Payne were saved.

St. Luke's church stands amongst mature trees in a churchyard by the crossroads at the east end of the High Street. It is easily missed as it is a rather low building and has no tower. The exterior is rendered and plain with lancet windows in an Early English style. The arcaded western portal around three doorways and the three-light west window were accompanied by a pair of tall pinnacles to make a grand west front similar to that at St. Peter, Upper Gornal. The pinnacles were taken down in 1912. The nave is of 1847 by William Bourne, though the stone apsidal chancel was added in 1878 by John Cotton, who also added the tower to St. Peter, Cradley. The interior fittings are mainly late nineteenth century, some of them from the time of Cotton's refurbishment of the church. The reredos was installed to commemorate Queen Victoria's diamond jubilee of 1897. There are several early twentieth-century stained glass windows. The west end has recently been reordered.

Much of the extensive graveyard lies to the south east of the church. Within it the war memorial is by the Bromsgrove Guild.

DARBY END   ST. PETER, ST. PETER'S ROAD

It is easy to miss this church which stands beside the canal bridge on St. Peter's Road close to the former mines and ironworkings of Bumble Hole. The Dudley Canal enters the five thousand yards of Netherton Tunnel a short distance to the east of the church by the picturesque ruins of Cobb's Engine House of 1831, which housed a beam engine used to pump over a million litres of water each day from the coalmines deep below into the canal. Nearby Baptist End records the presence of a dissenting congregation here from the 1650s.

The church is combined with the hall in a long, plain, red brick building with a steep pitched roof. The open bellcote at the east end denotes the church, which was built between 1910 and 1913 by public subscription to replace a mission church in the parish of St. Andrew, Netherton. The mission church met in the day school, using the school furniture for worship until new schools were built in 1888. The choir stalls from this church are in the present building which became a parish church in 1986.

DARLASTON   ST. LAWRENCE, CHURCH STREET

This ancient settlement remained little more than a village until the eighteenth century when coalmining was developed and ironworking began. The main products were gun locks, which were supplied to Birmingham's gun quarter, together with nuts and bolts. Many small firms were absorbed into Guest, Keen and Nettlefold (GKN) during the nineteenth and twentieth centuries. Rubery Owen also became important producers of components for bicycles, vehicles and aircraft. The town developed very quickly during the nineteenth century and became well known both for its iron foundries and its poor living conditions. Nevertheless, today a number of good Georgian buildings remain in the centre, although there has also been considerable twentieth-century redevelopment with the shopping centre and inner bypass, St. Lawrence Way.

The church stands at the north end of King Street, its spire being the main landmark in the town centre. There has been a church on this site since at least the twelfth century. In 1606 the timber belfry was rebuilt in stone, but the church was destroyed by fire in the early eighteenth century and rebuilt. In 1721 a new north aisle was added in brick and then the nave itself was rebuilt in brick in 1807. This was a plain Classical structure and had windows with cast iron frames which was replaced by the present building.

The church today is of 1871-2 by Archibald Paul Brevitt. It is an impressive red sandstone building with a west tower and spire, nave with aisles and clerestorey, north and south transepts and chancel. The tower and spire are very fine. The core of the tower dates from the Georgian rebuilding. Above the Decorated style bell openings, the traceried parapets house the clock faces of 1907 and are crowned with pinnacles, behind which the spire rises from an integral octagonal corona. This is possibly based on Patrington church in Yorkshire, and similar to the idea used by Julius Alfred Chatwin at St. Augustine, Edgbaston. At the west ends of the aisles are lean-to porches, but the aisles are tall and have two-tiered windows on five bays. In appearance it is similar to All Saints, Bloxwich. There is a Decorated style rose window to the south transept, whilst the east window

Darlaston, St. Lawrence from the south

has plate tracery. There is a Tudor style hall of 1931 to the west of the church.

The nave arcades have pointed Gothic arches on iron columns with spiral decoration, unusual for a church of this date. North and south galleries survive with arcaded decoration to the fronts. The chancel arch is of the early Decorated style with shafts carried by corbels carved with angels to the sides, and there is a similar smaller arch to the north chapel. There are impressive timber roofs throughout.

There are several memorial tablets including early nineteenth-century ones from the previous church. The pulpit is painted and has unusual cast iron steps. The chancel furnishings date from the early twentieth century. The stained glass in the east window commemorates vicar Joseph Hugill who died in 1842, and Brevitt the architect, who died in the year that the church was rebuilt, is commemorated in another window. At the west end is a large wall painting showing the Crucifixion. The tower contains eight bells.

DARLASTON   ALL SAINTS, WALSALL STREET

The parish was established in 1872 with the erection of this church as a memorial to Samuel Mills of Darlaston House and Whitton in Shropshire. He was the proprietor of Bills and Mills, one of the largest ironworks in the area. The church was built in the Early English style to the design of George Edmund Street and was constructed in brick with an aisled nave with bellcote at the west end, chancel and vestry.

The organ was by Bryceson and Morton. One window contained stained glass designed by Edward Burne-Jones and made by William Morris. However, the building had the misfortune to be the only church in Lichfield diocese to be totally destroyed during the Second World War. On 31 July 1942 it was hit by a bomb targeting the nearby factory of Guest, Keen and Nettlefold, leaving a crater fifty feet deep.

In 1952 a new church was erected on the site by Lavender, Smith and Twentyman. It is a large brick building, traditional in plan, with nave and chancel under a gently curving roof. The two bells are in a large open belfry placed on the south side at the division of nave and chancel, and to the east is a low chapel with apsidal end, whilst entry is gained through a porch at the south-west corner.

The light interior has contemporary furnishings with a large pulpit. The sanctuary is defined by a coffered ceiling. The style is similar to the contemporary church by the same architects at nearby Bentley.

DARLASTON   ST. GEORGE, THE GREEN

In 1844 a new parish was created for the growing population at the northern end of St. Lawrence parish. The congregation worshipped in the Sunday school building until 1852, when the new church was opened. It was an attractive building in the Early English style by Thomas Johnson of Lichfield with aisled nave, chancel and vestry, and a short tower with a conical roof at the north-west corner. At the west end of the nave was originally a substantial gallery, whilst the east window was a memorial of 1884 to Samuel Rubery of Rubery Owen. It was extended in 1885 and 1890, but closed in 1974 before being demolished the following year. Apparently some of the carvings were reused as garden ornaments in Wombourne, Staffordshire and Tenbury Wells, Worcestershire. The site of the church is now a garden, where there is a statue of St. George by Thomas Wright, erected in 1959 as a memorial to longstanding churchwarden, George Garrington.

DUDLEY   THE PRIORY OF ST. JAMES, THE BROADWAY

Dudley is a most dramatically situated town on top of a limestone ridge at heights of over 200 metres with views out across the Black Country and into Shropshire, Worcestershire and Staffordshire. Rich mineral deposits gave the town prosperity throughout its history. Coalmining, basalt and limestone quarrying, as well as glassmaking and ironworking were industries which expanded with the arrival of the canals in the 1780s and then the railway in 1850. Between 1801 and 1851 the population rose from about 10,000 to 37,000. Goods such as nails, anvils, vices, bedsteads, postboxes, iron parts for bridges and stations were made here. Life expectancy was short as a result of dire public health. Slum clearance improved the situation; it has however also led to the loss of many historic buildings. Having had a market since the twelfth century, Dudley assumed importance as a retail centre in the Victorian era, but the town has been fighting decline since the creation of Merry Hill Shopping Centre in the 1980s. In addition, the decline of its manufacturing base has been widespread during the twentieth century.

Administratively, Dudley has been the centre of the metropolitan borough since 1974, but it previously occupied the unusual position of being an outlying part of Worcestershire. There had been many detached parts of counties until reorganisations in the early twentieth century, but Dudley was a late survival. Historically this was complex, as the castle was in Staffordshire, whilst the parish churches have always been in the diocese of Worcester, and the priory was under the jurisdiction of the Bishop of Lichfield. Even today the ruins of the Norman castle dominate the town and particularly represent the power and influence of the Dudley family and their successors the Wards in the area through its late medieval and post-medieval history. The buildings in the bailey were rebuilt on a grand scale in the sixteenth century by the Duke of Northumberland, and although damaged during the Civil War only finally went into decline after the family subsequently moved to Himley Hall. After being used as a site for manufacturing for some years the castle was destroyed by fire in 1750. By the time of his death in 1823, the eighth Lord Ward had laid out the grounds as a pleasure garden, and the spectacular caverns from the mining of limestone beneath were later used for lavish entertainments. In 1937 the grounds were opened as the zoo with remarkable animal buildings by Tecton, which are similar to their previous work at Regent's Park, London.

The castle was held by William FitzAnsculf from the Norman Conquest, but by the twelfth century had passed to the Pagenals. Gervase de Pagenal was the most powerful lord in the area and it was he who founded the priory some time between 1149 and 1160. In the museum there is a fragment of carving from a tympanum of this date, which may be part of a scene showing St. Michael and a dragon, similar to Kingswinford. However, building was eventually completed through the patronage of the Somery family during the thirteenth century. Medieval tiles bearing their arms have been excavated in the chancel of the church. The priory remained small, frequently with less than four monks of the Cluniac order, and was subject to the rule of the important Cluniac priory at Much Wenlock, Shropshire.

Much in the shadow of the castle, the history of Dudley Priory was uneventful until it was dissolved in 1539. The surviving remains from the cruciform church include much of the aisleless Early English nave with lancet windows in the north wall and Decorated south and west windows and doorway. The south transept is possibly late Norman with an eastern arch which perhaps formerly opened into an apse, similar to that still found at Tewkesbury Abbey, but now leading into the expanded Perpendicular south-east

chapel with the remains of traceried windows and image niches. This is parallel to the chancel, the remains of which also appear to be Early English. Of the monastic buildings which were arranged around a cloister to the north of the nave, walls of the western range survive, along with parts of the Norman chapter house and reredorter in the eastern range. Above this was the dormitory which was accessed by a spiral stair, part of which can be seen leading from the north transept of the church.

Dudley Priory from the south-east

After the Dissolution the site passed to Sir John Dudley. By the end of the eighteenth century it was used as a tannery, and then for making thread, before fire irons were manufactured here leading to the construction of a kiln in the western range. With the building of the Tudor style mansion Priory Hall in 1825, the ruins were cleared of industrial remains and incorporated into the landscape park. However, the main carriageway approach was driven through the ruins, destroying much of the eastern

Dudley Priory from the south-west

end of the church. Since 1926 Priory Hall and the ruins have been owned by the local authority. A large stone coffin possibly from the grave of one of the Somery patrons was found on the site and is preserved in Priory Hall. Today the house serves as the registry office.

DUDLEY ST. EDMUND KING AND MARTYR, CASTLE STREET

St. Edmund, known locally as Bottom Church, is one of two churches of medieval origin in the town. The dedication to the ninth-century king of East Anglia suggests an Anglo-Saxon foundation, but first mention of the church is in a charter of 1180, when with St. Thomas it was given by Gervase de Pagenal as an endowment to the newly founded priory. The first recorded vicar was John de Clon in 1287.

The church is prominently positioned at the north end of the Market Place, close to the entrance to the Castle. The Georgian and Victorian buildings across the street give a sense of the scale of the prosperous market town. Little is known of the appearance of the medieval church, which was much rebuilt in the fifteenth and sixteenth centuries. However, it has been suggested that it was considerably larger than the present building. In 1646, during the Civil War, the church was demolished and the area around it cleared by Colonel Thomas Leveson, the Royalist governor of the castle, to prevent it being used as a shelter by Parliamentarian forces when the castle was put under siege. Only one simple memorial tablet to Frances Beaumont of 1644 and the grave of Lady Honor Dudley, now marked by a brass plaque, have survived from the earlier church.

Whilst St. Edmund remained in ruins services were held at St. Thomas, which took on the role of parish church from 1646, until the present church was erected in 1724 through the patronage of Richard and George Bradley. The architect is believed to have been Thomas Archer, whose finest work in the region is St. Philip's church (now cathedral), Birmingham. The church remained a chapel of ease to St. Thomas until it became a parish church once again in 1844. It is a stately Classical building of red brick with stone dressings, and has an aisled nave and long chancel with south organ chamber and vestry. The tall tower is central to the west front, and has pinnacles and parapet above round-headed bell openings. Below, the three round-headed west doorways have curved pediments. The west ends of the side aisles were altered to form

Dudley, St. Edmund from the southeast (top) and the west front (lower)

43

porches in the early nineteenth century and above the side doorways are oval windows. Over the main entrance a single ornamented curved pediment rests above a pair of blind round-headed niches, which may have been designed to take statues. The pediment is repeated to the south and north sides of the tower and above are glazed clock faces. The north and south walls of the aisles have four large round-arched windows between pilasters beneath a plain parapet, and there are further niches to the sides of the chancel. During the late eighteenth and early nineteenth centuries the west porch under the tower was used as the vestry before the present vestry was added in 1849. In 1864 there was a major restoration, when wooden

Dudley, St. Edmund showing the external niches to the chancel

tracery was inserted in the side windows. The present Venetian style east window is a twentieth-century replacement of the previous larger Victorian Gothic fenestration.

The interior of the nave is the same height as the side aisles, but divided from them by four bay arcades with round arches. The galleries were added in the early nineteenth century. Although the furnishings were much changed in the nineteenth and twentieth centuries, the pews, pulpit and galleries all contain eighteenth-century woodwork. The present pulpit was the gift of the Earl of Dudley in 1868. The fine tower screen has round arched doorways and Ionic pilasters. The organ case is made up with parts of the eighteenth century reredos. The floor has Minton tiles of 1864, at which date the east end was reordered and the organ moved from the gallery to an organ chamber. The long chancel now culminates in a high reredos behind the altar. There is much nineteenth- and early twentieth-century stained glass. The fine Christ in Majesty above the altar replaces a larger stained glass window of the Annunciation to the Shepherds by William Wailes of about 1870. Today the church is of the Anglo-Catholic tradition and so contains many remarkable statues of saints including St. Edmund, and a relic of the tree on which he was martyred.

There are numerous memorial tablets including those to the rebuilder George Bradley. One depicts a female figure standing by an urn. This commemorates Edward Dixon who died in 1806 and is by Thomas King of Bath. Another, by Peter Hollins of Birmingham, shows a woman seated by an urn and a medallion with the head of Thomas Badger who died in 1856.

A bell in the tower is of 1778, whilst the graveyard to the south of the church contains many fine eighteenth- and nineteenth-century memorials. To the north-west is an impressive statue of the first Earl of Dudley of 1888 by Charles Bell Birch.

DUDLEY   ST. THOMAS, HIGH STREET

Top Church, to use its local name, stands at the southern end of the High Street at a height of almost 250 metres above sea level, and its spire of 175 feet is a familiar landmark which is visible for miles around. The stonework was cleaned and the top of the spire rebuilt during the 1990s restoration and so the church is now an attractive pale grey colour. The surroundings today are twentieth-century shops which give a different appearance to the area from the elegant Georgian streetscapes depicted in paintings. To get a flavour of the pre-twentieth-century Dudley town centre now requires a visit to nearby Priory Street or Wolverhampton Street. As a result of road widening, the west end of the church stands right on the street and it is best approached via the gardens from the Inhedge for a clear view of the tower and spire.

Like St. Edmund's, this church was recorded in the twelfth century as in the gift of the priory. It is a site of ancient human activity, as was proven by the discovery of pre-Christian, possibly Iron Age, burials in part of the churchyard during recent restoration works. The medieval church consisted of a west tower, nave, south aisle and chancel, which had been refashioned during the seventeenth and eighteenth centuries with Classical windows and doorway. The church served as the parish church to the whole town until St. Edmund's was rebuilt in 1724 following its destruction in the Civil War.

The driving force for a new building at St. Thomas came in 1813 with the arrival of an evangelical vicar, Luke Booker, and an Act of Parliament to rebuild the church was passed in 1815. It had cost £24,000 by the time it was opened in 1818. The architect was William Brooks, who created a large Perpendicular aisled nave with short chancel and west tower with spire. The church represents a use of Gothic reminiscent of Francis Hiorn's church at Tetbury in Gloucestershire of thirty years earlier, and it has a design reflecting the uniform symmetry of other Georgian and early nineteenth-century churches. The plan is unusual in that the aisles widen out to form gabled transepts in the centres, with canted bays to east and west giving the church an almost octagonal shape in the style of many Wesleyan chapels of the period. This may reflect Brooks' non-conformist roots. The Perpendicular style is emphasised through a wealth of battlements and pinnacles

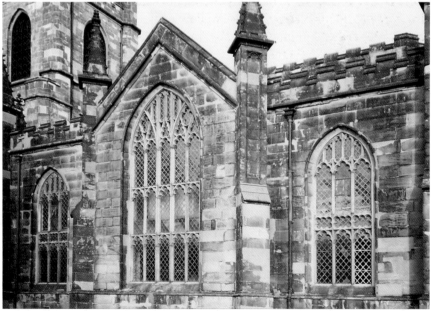

*Dudley, St. Thomas from the south-east (top)
and a detail of the south side*

to the parapets, as well as through the window tracery, which is in fact of ironwork. The simple vestries were added to the east end in 1951.

A small plain medieval crypt survives from the previous church, hidden from view beneath the east end. Access to the interior of Brooks' church is through the porch under the tower. The nave is divided from the aisles by slender piers and has smaller canted bays at the corners. The ceiling was replaced in the twentieth century and is a plaster tierceron vault without bosses. All three galleries survive to the south, north and west. The high three decker pulpit incorporates parts of the seventeenth-century one given to the previous church by ironmaster Richard Foley. However, to create space for the choir, it was lowered and moved from the commanding central position from which Booker delivered his powerful sermons. The box pews were also remodelled, and although the organ which fills the west gallery has been altered, it contains much from the original instrument by Thomas Elliot of 1819.

Most of the nineteenth-century stained glass was destroyed when a bomb fell nearby during the Second World War. However, the short chancel is dominated by the remarkable painted glass east window with its golden brown Ascension, in the style of Raphael, by Joseph Blackler of Stourbridge of 1821. Either side are cast iron commandment tables, with figures of Faith and Hope on the side walls above in canopied niches. The heavily carved reredos shows the Confession of St. Thomas. The sculpture of the Virgin was created

Dudley, St. Thomas — the east end

Dudley, St. Thomas — the east window

for the new Lady Chapel in 1977 by Arthur Rodley of Liverpool. The lavish Gothic font with carved baptism scenes has a tall wooden cover with saints' figures to the corners. It was bought by the Earl of Dudley at the Paris Exhibition of 1867, when he also acquired the extraordinary Italianate fountain for the Market Place. Both pieces are by James Forsyth, the Worcester sculptor of the great Perseus fountain at Witley Court.

A chalice and paten date from 1571 and the peal of ten bells dates from 1818. The graveyard has a good collection of eighteenth- and nineteenth-century memorials. The former vicarage to the east replaced a seventeenth-century building in the 1920s.

DUDLEY ST. AUGUSTINE, HALLCHURCH ROAD, HOLLY HALL

The parish of St. Augustine was formed out of St. Thomas in 1884 to serve the Holly Hall and Woodside area. The church, designed by Harry Drinkwater of Oxford, has a large aisled nave, with chancel, north organ chamber and vestry and south chapel. It is all in brick with stone dressings in the Early English and Decorated styles with mainly lancet windows. There is a baptistery at the west end with side porches. One proposed design shows a large south-western tower and spire, but no such tower was ever built and the church has a simple bellcote between the nave and chancel.

There is stained glass by the Camm family in the baptistery windows and glass in a further north aisle window by Florence Camm.

Dudley, St. Thomas — the font

Dudley, St. Augustine — from the north-west showing the baptistery (left) and from the south-east (right)

DUDLEY   ST. BARNABAS, MIDDLEPARK ROAD

The Russell's Hall area of Dudley is now dominated by the hospital. St. Barnabas parish was created in 1969 to serve the growth in housing here and the church is a contemporary building.

DUDLEY   ST. FRANCIS, LAUREL ROAD

The church, built in 1935, is a simple Byzantine style brick building in pleasant suburbia to the west of the castle. It is close to the limestone peak called Wren's Nest where there is a nature reserve famous for its geology including the numerous fossilised trilobites known as 'Dudley Bugs' now in museum collections across the world. Abraham Darby, the famous ironmaster, was born in 1678 at nearby Grove Farm, Heath Green.

    However, the church is best known for its association with footballer Duncan Edwards, one of the Manchester United players known as the Busby Babes, who was killed aged twenty-one in the Munich air disaster of February 1958. He is buried with members of his family in the nearby cemetery and was commemorated in 1961 by two stained glass windows in the church. These show him playing football beneath figures of St. Francis and St. George. A bronze sculpture of Edwards by James Butler was erected by the fountain in the Market Place in 1999.

DUDLEY   ST. JAMES THE GREAT, SALOP STREET, EVE HILL

The dedication of this church is taken from the medieval priory. It was completed in 1840 to designs of local architect William Bourne to serve the growing town to the south-west of the centre. The parish was formed out of St. Thomas in 1844.

    Situated in a sloping churchyard, the building is a large Early English style structure with lancet windows in grey limestone with an aisled nave and west tower similar to the Commissioners' type churches. The tower has characteristic long lancet bell openings and is topped by a parapet

Dudley, St. James the Great — the west front (left) and seen from the south-east (right)

and low pyramidal roof. The church was restored and extended in 1869, when the upper parts of the nave were heightened to provide a clerestorey with small quatrefoil windows, and the chancel, organ chamber and vestry were added.

The long interior has an impressive Early English style chancel arch and seven bay arcades to the nave with tall pointed arches on thin piers with carved foliage to the capitals. There are galleries with panelled fronts to the side aisles. The nave roof dates from the 1869 renovation. Many furnishings date from the building programmes of 1840 and 1869 and include the nave pews, pulpit and font. A wrought iron screen that divides the nave from the chancel commemorates Stewart Holland, vicar, and John Hughes, mayor, from the early years of the twentieth century. The former reredos is now in the west gallery. The east window glass of 1840 has been retained from the earlier chancel.

By the entrance to the churchyard is a large memorial with a broken column to John Stokes, a baritone who died in 1877. The memorial has a carved score of the song 'Life's Day' to the side.

DUDLEY   ST. JOHN, ST. JOHN'S ROAD, KATES HILL

At the top of a steep hill to the east of the town stands this large grey limestone church of 1840. At first glance it appears identical to St. James and it was indeed designed by the same architect, William Bourne. Initial funds for the construction of both churches were raised at a large fair in the grounds of the castle in July 1837, and the site was given by the first Earl of Dudley. The new parish was created in 1844, and the first vicar, Edward Noot, remained at the church for over sixty years until his death in 1905. However, St. John has been closed since 2002, when it was found to be structurally unsound, and its future is uncertain. The church has an aisled nave, chancel, south vestry, and west tower next to which a covered staircase provides access to the galleries. The nave has a clerestorey with quatrefoil windows and the tower, which once had battlements, is now finished by a plain parapet and low pyramidal roof.

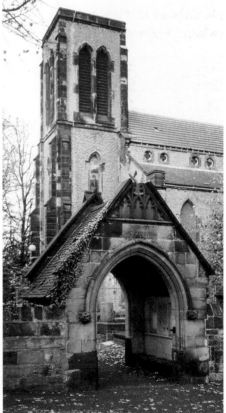

The interior also bears a striking resemblance to St. James, with arcades of seven bays with tall Gothic arches on slender

Dudley, St. John — seen from the south (left) and the tower and lychgate (right)

columns with foliage to the capitals. Here too the galleries survive to the north, south and west but with Gothic fronts. The wrought iron screen was installed in the chancel arch in 1888. There is a fine stone pulpit with statues of the Evangelists, a reredos carved with the Crucifixion, and a font designed in the Early English style by Thomas Grazebrook as a memorial to Edward Noot. There are several nineteenth- and twentieth-century stained glass windows, including a fine set of panels to the side aisles by James Powell of London, showing scenes from the life of St. John.

The church is approached through the Perpendicular style lychgate, erected as a memorial after the First World War. In the extensive graveyard which slopes down the hill from the north of the building is the plain stone memorial to William Perry, a canal man and English bare fist fighting champion from 1850 to 1857, known as the Tipton Slasher. He has also been commemorated by a statue erected in 1993 in the centre of Tipton.

DUDLEY   ST. LUKE, CHURCHFIELD STREET

Founded like St. Augustine as a daughter church of St. Thomas by zealous incumbent William Cosens, the brick church was built in 1878 to a design by John Middleton of Davies and Middleton. It had an aisled nave with chancel, south vestry and north organ chamber. After the church was closed and demolished in the late twentieth century, the dedication of St. Thomas was changed to St. Thomas and St. Luke reflecting the reunification of the parishes.

DUDLEY WOOD   ST. JOHN THE EVANGELIST, ST. ANNE'S ROAD

Dudley Wood, St. John — the west front

Dudley Wood lies south of Netherton, and some two miles from Dudley. It is part of the historic parish of Dudley which was an isolated part of Worcestershire until the twentieth century. The church is easily missed, standing on a bend in the road by the delightfully named Mousesweet Brook close to Cradley Heath. A prominent Methodist church opposite was demolished in 2006. At the opposite end of Quarry Road lies Mushroom Green, which remains one of the best places to get a flavour of a semi-rural Black Country village prior to twentieth-century development. This cul-de-sac of cottages and houses succeeded a squatter settlement on common land in the early nineteenth century. It was a nailmaking community from which small companies grew up also making chains. Kendricks' factory was the last to close in 1965. The restored brick building with characteristic chimneys and shuttered windows has been preserved as a small working factory by the Black Country Museum.

St. John replaced a mission church dedicated to St. Barnabas. It became a parish church in 1949 but was erected to designs of Sir Charles Nicholson in 1931. Nicholson was articled to John Dando Sedding and produced some fine Arts and Crafts churches, such as St. Luke, Grimsby in Lincolnshire or St. Paul, Yelverton in Devon. This is in the Byzantine style similar to several early twentieth-century churches in Birmingham. The interior is whitewashed and light with contemporary furnishings. Stained glass windows from St. Michael, Stourport, Worcestershire were installed here after that church was demolished in 1980.

ETTINGSHALL   ST. MARTIN OF TOURS, DIXON STREET

A manor at Ettingshall is recorded in Domesday, but there is little evidence of a medieval settlement today in this expanse of housing and industry to the south-east of Wolverhampton. There are also few reminders of the large steelworks which dominated the area until the 1970s, but many of the sites are now given over to service industry.

At the south end in the 1930s housing estates, the red brick church of St. Martin comes as a surprise. It was erected on substantial foundations over the site of a coal pit in 1938-9 to designs of Wolverhampton architects Lavender and Twentyman. Set in its own grounds, the view from the road is of the imposing west front with a cloister linking the church to the contemporary vicarage. The plain wide west tower has the appearance of a Romanesque French church, with four narrow round arched bell openings above a wide round arched doorway. The statue over the door is by Donald Potter. In many respects it is a traditional building with its tall six-bay nave which has round-headed windows, whilst the low side aisles, which extend a little beyond the west front, have square mullioned windows. The chancel is lower at the east end and has a brick cross on the east wall, with an oblong chapel to the south and vestries to the north.

The white painted interior is very similar to Lavender and Twentyman's contemporary church in Fullbrook near Walsall. It has tall round-headed arches to the tower, chancel and lower cavernous arches to the aisles. The openings from the chancel to the chapel by contrast are square. The large beams to the nave ceiling are impressive. The sanctuary has a panelled

Ettingshall from the west (left) and a detail of the west door (right)

ceiling with a canopy and curtain to the altar, which is next to the square sedilia and piscina. Most of the fittings, windows and ironwork are by the local firm of James Gibbons Ltd. There are original wooden furnishings including the altar, communion rails, choir stalls and pulpit carved with the Agnus Dei. The round stone font also by Donald Potter has dramatic figures to the sides and a wooden figure to the cover. Potter's apprenticeship to Eric Gill in the 1930s is strongly reflected in his work here.

ETTINGSHALL PARK   HOLY TRINITY, FARRINGTON ROAD

Ettingshall Park is in the historic parish of All Saints, Sedgley and lies to the west of the Birmingham Road close to Sedgley and the top of the ridge. It is now a large area of housing below the open space of the beacon. A nearby mission church of 1835 by Robert Ebbels was replaced by an Early English style church between 1870 and 1875 by local architect William Darby Griffin. It consisted of a nave with south aisle, chancel with transepts, vestry and organ loft. In turn this too was replaced by the present tall but plain brick church in 1961.

    The church was designed by Bryan Martin and built into the steep hillside, incorporating a hall and other functions within the structure. The church, which has a nave and chancel, is in the upper western part and has a simple bellcote on the north side. The interior, with its open roof structure and round-headed chancel arch, is similar to a nineteenth-century mission church, but the casement windows and attractive simple and quite traditional furnishings are reflective of the Arts and Crafts movement. There is a large organ on the gallery at the back of the church.

FINCHFIELD AND CASTLECROFT   ST. THOMAS, OAK HILL

Across the little River Smestow from the similar Victorian suburb of Compton, Finchfield is in the ancient parish of Tettenhall in the western districts of Wolverhampton. The area was mainly rural until the last quarter of the nineteenth century. Compton Hall, a large house of about 1840, stands amongst the many Victorian houses and few earlier cottages. William Morris refurbished the interior of the Hall in the 1890s for brewery owner Laurence Hodson, for whom he produced what is believed to be his last design of wall-paper, which he named Compton.

    St. Thomas was built in 1875 as a mission church to the recently completed parish church of Christ Church, Tettenhall Wood. It is a simple brown sandstone building of nave and chancel with plain Early English style windows to the chancel. The more utilitarian fenestration to the nave and bellcote at the south-east corner gives it the appearance of a small village school building. It was designed by local architect James Read Veall, who also produced the more elaborate St. Michael, Walsall. The church was closed in the late 1990s and remains derelict.

FINCHFIELD AND CASTLECROFT   GOOD SHEPHERD, WINDMILL LANE

Finchfield runs west into Castlecroft, where to the south of Castlecroft Road can be found an extraordinary group of timber-framed buildings in Castlecroft Gardens. These were erected by Major Kenneth Hutchinson Smith during the 1920s and 1930s, reusing much material from demolished historic buildings including St. Peter's Deanery House, Wolverhampton. The concept is sympathetic with the Arts and Crafts movement and may have been influenced by nearby Wightwick Manor.

The church of the Good Shepherd stands to the north in Windmill Lane. By contrast it is a plain, low brick building of 1955 by Lavender, Twentyman and Percy.

FULLBROOK ST. GABRIEL, WALSTEAD ROAD

Fullbrook is a large suburb on the south-eastern side of Walsall which grew up in the 1930s between West Bromwich and Great Barr. A new parish was formed in 1939, and the building of the church was funded by a bequest from John Laing, vicar at St. Michael, Walsall. St. Gabriel's church was designed by Lavender and Twentyman and consecrated in 1939. It has many similar features to their church at Ettingshall. The high brick nave is entered through a south porch with a wide round-arched doorway. The doors are painted deep red with circular white motifs. The church has low side aisles with mullion windows, but the clerestorey windows here are square headed. The square chancel is higher than the nave, almost like a squat tower to the east end, with four narrow windows to the sides and a blank east wall, decorated outside with a brick cross. The belfry turret rises from the south-west corner in the manner of a stair turret on a medieval tower. The church was extended to the west in 1971 to link to the hall and adjacent care home.

The white painted interior (see illustrations on pages 10 and 14) has low rounded arches to the side aisles similar to those at Ettingshall, and the chancel is well lit by the long side windows. There is a beamed ceiling to the nave and painted coffered ceiling to the chancel. Furnishings include a round font and twin rounded white pulpits to the sides of the chancel arch. The square sedilia and other chancel fittings are all contemporary. The church has a High Church tradition and there are many statues placed by the pillars of the nave in the manner of medieval side altars. At the back of the nave the organ is placed on a large gallery, which has been glazed below to provide a meeting space. There are furnishings and stained glass from the demolished chapel of the Good Shepherd at nearby Delves Green, a mission church of St. Paul, Wood Green, in part of the parish from which this parish was created, and where services were first held before St. Gabriel's church was completed.

FULLBROOK THE ANNUNCIATION, REDWOOD ROAD

This church was founded as a mission from St. Gabriel's church in 1958 for the Yew Tree Estate. It was designed by Hickton, Madeley and Salt as a purpose-built hall and worship space.

GREAT BARR ST. MARGARET, CHAPEL LANE

Close to the M6 and under the shadow of Barr Beacon, there is much about Great Barr that still gives the atmosphere of a rural community. The church stands in an attractive country churchyard at the northwest corner of Great Barr Park, which has until recently formed the grounds of St. Margaret's Hospital established in 1912. Much of the hospital has been derelict since its closure in 1997, and Great Barr Hall has been ruinous after serving for many years as the administration centre. The Hall, which stands close to the lake in the park, was built in the late eighteenth century for Joseph Scott, and is a splendid Georgian Gothic building with later Victorian additions. Scott leased the house to Samuel Galton and Great Barr became a regular meeting place later in the century for Matthew Boulton, James Watt and members of the Lunar Society, the great entrepreneurs behind much of the industrial development of the West Midlands.

St. Margaret's church was founded as a chapel of ease to Aldridge in the thirteenth century, and was only created as a separate parish in 1653. The brick tower dates from 1677, and to this a spire was added in the eighteenth century. It was all encased in stone in 1893. The body of the church was rebuilt in 1863

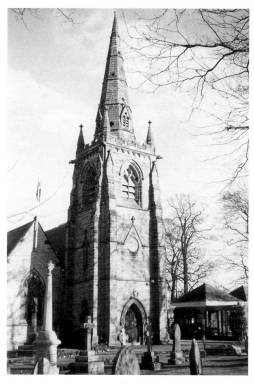

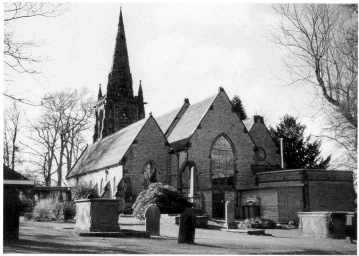

Great Barr from the south-east (above) and the tower and spire (left)

by William Darby Griffin of Wolverhampton. The nave and chancel have separate pitched roofs to the north and south aisles, which continue east as south chapel and north organ chamber. There is also a north vestry. The doorways and windows are all in the Decorated style. There is a late twentieth-century hall extension to the south-west.

Inside, the four bay arcades of the nave have round columns with carved foliage capitals, and pointed arches. The chancel arch, in similar style, is filled with a gilded wrought iron screen installed as a memorial to Sir Francis Scott who died in 1863. Many other nineteenth-century furnishings remain, including the marble pulpit which was designed by Walter Tapper as a memorial to Francis Henry Yates who died in 1895. Amongst the memorial tablets is one to Joseph Scott who died in 1828. There is good late nineteenth- and early twentieth-century glass to the windows, much of which is in memory of members of the Scott and Bateman families. Some earlier glass is collected together in the windows of the extension.

GREETS GREEN   ST. PETER, WHITEHALL ROAD

An unexpectedly rural-looking church stands in a large churchyard on the road between Greets Green and Great Bridge, the two communities which it serves. The name Great Bridge is derived from Greet Bridge over the River Tame and this area between West Bromwich, Tipton and Wednesbury grew up as a result of the ironworks that were served by the thriving canal network from the early nineteenth century.

A mission came here from Christ Church, West Bromwich in 1842, but the

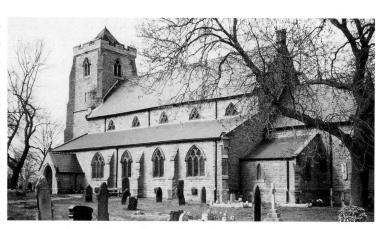

Greets Green from the south-east

church was not built until 1857 to the design of Thomas Johnson of Lichfield on land given by Sir Horace St. Paul and Edward Jones. Funding came partly from Queen Anne's Bounty. Greets Green became a separate parish in 1861. The church is of buff coloured sandstone and has a west tower, aisled nave with clerestorey and porch, and chancel with side chapel and organ chamber. The tower has battlements and a pyramidal roof, and in its Decorated style is similar to many mid-Warwickshire parish churches. There is a sanctus bellcote at the east end of the nave. The style of the doorways and windows is Decorated, with charming trefoil lights to the clerestorey. The church was badly damaged by fire in 1966, but was then sympathetically restored.

Most of the furnishings and glass date from the restoration in the late 1960s after the fire, but there remains a memorial to Sergeant-Major George Tilsley who died in 1864 and who had taken part in the Charge of the Light Brigade in the Crimea ten years previously.

HALESOWEN   ABBEY OF ST. MARY, MANOR FARM

The ruins of Halesowen Abbey are at the very southern edge of the town on private farmland. The house of Premonstratensian canons was founded in 1218 as a daughter house of Welbeck Abbey in Nottinghamshire. It remained small but gained further wealth in the fourteenth century through the acquisition of Dodford Priory near Bromsgrove, which had been a royal foundation, as well as through promotion of the cult of St. Kenelm. A legend grew up that this ninth-century boy king had been murdered at the instigation of his sister at nearby Romsley on the Clent Hills in Worcestershire, where there was a holy spring. St. Kenelm's church at Romsley attracted many pilgrims through the medieval period which provided a source of income for the abbey. After the abbey was dissolved in 1538 the site was sold to Sir John Dudley, who had recently acquired Dudley Castle, and the buildings were converted to a farm. Later in the century the estate passed to the Lyttletons of Hagley.

Today parts of the east end and south wall of the church, along with the excavated remains of the chapter house survive with parts of the refectory amongst more recent farm buildings. A building stands nearby which is believed to have been the abbots' lodging. It has a fourteenth-century roof, though most of the fabric is thirteenth century with the remains of Early English lancet windows, doorways and vaulting. There are also transomed windows suggesting sixteenth-century improvement to the lodging, similar perhaps to Abbey House in Tewkesbury. On a wall inside this building is preserved a small worn effigy of a fourteenth-century knight with crossed legs, probably from a heart burial, and similar to that at St. Mary, Tenbury Wells in Worcestershire. The knight is shown with his hand drawing his sword and his feet resting on an unidentified animal. There is also a thirteenth-century coffin lid carved with a kneeling figure, presumably the deceased, in front of the Crucifixion. Several medieval floor tiles with heraldic and animal designs found on the site are in the collections of the Worcestershire Archaeological Society at Worcester City Museum and the National Trust at Greyfriars, Worcester.

HALESOWEN   ST. JOHN THE BAPTIST, HIGH STREET

The town of Halesowen lies in a bowl amongst the hills with open Worcestershire countryside to the south. After the Norman Conquest estates here were held by the powerful Roger Montgomery, Earl of Shrewsbury, and Halesowen remained a detached part of Shropshire until 1844. The town developed as a market following the grant of a charter in 1232. Coal was mined here from the thirteenth century until 1948, and iron working became important from the Middle Ages. Heavier industry grew up to the north of the town, including the Coombeswood steelworks which was part of the firm of Stewart and Lloyd. Nailmaking was the main industry of the inhabitants, and particularly in the nineteenth century there was great poverty which was brought to national attention by a march of workers in 1852 to the other great nailmaking centre of Bromsgrove. The town still retains a few seventeenth- and eighteenth-century buildings, including timber-framed cottages in Church Lane. However, much of the centre was redeveloped in the second half of the twentieth century which led to the demolition of most of the earlier buildings.

The fine large medieval parish church stands at the heart of the town, its red sandstone tower and spire clearly visible from miles around. There was possibly a minster church here in the Anglo-Saxon period, but the earliest parts of the present structure are mid-twelfth century. At 117 feet long, the Norman church was the same length as it is today, but may have been cruciform, though evidence for transepts is not conclusive. There is a Norman west end to the nave which has a round-headed doorway with zigzag decoration to the arch and interlace to one of the capitals. To the sides are flat buttresses, whilst the thirteenth-century lancet west window is similar to the Early English lancets to be found at Halesowen Abbey. At the east end, the chancel has Norman intersecting blind arcading above the later window on the east wall. There is also a tiny circular window in the gable. It seems that this wall is of similar construction to the south wall of the south transept at Pershore Abbey. As at Pershore, the use of arcading is apparently connected with a barrel vault in the chancel which has disappeared, whilst the window was to light the roofspace above. The south doorway, possibly reset from a narrower aisle, is also Norman with zigzag decoration to the arch, and has recently been restored.

Other external features represent the expansion and alteration of the church during the later Middle Ages and the extensive restoration by John Oldrid Scott in 1883. The end windows of the south aisle and the east window of the chancel are early fourteenth-century Decorated, though the tracery to the east

Halesowen from the south-east

56

Halesowen, the east end

window was replaced in 1849. The outer south aisle was added in 1883 as a memorial to Richard Hone, vicar and archdeacon, and the rebuilt south chapel, east end and north vestry are also nineteenth century. The north aisle and north transept chapel are fifteenth-century Perpendicular, as is the turret for the rood loft stair. The north chapel was a chantry dedicated to St. Katherine. In the centre of the church the pitched roofs of the west end of the nave and the chancel at the east are divided by the tower which is placed part way along the nave, to the east of which is a short three-bay clerestorey with low pitched roof of fifteenth-century Perpendicular type. This unusual arrangement is not completely explained, but it seems that a central tower at a crossing to the west of the chancel arch may have been taken down and replaced by the present tower further to the west. There is no evidence, documentary or otherwise, for the collapse of a previous tower, but contemporary disputes with the abbot of Halesowen Abbey, patron of the church and thus responsible for the maintenance of the chancel, suggest that the rebuild in this position might have been a solution to an unresolved problem. The present tower rises three stages above the nave with Perpendicular openings and a higher north-eastern stair turret. It has battlements at the base of the tall slender spire with Perpendicular lucarnes.

Halesowen, the south door (left) and west door (right)

Inside, Norman work can be seen in the two remaining bays of the arcades at the west end of the nave. Large columns, both rounded and with multiple shafts, have scalloped capitals supporting plain round stepped arches. Small round-headed doorways on the north side appear to have given access to a west gallery, eventually removed by Henry Curzon in 1871. The chancel arch is also Norman. It is round headed with rope moulding, but was heightened first in 1838, and again in 1871 by Curzon. The east wall of the chancel has the shadow of a round arch which seems to be where the barrel vault abutted the wall. The vault must have been wide and impressive and these are rare remains of such a construction on this scale in a parish church, though a similar and smaller example can be seen in the crypt at Duntisbourne Rous in Gloucestershire. The association with Roger de Montgomery in the late eleventh century and then Henry II after the manor was forfeited to the Crown in the twelfth may go some way to explaining such fine architecture here. This may also be reflected in the presence of Romanesque Herefordshire School sculpture in neighbouring Pedmore, Hagley and Romsley churches, which makes its absence from this church more remarkable. Only the font survives with any elaborate carving and this has not been connected to the Herefordshire School. Part of the east wall of the former Norman north transept or aisle survives at the east end of the present north aisle, whilst one small Norman window can be seen inside on the chancel north wall. There are worn carved Norman corbels with animals reset in the south porch.

Halesowen, the nave looking west

The massive crossing arches and eastern nave arcades are fine Perpendicular work. The arcades have octagonal piers with moulded capitals and chamfered arches, whilst the lower part of the tower is a lantern with Perpendicular vault. The arches from the chancel to the south chapel are fourteenth-century Decorated. The arcade to the outer south aisle is Oldrid Scott's work of 1883. The roof to the western part of the nave contains early medieval timberwork, whilst that to the east is from the 1870s restoration.

The font under the crossing is most unusual. Of fine Norman work, the square bowl is carved with an interlacing design, with worn figures probably of saints at the corners. It stands on four round shafts with a central support in the manner of some West Country and Sussex fonts of this date. The rare design is perhaps a further reflection of the patronage of a leading Norman. A fifteenth-century head, possibly from the former churchyard cross, is preserved in the south aisle. It shows the Virgin and Crucifixion on opposite sides in the

Halesowen, the nave looking east

manner of crosses surviving at Tyberton and Madley in Herefordshire. Medieval tiles are displayed in the south aisle. No internal evidence survives for the rood screen and loft which ran from the external stair turret (see illustration on p.13) across the full width of the church in front of the chancel arch and dividing the north aisle from St. Katherine's chapel. The present Perpendicular style screen of 1923 is now in the south aisle. The plain stone sedilia in the chancel probably date from the fourteenth century. There are traces of medieval wall painting in the Norman chancel window splay. Reset above the chancel arch is a medieval carved corbel showing a hand with pair of scales, which may relate to a painted Judgment scene in which St. Michael is weighing souls.

A piece of timber from the bellframe is dated 1774 and is inscribed with the churchwardens' names, reflecting eighteenth-century alterations to the church. There are royal arms of George II and charity boards are preserved at the west end. Plans to rebuild the eastern parts of the church, which had become filled with box pews and galleries, were drawn up by Thomas Rickman, Richard Hussey and

Halesowen, the font

Francis Goodwin in the early nineteenth century but nothing appears to have been done as a result. It was between 1873 and 1878 that Sir George Gilbert Scott replaced the furnishings with the present pews and pulpit. In 1983 the north-west aisle was partitioned to house kitchen facilities and a shop by a glazed screen incorporating woodwork from a side screen in the chancel.

The stained glass in the east window is a memorial to Frances Hone by John Hardman of 1873. The west window is a memorial to local surgeon Edward Moore of 1875. The window at the west end of the north aisle was presented in 1884 by John Corbett, the Droitwich 'Salt King'. At the east end of the south aisle is a window commemorating the fourth Lord Lyttleton of Hagley. It shows Christ in Majesty surrounded by saints, prophets and other prominent biblical characters, whilst that showing archangels at the east end of the outer south aisle is a memorial to Thomas Attwood, son of the Birmingham member of Parliament. Other windows in this aisle commemorate the Hingley family, owners of the anchor and chain factory in Cradley, including Benjamin Hingley, Member of Parliament for this area of Worcestershire from 1885 to 1895, as well as James Grove, proprietor of a horn button factory in the town. The glass by Terence Randall in the north tower window is a Second World War memorial showing St. George.

There are many monuments including a worn effigy of a fourteenth-century priest. There are also two seventeenth-century brass plates and a memorial to Thomas Littleton who died in 1614. In the north aisle is the memorial to William Shenstone of the Leasowes, poet and landscape gardener, who died in 1763. It is an urn on a plinth which was intended to be placed in the churchyard, where there is instead just a simple stone.

The extraordinary large memorial to John Halliday, who also lived at the Leasowes and died in 1797, is by Thomas Banks. It was moved from the chancel in the nineteenth century and shows a cloaked man to the left of an obelisk, whilst to the right there is a kneeling woman with a naked boy. She is holding a small dog, which Halliday was trying to save when he died. There is also a hatchment to the Lea family of the Grange. A further tablet at the crossing commemorates the author Francis Brett Young, who was born in the parish in 1884.

The tower clock was installed in 1895, whilst the bells have been recast from two mentioned in 1497 along with those of the seventeenth and eighteenth centuries. The cross in the churchyard near the entrance is the former market cross from Great Cornbow which was moved here in 1908. It is possibly medieval but crowned with a ball in the seventeenth century. The war memorial by Harold Brakspear was erected in 1921.

HAMSTEAD   ST. BERNARD, BROOME AVENUE

On the border of Sandwell and Birmingham, north of Handsworth, the coalmining community of Hamstead now largely consists of housing estates. The colliery was worked from 1878 up to a depth of two thousand feet, and was the scene of a disaster in 1908 when a fire caused the deaths of twenty-six people who are commemorated in a memorial on Hamstead Road. The colliery closed in 1967.

A church dedicated to St. Paul was built in the Decorated style in 1891 on Walsall Road as a daughter church to St. Mary, Handsworth, the medieval parish church of the area. However, it lies within the City of Birmingham boundary and so is not included here. St. Bernard's church and hall, located within Sandwell, were built in 1963 to serve this growing residential area which eventually included the site of the colliery. It was then remodelled in 1973 by John Sharpe. There is an impressive tiled spire rising from the ground next to the brick and metal clad church building, which houses a large open space used for worship.

HASBURY   ST. MARGARET, HAGLEY ROAD

To the south-west of Halesowen town centre, Hasbury is one of a number of residential communities which grew up from the end of the nineteenth century on the edge of the urban area. There was a small hamlet here in the Middle Ages and the church takes its dedication from the ancient well of St. Margaret here. The church was built in 1907 to the designs of John Edward Knight Cutts and John Priston Cutts of London at a cost of £4,000. It is a large brick building with stone dressings, including attractive pinnacles to the corners. There is an aisled nave and chancel with western baptistery and porches in the Perpendicular style. Although there is no tower, there is a gabled bellcote over the division between nave and chancel. The stained glass window of the Annunciation was designed by Archibald Davies of the Bromsgrove Guild as a memorial to Percy Fox who died in 1949.

HAWBUSH   ST. PAUL, HAWBUSH ROAD

Hawbush is an area of housing estates between Brierley Hill and Wordsley. St. Paul's church was erected in 1954 as a mission church from Holy Trinity, Wordsley and is a typical brick building of its date. Recently refurbished, it combines church and hall use in the same building.

HIGH HEATH   CHRIST CHURCH

This area of housing to the east of Pelsall developed from the late nineteenth century. Christ Church was a mission church in the parish of St. John, Walsall Wood and built in about 1885. It was a rendered brick building in a mixture of medieval and Classical styles which closed in 1973. The congregation was merged with that of St. Mark, Shelfield and the church demolished.

HURST HILL
ST. MARY, GORGE ROAD

As the road ascends the ridge between Coseley and Sedgley, it passes through the village-like community of Hurst Hill, which is still surrounded by a number of fields and woods, as well as modern housing. The centre around the Old Gate Inn was noted in the early twentieth century for breeding homing pigeons. The parish was formed out of All Saints, Sedgley.

St. Mary's church was built in 1872 to the design of George Bidlake, and the chancel added in 1882 by Thomas Henry Fleeming. Both architects were from Wolverhampton, and Fleeming also designed nearby St. Chad, Coseley. Further work was undertaken in 1911. The church has an aisled nave with chancel and vestry, all in the Early English style. Inside can be seen early twentieth-century stained glass by Albert and Peter Lemmon of the Bromsgrove Guild.

The war memorial has recently been restored, as has the nearby bust on a shaft erected on the corner of Gorge Road and Hall Lane in 1914 as an unusual memorial to noted local doctor Isaiah Baker.

KINGSWINFORD
ST. MARY, HIGH STREET

Kingswinford was from Anglo-Saxon times a royal manor on the edge of the Forest of Kinver. In 1206 the manor passed to Ralph de Somery, Baron Dudley, whose family continued to hold it during the Middle Ages. The medieval parish encompassed a vast area including present day Brierley Hill, Brockmoor, Pensnett, Quarry Bank and Wordsley. The importance of glassmaking here since the eighteenth century is reflected in the presence of Broadfield House at the south end of the village, which houses the fine glass collection of Dudley Museums. Today the village is spread out along the main road from Stourbridge to Wolverhampton, with older cottages now amongst suburban houses and shops. To the east of the crossroads in the village centre, the High Street leads to the church, which is prettily situated behind a green surrounded by cottages close to the Court House. The mound to the east of the church is not a motte but a spoil heap which serves as a reminder that coalmining and ironworking was undertaken immediately around the village from the medieval period.

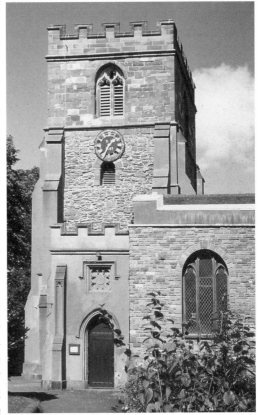

Kingswinford, the tower and porch from the south

The lower stages of the red sandstone west tower may be Norman, with round-headed openings which were perhaps for the former belfry. Above this the present belfry is Decorated with traceried bell openings and battlements, though a restoration of the seventeenth century is suggested by a stone dated 1668 inside the upper stages. The nave and aisles are eighteenth century with western porches. The north aisle dates from 1735 when it replaced a medieval chantry to the Corbyn family, whilst the south aisle had been added by 1808 and has Georgian round-headed windows to the south wall now filled with Gothic tracery. The exterior walls were rendered but are at present covered with stone cladding. The sandstone chancel has some thirteenth-century masonry,

Kingswinford, the Norman tympanum

but was much altered in the Victorian period. The church was closed from 1831, when it was abandoned in favour of a new, larger parish church at Wordsley, but reopened in 1846 after which much restoration was necessary. The large church room was added to the north-west corner in 1974.

The main entrance is through the west tower which forms a porch with a finely painted coved ceiling. The white interior appears uniformly Gothic as a result of the Early English style nave arcades which date from the nineteenth-century restorations. The earliest feature is the remarkable late eleventh-century tympanum which is believed to have been over the south doorway of the medieval church. It was reset in 1808 over the door in the south porch vestry. St. Michael is shown in dramatic relief killing a dragon, in the tradition of depicting saints overcoming evil beasts. He has long wings extending almost the whole width of the single stone. His costume is elaborately carved and he wears a belt with beads. He is holding a shield and is plunging his sword into the open mouth of the dragon below, which also has a long wing and is shown with a raised tail in coils. The eyes of both saint and dragon have sockets which may have contained coloured glass, similar to the beasts on the font at Holt in Worcestershire, and suggest that this would have been a most imposing coloured sculpture at the entrance to the Norman church. Although not considered to be by the masons of the Herefordshire School of Sculpture, there are striking similarities between this and the carvings at Kilpeck, Herefordshire and a connection with other local works ascribed to the School, such as at Pedmore, or indeed the fragment from Dudley Priory, cannot be ruled out.

Kingswinford, the font

There is a 'Breeches Bible' of 1605 and a medieval chest, whilst many of the more recent fittings reflect the High Church Anglican tradition started here during the incumbency of Robert Streeten from 1880 to 1921. The font of 1662 has a gilded Classical canopy of 1955 by Ninian Comper. The vicars' board, aumbry and sanctuary lamp were also designed by Comper in 1955, and in 1935 he designed the stained glass in a south aisle window showing the Presentation at the Temple. The lady chapel reredos depicting the Nativity was the gift of the Bagot family of Summerhill, whilst the window by Charles Eamer Kempe showing the Annunciation of 1907 is a memorial to William Bagot.

Some seventeenth-century memorial tablets to the Corbyn family are to be seen in the chancel, including that of George Corbyn dated 1654 with

Kingswinford, some of fine headstones (above)
and the cross, of which the shaft and base are medieval (right)

ravens on the coat of arms. At the time the Corbyns were the principal family in Pensnett. Eighteenth-century and later tablets include that of John Hodgetts who died in 1741. He was a wealthy landowner of Shuttend and brother of the vicar Thomas Hodgetts who rebuilt the north aisle. A further tablet in the chancel commemorates John Addenbrooke, founder of the medical training hospital in Cambridge, who was born in 1680 at Kingswinford.

Outside in the pretty churchyard the cross base and shaft are medieval, and the earliest of some fine sandstone headstones on the south side date from 1653 and 1655. Nearby is a bronze memorial to George Henry Dudley of 1914 by the Bromsgrove Guild. There is also a memorial to Joshua Hodgetts, who died in 1933. He was an amateur botanist who used his understanding of nature in designs for engraved glass. George Woodall, an acclaimed carver of cameos in glass vases and plaques who worked for Thomas Webb and Sons from about 1880 to 1911, was also commemorated following his death in 1925.

LANGLEY   HOLY TRINITY, TRINITY STREET

Langley parish was divided from Oldbury in 1845. The first church, Holy Trinity, was built in 1852 on land near the housing for those working in the coalmines and chemical works in the village. The sandstone building was designed by William Bourne and had the appearance of a small fourteenth-century village church. It consisted of a nave and chancel with north aisle, south porch and west bellcote. Details such as the cusps and ogees to the windows show the Decorated style being used to follow the ecclesiastical principles of the day, though the chancel with a priests' door appears to have been unusually small. Despite much local opposition the church was demolished in 1968.

LANGLEY   ST. JOHN, ST JOHN'S ROAD, RICHMOND HILL

This small brick mission church was opened in 1915.

LANGLEY   ST. MICHAEL, CAUSEWAY GREEN ROAD

In 1890 a new church and school were built in Langley Green on land given by Mary Barrs. Financial backing came from glassworks owner Alexander Chance and brewer Walter Showell. St. Michael is a brick building with stone dressings by Birmingham architects Frank Barlow Osborn and Alfred Reading. It has a large nave with clerestorey and side aisles, chancel at the east end with a chapel and an organ loft to either side. At the west end is a large porch with double doorway and, although there is no tower, the north-west pinnacle is constructed as a turret with spirelet to take a bell. The style is Early English to Decorated with mainly lancet windows, though some have cusped trefoil heads and the west window has geometrical tracery.

The spacious white interior has brick dressings used to good effect in the pointed arches of the nave arcades, which rest on round stone columns with moulded capitals. The chancel is divided from the nave by a wide open arch. The whole building reflects the Arts and Crafts movement, the influence of which is also evident in the furnishings including the fine wooden panelling to the chancel and the Nicholson organ. There are several stained glass windows of note. The finest is by Camm of Smethwick showing Christ with a group of children. Amongst them is a portrait of Gladys Pryor, daughter of the vicar, who died aged twelve in 1900, whom the window commemorates. The First World War memorial window shows St. George, Faith and Hope and lists the sixty-four men from Langley who were killed, whilst the death on the Somme of Cecil Lloyd is commemorated in a further window.

The church was closed in 2007 and its future is uncertain.

LAPAL   ST. PETER, HIPLANDS ROAD

The unusual name of this area on the eastern side of Halesowen is derived from the Anglo-Saxon personal name Hlappa, and perhaps refers to the holder of the estate. Today Lapal is a residential area close to junction 3 of the M5. It is separated from Halesowen by the Leasowes Park, which was landscaped from 1745 by the poet William Shenstone, with follies and

Lapal, interior looking north (left) and exterior from the south-west (right)

features of the type favoured by followers of the picturesque movement of the time. Lapal also gave its name to a tunnel on the Dudley Canal, which was closed due to subsidence in the early twentieth century.

A wooden church was built here in 1950, but replaced in 1964 by the present building in pale brick. It was designed by Peter Falconer, and was inspired by the then new Coventry Cathedral with its saw tooth arrangement of full length windows to the sides of the single structure of nave and chancel. The church is orientated north to south, rather than east to west and there is a large window at the back of the nave with a fibreglass spirelet above, with a blind wall behind the altar at the north end. A stone from the parish church at Halesowen is incorporated at the entrance. The interior is a light, attractive space with floors of green slate.

LONDONDERRY   ST. MARK, THIMBLEMILL ROAD

Londonderry Lane can be traced winding through the mainly 1930s suburban housing to the south-west of Smethwick. Some of the present parish was in that of Christ Church, Quinton, a Worcestershire village absorbed into Birmingham in 1909. St. Mark's church is located on an island site where Thimblemill Road is joined by Hales Lane. It was completed in 1936 and is an attractive red brick building with aisled nave and chancel without division designed by Frederick Randle to replace a previous mission church in St. Mark's Road.

LOWER GORNAL   ST. JAMES THE GREAT, CHURCH STREET

Upper and Lower Gornal are on the western side of the ridge between Dudley and Sedgley. Lower Gornal is sited in a bowl in the hills and is now, along with Gornalwood, mainly a pleasant residential area close to Himley Park. However, the name Gornal was synonymous with some of the hardest conditions of the Black Country in the nineteenth century. The last of the coalmines closed in the 1960s, but prior to that had been the main employer of the male population back into the early nineteenth century. The women of Gornal were also known for travelling across the region with their donkey carts from which they sold salt from Droitwich and crushed sand for scouring. The nearby Glynne Arms, usually known as the Crooked House, leans at remarkable angles and is a reminder of the problems caused to buildings by mining subsidence.

A strong non-conformist community developed in Lower Gornal, where the Zoar Methodist Chapel of 1906 still dominates the village centre, and even today there are at least four other recognisable chapel buildings near the main street. In the midst of these, where Church Street becomes Temple Street, can be found St. James in an extensive graveyard surrounded by mature trees. The first vicar, the remarkably named

Lower Gornal, the exterior from the south-west

65

Theodosius Theodosius, was a key influence in its foundation. Until 1814 he had been minister at Ruiton Chapel, a significant Independent Chapel and later Congregational Church near Upper Gornal. However, Theodosius was unsuccessful in his attempts to bring the chapel into the Anglican church, the matter ending acrimoniously, and he left to found this church. He died in 1853 and is buried in the churchyard. The story contrasts with those of St. Peter, Cradley (see above) and St. Thomas, Stourbridge (see below).

Land for the church was given by the Earl of Dudley and the earliest parts, the present nave and tower designed by Thomas Lee, were completed in 1817, apparently reusing materials from the demolished medieval church of St. Thomas, Dudley. The church dates from the time of erection of a group of churches in and around Dudley, several of which, including Netherton and Coseley, were designed by Lee. This building had porches added on the north and south sides in 1837 and was altered in 1863 when the chancel was extended, possibly by William Bourne. It was then restored in 1889 by Thomas Henry Fleeming, when the three-sided apse was added. The upper parts of the tower had to be rebuilt in 1930. The styles are Early English in the lancet windows to the nave and the plate tracery in the lower parts of the tower and chancel, Decorated in the bell openings, and Perpendicular in the apse.

The whitewashed interior retains its west gallery installed by a local architect, C. Marsh, in 1837. There are late nineteenth-century fittings including the font and pulpit, and the organ was installed in 1899. The Lady Chapel altar is a memorial to Bernard Keble, son of a vicar, who was killed in 1915 at Ypres, and his face is included as one of the soldiers on the painting. Further furnishings of 1903-4 are by Sir Ninian Comper. The north window of the apse has stained glass of 1903 also by Comper.

THE LYE   CHRIST CHURCH, HIGH STREET

Today, High Street, The Lye is bypassed to the north, and the busy road from Hagley to Dudley passes over the crossroads at the west end, the historic centre of a settlement which grew up on the high ground east of Stourbridge from the seventeenth century. A forge owned by James Folkes was operating by 1699, and ironworking was important here through to the twentieth century. There is little remaining in the town from before the nineteenth century, but the High Street retains several buildings of character, not least the former Unitarian Church of 1861 with its heavily battlemented tower. Lye and Wollescote was an independent urban district during the nineteenth century, and the nearby cemetery chapels of 1877-79 by Thomas Robinson also reflect great local pride. These have a fine spire which serves as a local landmark, and the chapels are currently being restored for office use.

Although the similarly prominent spire of Christ Church was removed in the mid twentieth century, the building is still a significant focal point in the street and stands at the back of a small square behind the war memorial of 1926, which has a statue of a soldier by George Brown and Sons. The church is constructed in brick,

The Lye, exterior from the south

and the west tower has battlements with finials by the corners. There is a wide nave, transepts and chancel to the east and church rooms to the west. Founded by glass manufacturer Thomas Hill who is buried at Oldswinford, the church opened in 1813 as a chapel of ease to that parish church. It was then extended in 1843 by Thomas Smith of Stourbridge, and the additions which attractively embrace the tower were to house stairs to the west gallery.

The interior has been cleared of old furnishings, including some box pews, yet nonetheless has a cheery, brightly coloured appearance. There were galleries installed by Smith to the west end and to the transepts. The stained glass in the small window at the west end would seem to date from the 1840s, but there is other fine stained glass of the early twentieth century, particularly in the Hill, Hodgkiss and First World War memorial windows.

MOXLEY   ALL SAINTS, CHURCH STREET

It is easy to pass through Moxley today, on the Black Country New Road between Bilston and Wednesbury, without realising it is a distinct settlement and home to some of the most significant ironworks of the

nineteenth and twentieth centuries. However, the striking sandstone tower and spire of the church is a familiar landmark by the junction with Moxley High Street. On the site opposite, where Curtin Drive is today, Moxley ironworks was founded by Daniel and David Rose in 1830 beside the Walsall Canal. The Victoria Works beyond was acquired by William Wesson in 1898 and became Wessons, a firm which continues today in the United States.

Moxley, exterior from the south

The parish of Moxley was created in 1845 out of St. Lawrence, Darlaston. The building of the church on the parish boundary with Wednesbury commenced in 1850, and was completed during the following year. The church has an aisleless nave and chancel with lancet windows and doorways with foliage capitals in the Early English style designed by William Horton of Wednesbury, who also designed the nearby church of St. James, Wednesbury. The tower and spire were added in 1877 as a memorial to Thomas Wells of Eaton Mascott Hall near Shrewsbury.

The choir stalls were the gift in 1884 of William Winn, whose shop in Darlaston was the first in the town to

Moxley, nineteenth-century gravestones including some of slate

have electric light. There are some good Victorian commandment boards and tilework. The altar was given in 1926 as a memorial to Albert Henry Brooks who was killed in 1918. Other memorials commemorate further First World War deaths and there is also a tablet to Thomas Wells whose family completed the steeple. Several slate memorials can be seen in the churchyard, which also contains the grave of industrialist William Wesson who died in 1936.

NETHERTON   ST. ANDREW, HILL STREET

The situation of this church to the west of the village is dramatic, at a height of almost 200 metres on a hilltop overlooking Merry Hill Shopping Centre. It almost suggests a medieval site, but although Netherton was a significant village on the road between Dudley and Halesowen from the Middle Ages, it was without a church until the nineteenth century, being served by St. Thomas, Dudley. Along with Dudley, Netherton was in the detached part of Worcestershire until the twentieth century. The village centre is a place of considerable character with several early nineteenth-century cottages, industrial buildings and chapels grouped in the streets around the Green. It is also well known for the Old Swan, a traditional Black Country pub with an extraordinary enamelled ceiling, known locally as 'Ma Pardoe's' after a celebrated licensee. The impoverished nailmakers of Netherton took an important part in the nailers' strike of 1862 to fight against the mechanisation of their trade.

St. Andrew's is a very good example of an almost unaltered Commissioners' church. It was erected between 1827 and 1830 to the designs of Thomas Lee, architect of the churches at Lower Gornal and Coseley. The site was given by the Earl of Dudley and the Church Commission paid for the building at a cost of some £8,000. It comprises a wide nave, short chancel and slender west tower with pinnacles. The church was restored in 1886 and again in 1913 after a pinnacle was blown down into the church. The eastern apsidal vestries were added in 1938. The church is faced with local Gornal sandstone, which now appears weathered and blackened. It is in a simple Early English style with lancets and wider pointed windows with some Perpendicular tracery.

*Netherton, from the south (top)
and across the churchyard from the east (lower)*

The seven bay nave is filled on three sides with galleries supported by iron columns. The area beneath the west gallery has been glazed to create a meeting space, but the remainder is filled with a splendid set of plain box pews of the same date as the church. The organ on the gallery dates from 1835 and is by Harrison of Rochdale. Other furnishings date from the incumbency of Canon Marriott in the later nineteenth century and include choir stalls, an alabaster reredos of 1883, alabaster pulpit of 1903, openwork wrought iron screen of 1892, font of 1879, and lectern of 1897. The stained glass includes an east window of 1865, and fine panels in the north and south aisles including two by Jones and Willis of 1911.

The impressive memorials which fill the extensive graveyard include those of Noah Hingley and his family, whose company manufactured ships' anchors, including that of the *Titanic*. John Barnsley, who made jews' harps and lifting gear, is also commemorated, along with the Grazebrook family whose factory supplied casings for bombs in the Second World War. The north-eastern part of the churchyard is the site of burials from the cholera epidemics of 1832 and the 1840s. The approach to the church is by an avenue which continues the line of Church Road up the hill to the war memorial at the east end of the church.

NORTON ST. MICHAEL AND ALL ANGELS, MAYNARD AVENUE

Until the early twentieth-century housing developments, Norton was a largely rural and agricultural area on the south-west side of Stourbridge. Indeed horse racing took place here during the nineteenth century around the present Racecourse Lane. St. Michael's church stands by a roundabout in the housing estates and is a replacement church for a building of 1929. This had in turn succeeded a mission church from St. Thomas, Stourbridge. The present parish was established in 1951 from parts of the parishes of Oldswinford and St. Thomas, Stourbridge.

The church is a low yellow brick structure with long windows breaking the solid walls. It is an octagon in shape with transepts to the sides, and has low pitched roofs sloping around a small square central lantern. The interior is light and brick faced, providing a hall-like church with small sanctuary.

OCKER HILL ST. MARK, OCKER HILL ROAD

A largely suburban area to the south-west of Wednesbury, Ocker Hill was much developed in the 1920s and 1930s. The parish was created out of part of Tipton and St. Mark's church was constructed in 1849. It is of blue Staffordshire brick, such extensive use of which is uncommon in a church building in contrast to canal and railway construction. The church has an aisled nave, chancel, south porch and vestry, though the tower was never built. It was designed by local architects George Ernest Hamilton and Henry Caulfield Saunders and is mainly in the Early English style. There are lancet windows as well as plate tracery, but the east window is in the Perpendicular style. From the outside this window appears to be overly short but it is designed to be integral with the blind arcading of the reredos inside. Both have cusped rectangular stone panels. The light interior has Early English style arcades with rounded columns and moulded capitals, with chamfered pointed arches.

OLDBURY CHRIST CHURCH, BIRMINGHAM STREET

The centre of Oldbury is now bypassed by main roads and despite much redevelopment still resembles a small market town, retaining several Georgian and early Victorian buildings, particularly in Birmingham Street. The medieval origins of the town have been confirmed by archaeological recording. Church Square around Christ Church has the sense of a close, derived from the mainly early nineteenth-century houses around it. Until 1844 a medieval chapel of St. Nicholas had stood in Church Street. The churchyard of this chapel later became the gardens by the Market Place.

The parish of Oldbury was created from part of Halesowen and Christ Church was consecrated in 1841. The church is a red brick building in the Early English style, with long lancet windows to the aisles and short chancel in the manner of a Commissioners' church. The tall north-west tower is a significant landmark in the urban sprawl as seen from the M5. It has lancets to the bell openings beneath pinnacles and a balustrade. The aisles have their own pitched roofs and the nave is lit by a clerestorey which is almost concealed from view externally. At the east end the aisles have pairs of lancets whilst the east window is a typical stepped Early English triple lancet.

The interior was divided in 1992 so that the west end of the church could be used as offices. Entry to the worship area at the east end is now by doors in the north-east corner. Inside, galleries to the side aisles meant that at its peak the church could hold 1,500 people. When built most inhabitants of the town were non-conformist, but it was nevertheless deemed sensible to build an Anglican church that could accommodate them all! The five bay arcades have simple Gothic arches, and the early Victorian feeling of the building is emphasised by plastered walls and flat ceilings which have a flavour of Gothic in their moulded ribs. At the east end are traces of stencilled decoration and some Victorian tiles. There is a Gothic pulpit and the mayoral chair recalls the days when Oldbury was a borough. The glass in the east window, showing the Adoration of the Magi, commemorates William Chance of the Smethwick glass manufacturing family who died in 1856. The clerestorey windows have glass of about 1840. A window showing the elements of life at the west end is of about 1910 by Thomas Camm of Smethwick.

A memorial on the north side of the churchyard commemorates Theodore Pearsall who died aged sixteen whilst training as a violinist at the Berlin Conservatoire. Oldbury was also the birthplace of organist and composer Sir Frederick Bridge in 1844. A Georgian cast iron milestone on the corner of the churchyard recalls the town's position on a main coaching route, as does the nearby Talbot Hotel of about 1840.

Oldbury, exterior from the south-west (top) and from the south-east (lower)

OLD HILL   HOLY TRINITY, HALESOWEN ROAD

It is somewhat ironic that the centre of Old Hill lies in a valley, but the road to Halesowen ascends a steep hill to the south towards Haden Hill Park. Here the restored sixteenth-century brick Haden Hall with its stepped gables stands adjacent to Haden Hill House of 1878, both seats of the Haden family. Much of the area is residential, but it was also noted from the nineteenth century for the making of gun barrels, nuts and bolts. The centre of Old Hill is now bypassed, giving some dramatic views of this imposing church. It had its origins in a group of dissenting members of the congregation of St. Luke, Cradley Heath led by Walter Bassano, who wished to establish a more Protestant place of worship as St. Luke's adopted High Church practice. The worship style has remained Evangelical throughout its history and a special 'Old Hill Church Hymn Book' was compiled in 1877. To accommodate the desire for a new church a parish was created from parts of St. Luke, Cradley Heath and St. Giles, Rowley Regis. The church itself was built between 1874 and 1876 to designs of J.T. Meredith of Kidderminster, but was almost immediately found to be too small and so the nave was extended to the west in 1877.

The church is constructed of Penkridge sandstone and has a large nave, transepts, short chancel, porch, and organ chamber. It is dominated by the south-east tower with parapet, pinnacles and a higher stair turret on the south-eastern corner. The long pairs of lancet bell openings are Early English in style, whilst the nave and transepts windows have a variety of designs of early Decorated style geometric tracery. Twentieth-century additions to the church on the north and west sides include the church centre of 1975.

The interior has been subdivided, but has a fine roof structure with some trusses of a hammerbeam type. Trusses are also arranged to intersect at the crossing, which has no arches aside from the Early English style chancel arch. It is similar to Martin and Chamberlain's church of 1888 at St. John, Sparkhill in Birmingham. The west gallery of 1877 was removed in 1974. The royal arms are of Queen Victoria. A memorial tablet to Walter Bassano was erected in the south transept following his death in 1903, whilst his wife Emmeline, who died in 1892, is commemorated in the chancel.

The original clock was replaced in the 1920s, though the bells date from 1876. Reflecting the church's emphasis on bible study and education, some impressive Tudor Gothic style Sunday schools were erected in 1879 at Old Hill Cross, funded by George Haden Best, a descendant of the Hadens of Haden Hill House. The schools were demolished in 1971.

OLDSWINFORD   ST. MARY, RECTORY ROAD

St. Mary's church, the ancient parish church of Stourbridge, now stands in an area of housing to the south of the town. In Church Road there is still a sense of the old village, and the church is next to the fine Georgian Swinford Hall and Rectory, which is one of the few pre-twentieth century parsonage houses still used for its original purpose in the diocese of Worcester. The present centre of the settlement, around the crossroads on Hagley Road, is dominated by Oldswinford Hospital. The central brick building with gables, star-shaped chimneys and turret represents the school modelled on Christ's Hospital, London, which was founded in 1667 by the industrialist Thomas Foley, owner of the manors of Oldswinford and Stourbridge. Still an important school today, the complex of buildings is in close proximity to Stourbridge College.

The church is probably on an Anglo-Saxon site, but the earliest surviving part of the present red sandstone building is the fourteenth-century tower with battlements and Decorated bell openings. The medieval spire was replaced in 1810, though after several repairs it was finally removed in 1982. Illustrations show the medieval church to have had a nave and chancel under one roof with side aisles. Much of the fabric dated from the thirteenth and fourteenth centuries, though it was much altered in the seventeenth and early nineteenth centuries. The body of the church was rebuilt in 1842-3 in the Commissioners' style by Robert Ebbels. There is now a large rectangular nave which has battlements and pinnacles, with seven long two-light Decorated style windows to each side. There is a north porch and a polygonal vestry to the south-west. At the east end the tall pinnacles of Ebbels' building were retained when Julius Alfred Chatwin rebuilt and extended the east end in 1898, with a chancel, vestry, organ chamber and side chapel, all in a Perpendicular style. The tracery to the east window is very fine. Alfred Timbrell, the rector, was behind these plans but his premature death in 1898 removed the driving force to rebuild the church. Subsequent plans to replace the nave were prepared by Philip Chatwin in 1910, and Giles Gilbert Scott in 1924 and 1939, but all were unexecuted, and the building remains with contrasting Commissioners' type nave and Arts and Crafts style chancel.

This contrast is particularly striking inside. The large, well lit wide nave retains a gallery to the west end supported by cast iron columns, though the side galleries were removed in 1955. The box pews survive and there are powerful trusses to the roof structure. Springers for proposed arcades can be seen to the sides of Chatwin's great arch, which opens into the chancel, beyond which is a side arcade to the chapel opposite an arch to the organ chamber. The carved capitals are by Bridgeman of Lichfield and the chancel has a fine wooden barrel roof. Several fittings date from the time of the rebuilding of the east end. The altar is of 1894, but has painted panels of Christ and saints including the Virgin and St. John by Gustav Hiller of 1898. The fine altar frontal on display was worked by Jane Goring-Bankes in 1898. The brass eagle lectern is also of

1898, whilst the pulpit with carvings of saints dates from 1903. The large organ is of 1901 by Norman and Beard.

The stained glass in the east window by Clayton and Bell, showing Christ in Majesty with the Virgin and Child surrounded by saints, is a memorial to Mary Webb of 1902. It was given by her husband Edward Webb, the seed merchant whose family established Webbs of Wychbold. A south window in the side chapel is a memorial to Robert Grazebrook, who was killed on board *HMS Cressy* in 1914. It shows Christ saving St. Peter from the sea

Oldswinford, the tower from the south (left)
and rectory from the east (right)

Oldswinford, the interior looking west (top) and east (lower)

Oldswinford, the Grazebrook window designed by William Morris and Co.

and was designed by William Morris and Co. The east window of this chapel is a memorial to rector Alfred Timbrell, who died in 1898, whilst the other on the south side commemorates ironmaster James Evers Swindell, whose extraordinary castellated and timber-framed house, the Castle, is in Church Road. The heraldic glass in the opening from the chancel to the south chapel is from the former east window and shows the arms of Bishop Pepys, rector Charles Craufurd, and the Lyttleton, Foley and Dudley families, who were patrons at the 1842 rebuilding.

The church is rich in memorial tablets reflecting its role as the historic parish church to the large area of Stourbridge with its thriving iron and glass industries. Amongst the earliest are those at the chancel steps to ironmaster Richard Foley who died in 1657, and his son Robert who died in 1676. It was Richard's eldest son, Thomas Foley, who founded Oldswinford Hospital. By the end of the seventeenth century the Foleys had moved away from the industrial area to Witley in Worcestershire and Stoke Edith in Herefordshire. The Foley family home in Stourbridge became the Talbot Hotel, and from 1696 the tenant was Daniel Clarke, who is also commemorated on a tablet in the nave. Other tablets are to members of the Hill and Rogers families who were glass manufacturers, and to the Hickman family whose works produced fireclay bricks. A Dutch artist, Lodvick Verelst, who died in 1704, has a tablet in the nave, whilst the larger memorial in the side chapel with a bust is to ironmaster James Foster who died in 1853 and is by Peter Hollins.

The three earliest of the eight bells in the tower date from 1686, whilst the clock was installed in 1868. Outside, the extensive churchyard contains many significant memorials. The churchyard's northern gates and walls were the gift of Ernest Stevens in 1930, Stevens using his fortune from making metal buckets, dustbins and enamelled baths to fund the establishment of parks and the gift of significant buildings for the use of Stourbridge people.

PEDMORE   ST. PETER, PEDMORE LANE

Pedmore lies on the southern edge of the borough of Dudley between Hagley and Oldswinford. Until the early twentieth century this was a largely rural Worcestershire community, which then became absorbed in the suburban growth of Stourbridge. There is today little feeling of a village, but the church, Old Rectory, and Pedmore Hall stand towards the eastern edge of the housing, close to the open countryside of Wychbury Hill. The manor was acquired by the Foleys of Stourbridge in 1668, revenue from which was used to endow their school at Oldswinford. To this day the Feoffees of Oldswinford Hospital are patrons of the benefice.

The red sandstone church is behind the Foley Arms, hidden from view from the busy junction of the roads from Stourbridge and Dudley to Hagley. Today most of the exterior of the aisled nave, chancel, porch and vestries dates from the rebuilding completed in 1871 by Worcester architect, Frederick Preedy. However the fifteenth-century Perpendicular west tower remains, with a fine west window and bell openings, topped with a pyramidal cap behind a Georgian parapet. The medieval church consisted of a Norman nave and chancel, all of the same length as the present nave, together with a fourteenth-century south aisle.

The present south porch houses the reset Norman doorway. This has a fine tympanum showing Christ in Majesty surrounded by a mandorla, which is supported by the symbols of the four evangelists. The figures and the lion have similar characteristics to work of the Herefordshire School of Sculpture, with large almond-shaped eyes and prominent toes and claws, as can be seen on sculpture at Kilpeck and Brinsop churches in Herefordshire. Stylistic links to sculpture from Reading Abbey have also been suggested for the lion shown with its face turned to the viewer. This perhaps reflects a link through Leominster Priory, where there is also fine surviving Herefordshire

Pedmore, the tower from the south

School sculpture, and which was refounded in 1123 by Henry I as a daughter house of Reading. The mandorla ends in two grotesque heads at Christ's feet, possibly a rendering of the triumph of the church over the forces of evil. This was a popular theme in early carving and it would have made a dramatic and

Pedmore, the Norman tympanum which has similarities to work of the Herefordshire School of Sculpture

thought-provoking image at the entrance to the church. The beaded design of the mandorla and the drapery of Christ's robes are also similar to those on the fragment of another tympanum at Chaddesley Corbett just east of Kidderminster, yet quite different from the much simpler Christ in Majesty on the tympanum at Romsley. Both of these are also attributed to the Herefordshire School. The surrounding arch of the doorway has incised chevrons and lozenges to the moulding, and although the jambs are nineteenth century the scalloped capitals are Norman.

A further fragment of Herefordshire School Sculpture survives inside. On the north wall under the tower is reset part of a mask of a cat-like beast with beaded tendrils protruding from its mouth, of which that on the left survives to form a medallion around what might be either foliage or part of a further creature. The style is reminiscent of the carvings of the Green Man at Kilpeck and Brinsop. The sockets in the eyes were possibly filled with coloured glass and are similar to the eyes of the beasts on the font at Holt, Worcestershire. To the side of the panel is part of a carved bird.

On the north side of the chancel the plain former Norman chancel arch has been reset to form the entrance to the organ chamber. In the south aisle a Decorated piscina from the fourteenth-century Lady Chapel has also been reset, whilst the Perpendicular octagonal font with traceried panels appears to be fifteenth century. There are some fragments of medieval glass in the vestry, including parts of the arms of the Arderne and Clare families. The seventeenth-century clock mechanism also remains, whilst the eighteenth-century bells have subsequently been recast. Most of the fittings date from Preedy's rebuilding and include good examples of his Gothic Revival designs in the pews, choir stalls and pulpit. The reredos contains mosaics from Preedy's workshop. The stained glass in the east and south chancel windows is also by Preedy.

PELSALL   ST. MICHAEL, HALL LANE

Between Bloxwich and Brownhills, the pleasant open greens of the centre of Pelsall are an unexpected surprise. The village grew up around ironworking and coalmining from shallow deposits. Nailmaking was also important from the eighteenth century and industry was supported by the construction in about 1795 of the Wyrley and Essington Canal. An interesting reminder of the industrial past is the cast iron fingerpost on the crossroads at the north end of the village.

Pelsall, the west front (left) and from the south-east (right)

There was a chapel of St. Peter on Paradise Lane in the fourteenth century which was rebuilt in 1763, though nothing remains today apart from some gravestones in the former churchyard. The present church stands in a prominent corner position on the edge of Pelsall Common. It is an attractive brick building with nave, short chancel and transepts of Commissioners' type in the Early English style of 1843-4 by George Hamilton. To this, the west tower with twin lancet bell openings, battlements and tall pinnacles was added in 1875, while the chancel was extended in 1889 by Thomas Henry Fleeming with an unusual five-light east window. The church has recently been extended on the south side with new rooms and a large entrance.

The long whitewashed interior has a wide Perpendicular style chancel arch as well as a delicate gallery at the west end. The 1844 triptych reredos with commandment boards under imposing crockets is displayed on the north wall. Other fittings including the stone pulpit are late nineteenth or twentieth century, and there is a recent mural in a blocked nave window showing Lichfield Cathedral. The stained glass in the east window is a memorial to John Charles of Pelsall Hall who died in 1901, whilst much of the other stained glass dates from the 1950s.

Outside in the churchyard a memorial commemorates the twenty-two men and boys, the youngest of whom was just thirteen, who died in the Pelsall Hall Colliery Disaster of 1872, when the mine was flooded.

PENDEFORD   ST. PAUL, WHITBURN CLOSE

To the north-west of Wolverhampton, Pendeford is now a large area of housing and industrial development close to the M54. This was rural countryside until the twentieth century, when it became the location for Wolverhampton Airport and the Boulton Paul, later Dowty, aircraft works. In the medieval period Pendeford was a manor in the parish of Tettenhall, but the seventeenth century Pendeford Hall, home to the Fowler and Butler families, was demolished in 1968. To the west of the canal is a seventeenth-century dovecote, part of the manorial estate of Barnhurst. A hall used for services, which were held from St. Michael, Tettenhall as housing estates expanded in the 1970s, was known as the Dovecotes Centre.

The present St. Paul's church and centre opened in 1982. It is a curving brick building with sweeping roofs designed by Nick Woodhams, similar to the new St. John, Pleck in Walsall. The church houses the Norman font that had been at St. Michael, Tettenhall. It had been removed from that church in the nineteenth century and placed in the churchyard, and thus survived the fire of 1950 which destroyed the church. The plain bowl has an attractive interlace design to the rim and sides.

PENN   ST. BARTHOLOMEW, VICARAGE ROAD

On the south-west side of Wolverhampton, Penn is set high on a hill from which its Welsh name is derived. Although suburban, the old village centre at Upper Penn around the church still retains much of its rural character, and Penn Hall in Vicarage Road is a fine Georgian building that is now part of a school.

Evidence for Saxon worship on the site can be found south of the church with the excavated remains of a circular preaching cross base, which probably dates to the early eleventh century. It is associated with Lady Godiva, wife of Earl Leofric of Mercia, who held land here before the Norman conquest, and is said to have set up preaching crosses on her estates. It is similar to the cross base at Bushbury, and a parallel to the great cross at St. Peter, Wolverhampton. The church itself is a large attractive building with many rooflines, and the west tower is a focal point to the small square and green in the village centre. The fifteenth-century tower was encased in brick in 1765, and has Georgian Gothic windows, bell openings, battlements and pinnacles. The nave, aisles, chancel, vestries, organ loft, and church rooms all have separate pitched roofs and the walls are a mixture of stone and brickwork. Much of the nave is medieval, and the blocked window on the north wall of the north aisle may date from the church erected at the end of the twelfth century by Hugh de Byshbury. Could the north aisle incorporate the Norman church as at Ribbesford in Worcestershire? The south aisle is by local architects Edward Banks and William Evans of 1845. The aisle was extended eastwards, and the chancel was added in the Decorated style with traceried windows in 1871 by Edward Graham Paley, who is best known for his great Perpendicular style churches in the Lancashire area, particularly as part

Penn, the remains of the Saxon cross

of the firm Paley and Austin. Paley's brother was vicar here, so this is an unusual southerly example of his work. The previous chancel had been rebuilt in 1799. An inscription on the organ chamber records the work of the local architect J. Lavender in 1901. The western vestry is a charming brick addition of 1828, whilst the main vestry was added in 1958, and the attractive northern extension with church rooms and offices dates from 2000.

The west tower also serves as the entrance and leads to the aisled nave. Two bays of the northern arcade are late thirteenth century, whilst the rest is Perpendicular. The remainder of the arches, including the broad chancel arch, date from the nineteenth-century alterations. There are fine timber roofs throughout, and the tower has fifteenth-century internal timbers. The octagonal font is Perpendicular with traceried panels to the lower parts. The bowl was recovered from the churchyard in 1850. The seventeenth-century pulpit

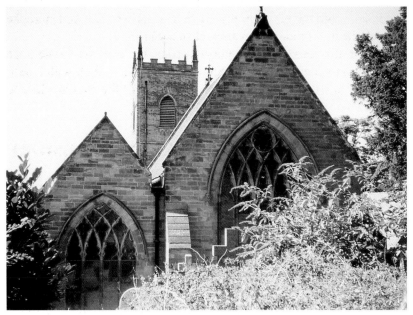

Penn, the east end

was remodelled in the nineteenth century. Indeed most of the other furnishings are of the nineteenth and twentieth centuries, but the brass name plates from the eighteenth-century box pews are preserved in the south aisle, and the west gallery of 1765 is a good survival. The screen between the aisle and chapel dates from 1918, and is a memorial to Alfred Hickman, ironmaster and Member of Parliament for Wolverhampton. The screen between the chancel and side chapel was made up in 1979 from the rood screen which had been given in 1897 to commemorate the diamond jubilee of Queen

Penn, the memorial to John Marsh by John Flaxman

Victoria by the Twentyman family of the Wolverhampton architectural practice, Lavender and Twentyman. The organ by Walker was installed in 1871. The nineteenth-century tiles are copies of medieval designs from Westminster Abbey. There is much nineteenth-century stained glass, including windows by Clayton and Bell in the south aisle, and a grisaille window of 1902 in the vestry.

The fine collection of memorials includes a tablet of 1802 to John Marsh by John Flaxman. A woman in mourning is shown below a cameo portrait of Marsh, in a manner typical of the date. Similar is the memorial to Eleanor Bradney who died in 1817, which shows a figure of Hope, and is by Joseph Stephens of Worcester. Ann Sedgwick of Penn Hall is represented by a framed portrait bust. A tablet to Richard Evans of 1734 commemorates his gifts to

Penn, the tower from the west with the churchyard cross

the parish, whilst that to Ellen Pershouse commemorates her as a donor towards the cost of the Georgian chancel. A wooden cross formerly on the grave of vicar Oswald Addenbrooke Holden commemorates his death in action whilst in France as an army chaplain in 1917.

The bells in the tower include one from the seventeenth century. Outside, the entrance to the large graveyard is dominated by the churchyard cross which has a thirteenth-century base and shaft with a head carved in the medieval style in 1912. At this time the base was moved from south of the church, close to the Saxon remains.

PENN FIELDS   ST. PHILIP, CHURCH ROAD, BRADMORE

The centre of Penn Fields represents the character of the growing nineteenth-century residential areas of Wolverhampton towards Penn. Smaller Victorian cottages mix with substantial villas and more recent housing to make pleasant streets, amongst which can be found St. Philip's church.

This large brown sandstone building has a chancel, transepts, vestry and an aisled nave without a clerestorey. The south-west porch tower has a parapet to the top and a higher octagonal stair turret. It is all in the early Decorated style, and was designed in 1858-9 by William Darby Griffin and John Weller, who were also architects of the demolished St. John, Pleck in Walsall.

The interior was reconstructed in the 1990s to provide offices and meeting rooms on two lower levels in the body of the church. The worship space is therefore now at roof level and accessed by a large staircase at the west end of the nave. The roof structure is clearly visible with its large traceried trusses. The nineteenth-century furnishings have been largely dispersed, but the reredos with traceried panelling is still at the east end of the ground floor of the former chancel, whilst the commandment boards are by the east window. There is much later nineteenth-century stained glass throughout the building, including some with geometric designs from the transepts now in the screen at the west end of the worship space.

The church stands at the east end of an expansive graveyard. The war memorial with a statue of a soldier stands opposite the church.

PENN FIELDS   ST. AIDAN, MOUNT ROAD

A small mid twentieth-century mission church and hall built to serve the growing housing estates to the east of Penn Road on the south side of Wolverhampton.

PENN FIELDS   ST. JOSEPH, COALWAY ROAD

This modern brick church and hall was erected in 1989 to be at the centre of the Merry Hill estate to the west of St. Philip. The attractive design by George Sidebotham appears to be based on a nineteenth-century school building, and the fleche to the roof of the church makes a landmark feature.

PENSNETT   ST. MARK, VICARAGE LANE

On the slopes of the hill to the west of the vast complex of Russell's Hall Hospital, Pensnett is a former mining village with several streets of small Victorian terraced houses. However, it is an ancient settlement which was once part of the vast parish of Kingswinford. The name Pensnett is derived from the Welsh for 'wood on a hill'. Perhaps this is a reference to the woodlands which became the core of Pensnett Chase, a

Pensnett, from the south-east

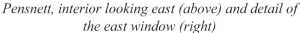

Pensnett, interior looking east (above) and detail of the east window (right)

medieval royal forest, of which vestiges survive in the open ground around the present church. In 1619, Dud Dudley conducted some early experiments into using coal to smelt iron in Pensnett Chase as at Cradley, but it was not until after the Chase was enclosed in 1787 that mineral working was undertaken on a large scale here. Ketley bricks and Dreadnought tiles were also made in the village.

The Earl of Dudley held the mineral rights at Pensnett and indeed gave the land for the site of the church in 1846. It is a tall cruciform building known locally as the 'Cathedral of the Black Country'. There is an aisled nave and clerestorey, transepts and chancel with side chapel and organ chamber, all of local yellow sandstone, though this is now blackened. It would have been an even more commanding structure had the intended south-west tower and spire ever been built. The architects were John Macduff Derick and Lewis Stride. Derick was an Irishman who had recently built the Anglo-Catholic church of St. Saviour, Leeds for Dr. Edward Pusey of the Oxford Movement. This church is a rare survival of Derick's work and was completed in 1849 at a cost of £6,700. It is in the Early English style with numerous lancet windows, a rose window over the three lancets at the east end and details carved with foliage to the doors and arches. The present homely tower with square bell openings and pyramidal roof was added in the early twentieth century.

The interior is fine, lofty and spacious, not least as a result of a successful reordering in 2006 to provide meeting rooms and facilities. Whitewashed walls contrast with pink stone arcades and a new stone floor. The easternmost arches of the arcades are larger as they act as entrances to the transepts. There are good Victorian furnishings to the chancel as well as the wooden screen and pulpit with painted panels. The Lady Chapel beside the chancel was intended as a private chapel for the Earl and Countess of Dudley. A case in the south aisle contains a sword owned by William Gladstone, the Prime Minister, and made at the works of his brother-in-law at nearby Gornal.

Apart from the east window of 1862, the stained glass is mainly twentieth century. In the south aisle, the figures of Saints Paul, Luke and John of 1937 are by Florence and Thomas William Camm of Smethwick. The east and south windows of the Lady Chapel and a north aisle window are of 1938 by Charles Eustace Moore of London. The south transept window commemorates Richard Morris, policeman at Pensnett from 1904 to 1930, whilst the north transept window has glass by Bryan Thomas of 1966 celebrating the history of Lichfield Diocese, in which this parish was situated until it was transferred to Worcester in 1993. Other windows contain good grisaille glass, whilst those in the south-west corner are by Celtic Studios of Swansea.

The splendid view from the west doorway looks across to the Shropshire Hills. The vast churchyard slopes steeply away from the church and is entered through a large stone lychgate contemporary in style to the church itself.

Pensnett, Moore glass in the north aisle

PHEASEY   ST. CHAD, HILLINGFORD AVENUE

Barr Beacon at a height of 700 feet has panoramic views across the neighbouring counties from the public park around the peace memorial pavilion on the summit. To the south, Pheasey is a large mid twentieth-century housing estate situated between the parkland of Great Barr Hall and Queslett Road. The name Pheasey seems to be derived from the surname Vesey after the family who held land here in the sixteenth century, though any connection with the philanthropic Bishop Vesey of Sutton Coldfield is unclear. The Methodist church and St. Chad's church combined in 1995 into a new ecumenical church building which was erected on the site of the mission church of St. Chad and is more often known as the Beacon Church.

St. Chad's church began as a wooden building, in fact a former air force hut, and was a chapel to St. Margaret, Great Barr. Today it is a yellow brick structure with curving outer walls arranged at interesting angles, concealing window openings in between. The space inside is light with white walls and the low ceiling allows for a central lantern. The building is combined with a community centre.

PLECK AND BESCOT   ST. JOHN, SCARBOROUGH ROAD

To the north of junction 9 of the M6 the combined suburbs of Pleck and Bescot are a largely residential district on the approach to the industrial areas of central Walsall. However, Bescot is also home to the stadium of Walsall Football Club.

The parish of St. John was created in 1860, whilst the church was erected in 1858 to designs of local architects William Darby Griffin and John Weller. It was built in the Decorated style and consisted of an aisled nave with north porch, transepts and chancel with vestry and organ chamber. In 1907 a new bell turret had to be built following the destruction of the previous one in a storm in 1895. Continual structural problems led to the demolition of this church in 1976 and the construction of the present building. Other work by Griffin and Weller includes churches at Penn Fields and the chancel of St. James, Wednesbury. The new church is simple and of its period with a wide interior and sweeping slope to the roof. It was altered to enhance community use between 1996 and 1998.

Whilst most of the furnishings are late twentieth century, the Victorian stone reredos showing the Last Supper is incorporated in the brickwork behind the altar, and the font together with some stained glass windows were retained from the old building. However, many of the Victorian furnishings including the screen were not reused.

QUARRY BANK   CHRIST CHURCH, HIGH STREET

Quarry Bank from the south-west

To the south-east of Brierley Hill in what was a remote part of Kingswinford parish until the nineteenth century, Quarry Bank grew up as a centre of nail- and chainmaking. The long High Street runs east from the main Dudley Road at Merry Hill, where the shopping centre has all but engulfed the town. To the south a pleasant park was set out by Stourbridge philanthropist Ernest Stevens in the early twentieth century.

Christ Church, by the junction of High Street and Park Road, is a striking building which comprises a nave, transepts and chancel with a bellcote at the west end. It is built of yellow fireclay bricks, in a similar manner to Holy Trinity, Amblecote. The architect was Thomas Smith of Stourbridge, who also designed the neo-Norman St. John, Brockmoor, but here he used the Commissioners' type Early English style with lancet windows. The chancel was extended in 1900. The hammerbeam roof is an unusual feature of the interior and there is some good modern glass.

ROWLEY REGIS   ST. GILES, CHURCH ROAD

High on the hills above the Stour Valley, Rowley Regis is famed for the quarrying of Rowley Rag, a form of hard-wearing basalt used for road surfaces across the region. The village was also a centre for coalmining, along with nail- and chainmaking, whilst jews' harps made there were exported all over the world. Terrible working conditions of women and children were particularly noted here in the 1860s by Elihu Burritt, the American Consul in Birmingham, on his visit to the brickworks towards Old Hill. Today Rowley is mainly residential, and the centre of urban activity has largely moved to Blackheath. The name Regis indicates that land here was held by the Crown during the early Middle Ages, as at Kingswinford.

The church has been rebuilt several times since the 1830s, but its dedication to St. Giles, a less popular saint in the nineteenth century, is perhaps a clue to the antiquity of the site on the hill top. The medieval church was a chapel of ease to Clent, which was then in Staffordshire. Illustrations show this church to have had a nave and chancel with south porch and west tower. The nave seems to have been altered during the eighteenth century with dormers inserted in the roof, probably to light the several recorded galleries. Tracery was removed from the windows, a feature that can still be seen today at Hanbury, Worcestershire.

The chancel had battlements, seems to have retained its Decorated windows and had a Perpendicular priests' doorway. However, the tower appears to have been much altered in the post-medieval period, perhaps like St. John, Tipton, with the insertion of round-headed windows and bell openings, although it was crowned with gargoyles, battlements and pinnacles suggesting medieval work.

By 1800, when George Barrs was appointed curate, the church was in a very poor state with many repairs in brick to the fabric. Barrs pressed for the church to be rebuilt and in 1838 the body of the old church was demolished. A new building by William Bourne, who also designed St. Luke, Cradley Heath, was completed in 1841 shortly after Barrs' death. The medieval tower had to be replaced by 1858, but by 1894 the church was unsafe as a result of subsidence from mining and was again demolished, with the exception of the tower which was reduced in height. In 1904 the building of a new church commenced, but was not completed until 1907. This was in red brick with an aisled nave and chancel

with short, low transepts, and the existing west tower. It was all in an Arts and Crafts Perpendicular style with many square-headed windows, particularly in the clerestorey, and low pitched roofs. However, in June 1913 the building was destroyed in a huge fire which just left the outer walls standing, even the font and memorials to the Haden family from the old church were damaged. The cause is unknown, but an unsubstantiated legend grew up that the fire was started by members of the suffragette movement. A further suggestion has been it was started by local steelworkers, angry at a lack of support from the vicar.

Rowley Regis from the north-west (top) and a detail from the south-west with the porch in the foreground (lower)

The salvaged outer walls and tower remained as a ruin until 1920, when rebuilding commenced following the First World War to designs by Birmingham architects Arthur Stansfield Dixon and William Holland Hobbis. The tower was replaced by the present structure, with double bell openings and large parapet, and whilst some of the 1904 walls were retained, particularly in the transepts, the style of the building was changed externally more to Early English. A new porch with lancet blind arcading over the pointed arch of the doorway was added to the south-west corner.

The interior is more reminiscent of Hobbis' southern European style work and Dixon's churches modelled on early Christian basilica designs, such as St. Basil, Deritend in Birmingham. White walls are offset by brick to the arcades. There are fine fittings, including much of the woodwork from the 1930s. The Lady Chapel in the south-east corner was made into the baptistery, and contains the font and a medallion of glass showing a portrait of Thomas Pittaway who died aged twelve in 1928. The adjacent window shows Faith, Hope and Charity, and the arms of the dioceses of Worcester and Birmingham, whilst that in the fine east window shows Christ with St. Faith, St. George, St. Michael and St. Giles. All these windows are by Benjamin Warren of Birmingham. The baptistery also houses memorial tablets that have survived from the previous churches including those to the Haden family and Tycho Gaunt, a Birmingham surgeon who died in 1814.

The bell of 1684 in the tower, which survived the fire, was recast along with the others in 1984. The large churchyard is entered through the lychgate of 1933, but contains a number of headstones of the eighteenth and nineteenth centuries to the west of the church.

RUSHALL

ST. MICHAEL, LEIGH ROAD

Rushall, St. Michael from the west

Today the older centre of Rushall is easily missed just off the Aldridge Road on the north side of Walsall. The church and Rushall Hall stand side by side on a low hill, though it is the Hall that still displays evidence of medieval history. Although the house itself is a replacement of the nineteenth century, the fifteenth-century fortified gatehouse and curtain walls remain as a complete surprise in this suburban setting. The house was held by the Harpur family until the sixteenth century, when it passed to the Leighs, who improved the defence of the house during the Civil War. It was then the property of the Mellish and Buchanan families from the eighteenth to the mid twentieth centuries.

The medieval church was a chapel of ease to Walsall in the thirteenth century, but was rebuilt as a parish church in the late fifteenth century by the Harpurs. The plain square medieval west tower was retained when the church was rebuilt in 1854-6 by James Cranston, who was also noted for his greenhouse designs and the architecture of the exotic spa and market buildings at Tenbury Wells, Worcestershire. The tower was replaced by the present south-west porch tower with tall spire in 1867-8. These are in the Early English style with elongated lancet lucarnes to the base of the spire. Cranston's church has a wide nave with sweeping roofs, transepts and chancel. The style is Early English to Decorated, as shown in the tracery of the east and west windows.

The interior has massive roofs to the nave and transepts which meet in front of the chancel arch. Although there is a bench dated 1661, many of the fittings are late Victorian, whilst the fine rood beam is a memorial to John and Catherine Rubery of 1926. On the transept walls and above the chancel arch is a fresco painted in 1905-6 by Reginald Frampton showing the four Archangels and the Heavenly Choir. These recently restored paintings, considered to be Frampton's best surviving

Rushall, St. Michael, the medieval cross base

work and clearly influenced by the pre-Raphaelite movement, are a memorial to a former chorister, Frank Child, who died aged twenty-two. Other similar work by Frampton can be seen at Birstall in Yorkshire and Ranmore in Surrey. There is also much nineteenth- and early twentieth-century stained glass.

A large community room was added to the south of the church in the 1980s. Next to it in the graveyard is the resited base of the medieval octagonal churchyard cross which has the date 1829 inscribed on the side, perhaps recording a time when it was repaired. There are also some good eighteenth- and nineteenth-century headstones.

RUSHALL   CHRIST THE KING, LICHFIELD ROAD

A 'tin tabernacle' of 1887 was built of timber and corrugated iron as a mission church from St. Michael for the miners of this western part of Rushall, and is an increasingly rare example of such a church still in use today.

SANDWELL   PRIORY OF ST. MARY MAGDALENE

Sandwell Valley with its country park lies to the east of West Bromwich and is bisected by the M5 motorway. However, it survives as an important green space and one of the few areas of rural character in the borough of Sandwell, to which it has given its name. To the north-east of junction 1, close to Sandwell Park Farm, the Sand Well or *fons sanctus* is a spring which became venerated as a holy well during the early Middle Ages, and alongside which a hermitage was established. Flint tools dating back to the Mesolithic period and Bronze Age have been excavated here, showing prolonged human activity around the site.

The Benedictine priory was founded before 1190 by William de Offney, a tenant of Gervase de Pagenal of Dudley Castle. Always a small monastery, it increased its wealth by taking possession of the church at West Bromwich from Worcester Cathedral Priory in about 1230. Little else is known of its history until it became one of twenty-one monasteries to be dissolved in 1524 to fund the foundation by Cardinal Wolsey of Cardinal's College, now Christchurch College, Oxford. The buildings seem to have been in ruins within a couple of years and were made into a house by the Whorwood family. The property was purchased by the Earl of Dartmouth in 1705 and rebuilt as Sandwell Hall, which was occupied by the Dartmouth family until they moved in 1848 to Patshull Hall near Wolverhampton. The hall was eventually demolished in 1928, but the estate was purchased by the then borough of West Bromwich to remain an open space. A remarkable stone Classical temple-like gatehouse of 1705, possibly by William Smith of Warwick, can still be seen on the motorway roundabout.

The remains of the priory, together with those of the hall, were excavated during the 1980s. Foundations and low surviving walls of the church, including a stone coffin, along with the walls of the cloister and some of the monastic buildings, have been uncovered. The pools to the west represent the medieval monastic fish ponds.

SEDGLEY   ALL SAINTS, VICAR STREET

Sedgley, the spire

At a height of some 224 metres above sea level, the centre of Sedgley is only some five metres lower than the summit of Bredon Hill on the opposite side of Worcester diocese. The tower erected by Lord Wrottesley in 1846 on the nearby Beacon is a noted landmark. Once the centre of a large parish and manor, which included Gornal, Coseley and Ettingshall, the town of Sedgley remains a thriving community at an important crossroads. In the nineteenth century it was noted for the manufacture of iron nails, locks, and other wrought iron goods. Several Georgian buildings survive including the Red Lion and Court House on the Bull Ring, whilst the nearby Roman Catholic church of 1823 is possibly the earliest example of a prominent Catholic church building with a tower in England. It replaced a church of 1789 in Sandyfields, and a Catholic boarding school for boys had been opened in Sedgley Park in 1763. There remained a strong Catholic presence in the area following the Reformation.

The blackened sandstone tower and spire of All Saints form another significant landmark in the town. On the approach to the church along Vicar Street, it is apparent that their position on the south side of the aisled nave and chancel is unusual. The core of the tower is medieval, and may possibly even be Norman, as a church is known to have existed here in the twelfth century when it was held by Dudley Priory. The tower was recased when the body of the church was rebuilt between 1826 and 1829 by Thomas Lee at a cost of £10,800 for the Earl of Dudley, at a similar time to the building of other churches by Lee for the Earl in Netherton and Coseley. It is a fine building with long early Decorated style windows to the sides, and large five-light windows at the east and west ends of nave and chancel. Battlements and pinnacles embellish the parapets and hide low pitched roofs and are also at the base of the spire in the manner of a Perpendicular church. The entrance is through a short porch at the west end.

The elegant, light, painted interior is also in the Perpendicular style, with piers of clustered shafts without capitals and an elaborate plaster tierceron vault. Parallels have been drawn between Lee's interior design and the church of St. Andrew Undershaft in the City of London, which could have been the inspiration. There were galleries around the nave and aisles, but the interior was remodelled and galleries removed in 1883, reducing the seating capacity by almost a quarter. The box pews and other furnishings from 1829 have also disappeared, but the pews remaining at Netherton church give an impression of how this interior would have originally appeared. The present stone pulpit and the low chancel screen were

installed in 1901, whilst the lectern dates to 1902. The panelling from the Pursehouse pew of 1626 in the north aisle was returned here from Priory Park in Dudley. It had been moved there from the earlier church when the woodwork from family pews was redistributed to houses on the Earl of Dudley's estates at the time of the rebuilding. In 2003 the west end of the church was successfully reordered to give room for kitchen facilities.

In 1970 the present stained glass in the east window replaced the glass of 1830; this had depicted the apostles and coat of arms of the Earl of Dudley, and had been installed by Hemle of Freiburg, Germany. The First World War Memorial window of 1921 is by Pearce and Cutler of Birmingham. There are also two important late twentieth-century windows in the north aisle. The Fellows memorial window (see rear cover) is by Rosemary Rutherford, a Suffolk artist whose premature death in 1972 meant that few commissions were completed outside her home area, and this window installed in that year shows the Virgin and St. Hubert. The more abstract Hives memorial window of 1975 representing the Resurrection is by Alan Younger, whose glass is also to be found in Durham, Chester and St. Alban's cathedrals (see left).

Several of the memorial tablets and brass plates are preserved from the previous church. These include an inscription to Edward Pursehouse who died in 1685, and another to Michael and Catherine Nickins. She is recorded as the daughter of Matthew Hale, Lord Chief Justice to Charles II.

The clock is of 1829 by Taylor of Oxford, and six of the eight bells recast in 1975 are dated to 1720. There are good nineteenth-century memorials in the graveyard. The fine gabled seventeenth-century vicarage was demolished in the late twentieth century.

Sedgley, the Hives memorial window by Alan Younger

SHELFIELD   ST. MARK, GREEN LANE

A mission church to the Shelfield area from St. John, Walsall Wood was founded in 1895 in School Street. The church was replaced by the present dual purpose building of church and community hall in 1965, which also succeeded Christ Church, High Heath. It is a plain brick structure, typical of its period, laid out as a nave and chancel recently enhanced by the introduction of simple stained glass windows with symbols of the Church and St. Mark.

SHORT HEATH   HOLY TRINITY, COLTHAM ROAD

Now a mainly residential area to the north of Willenhall, Short Heath was an area of woodland within the royal forest of Cannock Chase, until coalmining and ironworking developed here during the eighteenth century. Today, remains of spoil heaps in the open spaces amongst the houses and a branch of the Wyrley and Essington Canal serve as reminders of the area's rich industrial past.

Holy Trinity stands at Lane Head close to the canal, and the parish was formed out of St. Giles, Willenhall to serve the growing population of this area. It is a dark red sandstone Commissioners' style church of 1854-5 by Wednesbury architect William Horton, which consists of an aisled nave, chancel and vestries, with a porch and bell turret to the north side. The style is Early English with plate tracery to the windows and a fine west doorway in a portal. The stained glass in the east window is a memorial to the first vicar, W. Rosedale, whilst the large memorial by the entrance commemorates Enoch Dutson.

SMETHWICK   OLD CHURCH, CHURCH ROAD

Smethwick is an expansive urban area on the south-east side of Sandwell. Although the place name is of Anglo-Saxon origin and means 'the place of the smith', large scale industrial development took place from the early nineteenth century following the opening of the canal and the Soho Foundry in 1796 by James Watt and Matthew Boulton to manufacture parts for Watt's patented steam engine. Although the foundry site in Foundry Road on the Birmingham border has since been redeveloped, it is seen by many as one of the cradles of the industrialisation of the Black Country. The arrival of the steam engine allowed iron to be smelted on the coalfields rather than needing to be close to running water to power machinery, and it was with this development that the Black Country flourished. Smethwick became a significant town which spread first along the canal, and then the railway and main road. The development of this part of the Galton Valley has left some particularly significant industrial archaeology, such as the Galton Bridge of 1829 by Thomas Telford, which with its span of one hundred and fifty feet was the largest canal bridge in the world at the time of its construction.

However, to the south of the present town centre, there is evidence of an earlier Smethwick, which until the nineteenth century was part of the parish of Harborne. In 1719 Dorothy Parkes, daughter of a Smethwick landowner, endowed a trust with land to build a fully furnished chapel with graveyard within three years of her death. She also laid down the terms for appointing a minister and for erecting a parsonage. She died in 1728, and the present church was consecrated in 1732. It had no dedication and was known as Parkes' Chapel until the erection of Holy Trinity in 1838, when it became referred to as the 'old church'.

Smethwick, Old Church from the south-east

During the eighteenth century, disputes with the authorities over marriages and burials here were finally resolved when Smethwick became a separate parish in 1842. The Trustees of Parkes' Charity remain the patrons.

The Classical style church is an attractive surprise in the suburban setting of Church Road. It is of red brick with stone dressings, and consists of a battlemented tower at the west end of a wide nave with just an apse to the east. The four bays of the nave are marked by large, simple, round-arched Georgian windows with prominent keystones. The bell openings on the tower are of similar design. Either side of the apse the east wall of the nave has a doorway with a round window above. The doorway on the south side is now blocked, whilst that on the north led to a nineteenth-century vestry, which was replaced in 1963 after a fire.

The spacious interior has a gallery at the west end supported by wooden Doric columns. It was added to provide extra seating in 1759, but the box pews and three decker pulpit were then removed between 1868 and 1883 whilst Edward Addenbrooke was vicar, when new seating, choir stalls and an organ were installed. The round chancel arch stands between pilasters. A memorial tablet to Dorothy Parkes on the south side of the arch is complemented by one on the north to John Hinckley who died in 1740.

The church possesses a chalice of 1732, whilst a bell of the same date remains in the tower, with the clock added in 1932. The attractive churchyard, surrounded by brick walls, was extended several times during the later nineteenth and early twentieth centuries, and is entered by the lychgate of about 1890. The Georgian parsonage was demolished in 1929.

SMETHWICK   HOLY TRINITY, NOW THE CHURCH OF THE RESURRECTION, HIGH STREET

This is the church at the centre of the town of Smethwick. It stands in a large open rectangular churchyard bounded by four streets on the side of the hill to the south of High Street. The centre of Smethwick suffered badly from the creation of the ring road in the late twentieth century when the majority of buildings on the north side of the street were demolished, leaving just the tollhouse of 1818. The broken streetscene of this lower part of the town centre has the Sikh Gurdwara with its shining golden domes as the most prominent landmark, yet the smoke blackened church also benefits from a more visible setting.

Smethwick, Holy Trinity from the south-west

Holy Trinity was consecrated in 1838 to serve the growing population of the northern end of Smethwick. Land was given by J.W. Unett whilst the building was largely funded by the first vicar, Thomas Simcox. The Early English style west tower and spire of dark Staffordshire sandstone has lancet bell openings and the main west doorway, and is the only part which remains from the original church designed by Thomas Johnson of Lichfield. The body of the church, which was cruciform, was replaced in 1887-89 by Henry Francis Bacon, who reused much of the stone from the previous building to create the present Early English and Decorated style nave and chancel with aisles, which have separate pitched roofs. There is a south porch and north-east vestry, and in 1934 further daylight was brought to the nave through the addition of attractive dormer windows.

Several other churches were opened as mission chapels and became separate parish churches through the later nineteenth century as the population of Smethwick increased.

Smethwick, Holy Trinity — the carved reredos (above)
and alabaster font (right)

Ironically as these churches have closed through the later twentieth century their parishes have been absorbed back into that of Holy Trinity, which was rededicated in 1996 as The Church of the Resurrection. Some of the key contents from these other churches are now to be found here. The church has been reordered since the 1980s, and partitioned to subdivide the internal space to form an entrance lobby at the west end, a fine worship space in the nave and chancel, with a glass screen to the south aisle, and a new internal wall to the north aisle and former organ chamber. The chancel arch and arcades are Early English in style with rounded columns and carved foliage to the capitals. There are elegant timber roof structures. There is fine stained glass to the east window (see rear cover), and further panels in the glass screen. The window by T.W. Camm is effectively illuminated in the western partition. A Perpendicular style painted screen from St. Stephen's church of the Arts and Crafts movement, perhaps inspired by those in East Anglian medieval churches, is now in the south aisle. Other nineteenth-century furnishings include the sumptuous carved reredos, pulpit and alabaster font.

An extraordinary feature of the churchyard is the external pulpit on the south side which was erected for open air services by the 'Brotherhood', a men's organisation founded before the First World War by the vicar, J.H. Newsham. The 'Brotherhood' also erected the substantial stone lychgate at the west end.

Smethwick, Holy Trinity
— the outdoor pulpit

SMETHWICK   ST. ALBAN, ST ALBAN'S ROAD

In 1904 a mission church funded anonymously (but since known to have been by George F. Chance) and dedicated to St. Alban was built in Silverton Road to replace a mission room in a nearby former printing works. A new church was then completed on land given by Samuel Henry Dibble at the corner of Devonshire and St. Alban's Roads in 1906, and the earlier building became the church room. Chance also gave the land next door for a vicarage in 1910. The red brick church has stone dressings and was designed in a late Perpendicular style by Frederick Beck of Wolverhampton. The aisled nave and chancel present a fine west end to the street with a bellcote above the west windows and a polygonal west baptistery with crenellation to complement the small corner annexes to the aisles to either side of the pair of west doorways.

Although closed as a church, it was converted to a community centre in 1984, thus continuing to fulfill the aims of Dibble in founding a parish room and a school.

SMETHWICK   ST. CHAD, SHIRELAND ROAD

The first St. Chad's church was opened in 1882 as an iron mission chapel in the parish of the Old Church. It was on the corner of Shireland and Edith Roads, close to the boundary with Edgbaston. This was replaced by a new church in 1901 with an endowment from Mitchell and Butler, whose vast Cape Hill brewery at the opposite end of Edith Road has only recently been cleared for a housing estate. The Early English style church was designed by local architect F.J. Gill and had an aisled nave and porch, chancel with vestry and organ chamber, with bellcote at the north-east corner. It was closed in 1968 and demolished three years later. A new parish had been formed in 1902 but was united with that of St. Matthew in 1970.

SMETHWICK   ST. JOHN THE EVANGELIST, FOUNDRY LANE

In 1910 a mission church in Foundry Lane replaced a non-denominational mission room of 1894 at a former factory in Slough Lane. It closed in 1967.

SMETHWICK   ST. MATTHEW, WINDMILL LANE

St. Matthew's church stands in an attractive churchyard with mature trees beside Windmill Lane, though it is now overlooked from the north by a group of 1970s tower blocks. To the south the smaller scale terraced houses give a good sense of the earlier context for this church. The site was given by J.W. Unett, who is commemorated in the name of the nearby street. The parish was formed in 1856 out of that of the Old Church, and received £100 from Queen Anne's Bounty. The church was built in 1855 to the designs of Joseph James and is of sandstone with limestone dressings. There is a large aisled nave with clerestorey, north and south porches, and chancel with organ chamber. A vestry was added in 1892. At the west end the wall is divided by a large buttress supporting the fine double bellcote. The pair of west windows and the east window have good fourteenth-century style tracery and the church is in the Decorated style.

Inside the nave arcades have round columns supporting pointed arches, and a good timber roof supported by corbels with carved angels. There are mouldings and carvings to the window surrounds and chancel arch which include ballflower decoration. Indeed, all effectively use fourteenth-century details. The furnishings were largely given by the Mitchell family of Mitchell and Butler and include the alabaster chancel rails and pulpit, font and floor tiles. The alabaster reredos and east window glass commemorating Harry Mitchell, who died in 1894, were funded by public subscription.

SMETHWICK   ST. MICHAEL AND ALL ANGELS, CROCKETTS LANE

The first church in this area of Smethwick to the north of Victoria Park was a mission church in Brook Street, which occupied part of James Middleton's Britannia Bedstead factory. The new church in Crocketts Lane was consecrated in 1892, funded largely by J.H. Chance. The new parish was formed in the following year.

The large red brick church was designed by Arthur Edmund Street, who took over the practice of his father, George Edmund Street, in 1881. It was in the Early English style with chancel, aisled nave with clerestorey and north transept, and had a west baptistery with two porches in the manner of Julius Alfred Chatwin's Birmingham churches. There was no tower, but the slope of the site allowed for a vestry and parish room under the east end. The exposed brick of the interior was similar to Street's church of St. Paul, Worcester, and had arcades of square but chamfered piers with unusual rounded arches. The organ was moved in the 1930s allowing a Lady Chapel to occupy space on the south side of chancel as a memorial to Charlotte Evans of the glass manufacturing family. The church was closed and demolished in the late twentieth century and is a great loss to the town.

SMETHWICK   ST. PAUL, ST PAUL'S ROAD

A mission church to West Smethwick was founded in 1850 and met in the schoolroom at Chance's Glassworks. The Chance family and their glassmaking factory have been synonymous with the growth of late nineteenth-century Smethwick. Even today the factory, which is being renovated, dominates views of the town from the M5 viaduct, with a seven-storey workshop at the centre of the site where glass manufacture began in 1824, and where glass for the Crystal Palace of 1851 was made. The family were great benefactors to the town, with many buildings and features taking their name, such as Chance's Park.

The parish of St. Paul was created from part of Harborne. The church, successor to the mission in the school, was consecrated in 1858. It was constructed of Stourbridge fireclay brick in the Early English style to designs of G.B. Nichols of West Bromwich. It had a nave and apsidal chancel with transepts. The transepts had turrets to the eastern corners which contained staircases giving access to galleries inside. There was also a west gallery which originally housed the organ. A north-west tower was surmounted by a spire, which was replaced with a green fibreglass structure in 1961 designed by Peter Falconer. The church was destroyed by fire in 1963 and replaced by a smaller structure in 1966 by Denys Hinton, which incorporated part of the transepts and north wall of the old church. The tower and spire were also retained. Although the new church was much acclaimed as good architecture, it was closed and demolished in 1996, when the top of the tower and the unusual early example of a fibreglass spire were removed to Avoncroft Museum of Buildings near Bromsgrove, where they are now a landmark beside the A38.

SMETHWICK   ST. STEPHEN, CAMBRIDGE STREET

A brick mission church was built in 1882 in Cambridge Street, North Smethwick, which was an area of terraced housing near the coalmines on the border with West Bromwich. A new church was completed on the adjacent site in 1902, and the mission church survived as the parish hall until 1932. The red brick church with an aisled nave and chancel was designed by Wolverhampton architect, Frederick Beck, and had a bellcote at the east end of the nave. It was closed and demolished in the late twentieth century and the site redeveloped for housing. The churchyard walls can still be seen at the corner of Cambridge Street and Sydenham Road.

STAMBERMILL   ST. MARK, STOURBRIDGE ROAD

A mill on the River Stour at Stanburn to the west of The Lye is first recorded in the sixteenth century. In 1882 Stambermill viaduct was constructed here to carry the railway across the Stour valley. Since St. Mark's church was demolished in 1987, this remains as the principal landmark of the area. The church had been built as a chapel of ease to St. Thomas, Stourbridge between 1869 and 1871 to succeed a mission held in the local school. The land was the gift of brick manufacturer Francis Tongue Rufford and the church designed by Stourbridge architect Thomas Smith. It had an aisled nave with bell turret at the east end, three-sided apse to the chancel, along with a vestry and north porch. The use of iron for the pillars and to strengthen the arches in the arcade was an unusual feature, particularly at a time when iron was generally not considered a suitable material for Gothic church construction, but rather more appropriate for factories or railway stations. It seems that concern about the potential effects of mining subsidence was the main influence on the decision to use it here.

The son of a local jeweller, Edwin Morris, who became Archbishop of Wales in 1957, attended this church as a boy and started the local scout troop. After the church was closed in 1985 the parish was united with Christ Church, The Lye. The site is now occupied by the houses of Stambermill Close.

STOURBRIDGE   ST. THOMAS, MARKET STREET

Stourbridge grew up in the early Middle Ages around a crossing point on the River Stour in the parish of St. Mary, Oldswinford. The settlement became a market town with rights confirmed by a charter of 1482, but developed significantly from the seventeenth century as a glassmaking centre, pioneered by immigrant families particularly the Tyzacks and Henseys from Lorraine. The town's glass became world famous, its manufacture taking place mainly to the north of the town in Amblecote and Wordsley in the area now delineated by 'the Crystal Mile'. This industrial base, coupled with the simultaneously developing iron industries, particularly that of the Foleys, placed Stourbridge amongst Worcestershire's most prosperous towns of the eighteenth and nineteenth centuries. Today it remains a fine place with a heritage of Georgian and Victorian buildings in the present centre and towards the historic core at Oldswinford.

In 1430 a chantry chapel dedicated to the Holy Trinity was founded by Philip Haley in Lower High Street. It was dissolved in 1547, and on the site was built the King Edward VI Grammar School, later attended by Samuel Johnson. St. Mary, Oldswinford remained the parish church of the town until the eighteenth century. In common with many industrial towns there was a growing number of non-conformists including the Quakers who, under the leadership of ironmaster Ambrose Crowley, founded a meeting house in 1689. This survives today as a peaceful haven by the busy ring road and is the oldest remaining place of worship in the town centre.

In the early 1700s a group of local industrialists initiated a public subscription fund, of which they became trustees, to fund a new Anglican church for the town. The fund was soon boosted by a bequest from a clothier, John Biggs. The aim was to provide free pew seating for the poor of the town, which was not available at the parish church. Construction of the new church began in 1728 and was completed in 1735. However, George Wigan, rector of St. Mary, and Thomas Foley the patron, attempted to install their preferred curate to minister at the new church. This resulted in much local dissent and the continued independence of the church with the incumbents being installed through fiercely contested local elections. The first minister was Walter Hickman, the son of one of the trustees. Two parliamentary bills attempting to formalise the organisation of the new church as a chapel of ease were defeated, and disputes between the trustees of St. Thomas and the parish church continued, until a new parish of Stourbridge was finally created and the church consecrated in 1866.

St. Thomas' church is a splendid Georgian brick building, though the architect is unknown. The aisled nave is the earliest remaining part from 1735 with round-headed windows to the sides. There were entrances at the east end to each side of a short, square chancel. The tower was added with balustrades and urns to the corners in 1759, followed by further alteration to the church in 1836. In 1890 the sympathetic western porches and curving eastern apse were added by William Henry Bidlake in partnership with John Cotton. The vestry was added in 1912 and the adjacent church hall erected in 1914 to make an attractively uniform group of buildings.

The church is very much in the style of James Gibbs and comparisons have been made with his church at St. Martin-in-the-Fields in London. The four bay arcades with wooden Tuscan columns and canted rounded arches support a curving ceiling to the nave with fine plaster decoration. There are individual tunnel vaults to the bays of the side aisles divided by moulded cornices. The gilded plaque of the Holy Ghost towards the east end of the ceiling has also been compared with one at St. Peter, Vere Street in London, which was also designed by Gibbs and where the plasterwork is by Giovanni Bagutti, to whom the plasterwork here has also sometimes been attributed. The height of the original box pews is indicated by the square bases to the columns, though the present pews were installed in 1836, when the side galleries were also added. A west gallery with the organ by George Pike was erected in 1809, though the organ with its fine Classical style case was moved to the south of the chancel in 1889.

The choir stalls date from 1891, whilst the screen of the same date dividing the chancel from the vestry was designed by Bidlake and made by Jones and Willis. The mosaic reredos showing the Crucifixion is a memorial of 1916 to Mary Ann Fiddian.

The base of the pulpit is by Charles Bateman of Birmingham of 1913, with the upper parts with Classical style arches by Robert Bridgeman of 1978. The Classical style reredos in the Lady Chapel was designed by Stourbridge architect John Homery Folkes, and made by Robert Pancheri in 1963, who also built credence tables for the church.

Stourbridge, St. Thomas. The east end (top)
and from the south-east (lower)

Stourbridge, St. Thomas. The interior looking east (top) and west (lower)

The stained glass in the east windows showing the Ascension in the centre, with the Nativity and the Annunciation to the sides, was given by Charles Collis in 1891 and designed by Samuel Evans of Smethwick. Four windows in the north and south aisles showing scenes from the life of Christ are by members of the Bromsgrove Guild, possibly including Archibald Davies. The glass in the west window showing St. Thomas is of 1836 and was moved from the east end when the new chancel was erected and the west gallery removed.

The tower clock was installed in 1878 by Charles Frodsham. There are ten bells, of which three date to the time of the building of the tower in 1759.

STOURBRIDGE   ST. JOHN THE EVANGELIST, ST JOHN'S ROAD

Just visible from the ring road on the approach to the junction with Hagley Road, St. John's church is located next to Stourbridge Town Station. It was erected to serve a growing population in St. Thomas' parish and a separate parish was created. The cost of building was partly borne by the Earl of Dudley. The red brick church was designed by George Edmund Street in 1860-61 in the Early English style with lancets and plate tracery to some windows. It has an aisled nave with clerestorey and bell turret. The chancel was restored after a fire in 1908. Since 1978, when it was declared redundant, the church has been used by the United Reformed Church who previously had a church in Lower High Street.

The arcades have round pillars with capitals. Stained glass in the east window shows scenes from the life of St. John, whilst that in the west has Christ and Old Testament figures above portraits of typical servicemen of different backgrounds — this is a memorial to the First World War.

THE STRAITS   ST. ANDREW, THE STRAITS

An area of former mines in the valley to the north of Lower Gornal, The Straits has been transformed during the twentieth century into a residential district with little visible evidence of its industrial past. Nearby Baggeridge Country Park was established in the early 1980s on the site of the last colliery to operate in the Black Country, next to the extensive Baggeridge brickworks.

The first mission church was damaged by mining subsidence and had to be replaced by the present building in 1914. It is an excellent example of a mission church of this date with a white painted nave and hall, and a short spire at the west end. Since 2006 the building has also been used by The Straits Free Church and has been extensively refurbished to adapt it to shared use.

STREETLY   ALL SAINTS, FOLEY ROAD EAST

The borough of Walsall adjoins the beautiful expanse of Sutton Park at Streetly, which developed following the opening of a station in 1879. This is an area of many large houses, including some good examples of Arts and Crafts architecture. The main road from the north-east to the south-west follows the line of the Roman Icknield Street, from which Streetly takes its name. A little to the west of this road, All Saints' church was built as a chapel of ease to St. Margaret, Great Barr to serve the eastern part of the parish. Streetly only became a separate parish in 1918.

The church is a long, low, red brick structure of which the earliest part, now the south aisle and Lady Chapel, was erected in 1908-9. It is in the Perpendicular style favoured by the Arts and Crafts movement, and has a short bell turret at the west end. The church was greatly enlarged in 1954 with a new nave and chancel to the north. To the north of this a new hall was added in 1975, and finally the west end of the earlier

Streetly from the south-west

south aisle was adapted to form an entrance lobby in 1985. The ensemble is nonetheless coherent and attractive.

Inside, the church is white painted, light and spacious. The nave has fine Perpendicular style arcades, with chamfered stone piers rising without capitals to brick arches on the south, and blind stone arches on the north side. The font is of 1909, whilst the lectern is a war memorial of 1916, and the pulpit of 1937 is by Bridgeman of Lichfield. The embroidered reredos of 1963 in the chancel, and that in the side chapel of 1965, are by Elizabeth Ward of Worcester. There is good twentieth-century stained glass, particularly in the south aisle. The east window shows depictions of sacrifice, whilst that to the south shows the childhood of Christ.

Outside in the churchyard, beyond the lychgate of 1952, stands the large war memorial of 1920 by Thomas Mewburn Crook with a life size figure of Christ. One of Crook's most noted pieces is the statue of the Welsh military hero, Sir Thomas Picton, in Cardiff City Hall.

TETTENHALL   ST. MICHAEL AND ALL ANGELS, CHURCH ROAD

A separate village until the nineteenth century, Tettenhall is now a leafy suburb on the west side of Wolverhampton. The church is by the green and surrounded by a number of pre-Victorian houses and cottages from the village which developed along the Holyhead Road during the eighteenth century. It is a place of ancient origins, and tradition claims that the church was founded by the Anglo-Saxon King Edgar to celebrate the victory of Edward the Elder over the Danes at a battle in Tettenhall in 910. However, Wednesfield also claims to be the battle site. By the time of the Norman Conquest Tettenhall was a royal manor, like nearby Kingswinford, and so has also been known as Tettenhall Regis. The church remained one of several free chapels on royal estates in Lichfield diocese, including Gnosall, Penkridge and St. Peter, Wolverhampton,

Tettenhall, St. Michael and All Angels from the south

all of which became collegiate churches. The presence of so many colleges may have been part of a royal strategy to curtail the power of the bishops of Lichfield, whose diocese covered a large area. Tettenhall had four vicars and two chantry priests by the end of the Middle Ages. At the Dissolution of the chantries in 1547 the college property passed to Walter Wrottesley who lived at Wrottesley Hall, and whose family maintained the privileges of the deans of the college, including the right to hold a court, until the nineteenth century.

The medieval church was destroyed in a fire in 1950, with the exception of the

Perpendicular tower with gargoyles and battlements. It was a mainly thirteenth-century building, with an aisled nave and chancel. The nave had a fine Perpendicular clerestorey, whilst the south aisle had been enlarged and rebuilt in 1825 by Edward Haycock of Shrewsbury, and then further rebuilt in the Decorated style with a porch by George Edmund Street in 1882-3. This fine vaulted Perpendicular style porch was the only other part of the building retained after the fire, though some damaged stone was reused internally to fill the nave columns.

The church was rebuilt between 1950 and 1955 by Liverpool architect Bernard Miller, using Henry Willcock as builder. This design owes much to the Perpendicular style churches of the Arts and Crafts movement. There is an aisled nave and chancel with lower Lady Chapel at the east end, with organ chamber and vestry to the sides. The architectural style and the use of sandstone is in keeping with the surviving remains of the earlier church. The nave clerestorey is Perpendicular in style, but the windows to the side aisles set in gables have reticulated tracery and transoms, as well as blind panels to the sides. However, the squared design with strong diagonal lines is similar to that used by William Lethaby at Brockhampton, Herefordshire and echoed in the work of his pupil Randall Wells at Kempley, Gloucestershire. The east window to the Lady Chapel is more of a traditional Decorated style. At the east end of the south clerestorey wall is a square sanctus bell turret with chimney.

The interior is spacious and light with stone facing. It seems at first glance like a medieval church with the wide nave divided from the aisles by pointed chamfered arches on round columns, but the style of the foliage detail to the capitals is more Art Nouveau than medieval. The Lady Chapel arch is of simple Perpendicular type by contrast, whilst the tower arch is restored medieval Perpendicular. The tracery to the side windows, and that on the west wall of the nave beside the tower, further dispels the illusion of a medieval church, as does the angular tracery to the roof trusses.

The cylindrical font is covered in a mosaic design by Hungarian artist G. Mayer Marten and represents Christian unity through baptism. The nave light fittings are designed to resemble bells and chalices. The altar has always been placed west of the Lady Chapel arch although the east end of the nave was reordered in 1985, when Miller's low wall dividing the nave and Lady Chapel was removed and replaced by a medieval style screen. The stone pulpit and lectern remain, and the effect is now more that of a medieval chancel than a separate Lady Chapel at the east end. The carved angel corbels at the east end are by Alan Durst of London, whilst the sculpture of the Virgin and Child in the Lady Chapel was carved by Helen Cromarty. The bee, emblem of the architect, Miller, was used in the design of the communion rails. Most of the other furnishings are to Miller's designs, whilst the stained glass in the east window representing Christ in Glory is by George Cooper Abbs of Exeter.

Along with the other contents of the earlier church, the Wrottesley memorials were destroyed in the fire, though the family vault remains beneath the east end of the church. The absence of wall tablets is a feature of the interior. However, the graveyard contains a variety of memorials of which the earliest are seventeenth century, such as the headstones to Mary Dykes and Will Dix. The fine timber-framed lychgate of 1890 at the southern entrance was damaged when the fire appliances were attempting to reach the church in 1950.

TETTENHALL CHRIST THE KING, PENDEFORD AVENUE, ALDERSLEY

On the north side of Tettenhall, Christ the King is a mission church in part of the parish of St. Michael. It was designed by George Sidebotham in 1956, and has brick walls with large windows and wide sloping roofs. Outside, the bell in a simple frame is dated 1604 and comes from the parish church. When new bells were installed there, this bell was taken to St. Mary, Wolverhampton in 1841, but returned to be used at the temporary church built to accommodate the congregation of St. Michael's church following the 1950 fire, before its subsequent use at this church.

TETTENHALL WOOD   CHRIST CHURCH, CHURCH ROAD

This suburban area south-west of Tettenhall takes its name from woodland which was part of the royal Forest of Kinver during the Middle Ages. The open common land was enclosed in 1809 — this led to the development of the village, and the core of this survives today. By the end of the nineteenth century the area was developing as a residential suburb, along with Compton to the south. Sir Geoffrey Mander, who made his fortune from paint, built Wightwick Manor immediately to the west. This is a treasure of the Arts and Crafts movement, with fine timber and brick architecture by Edward Ould and fittings by William Morris and other pre-Raphaelites. Its influence can be seen in the architecture and craftwork of many buildings in the area.

Christ Church began as a mission from St. Michael's church, which first met in the school in 1844. It was erected between 1864 and 1867 to designs by Birmingham architects John Jones Bateman and Benjamin Corser. Faced in local sandstone, it is in the Decorated style, and has a wide nave with chancel and gabled polygonal apse at the east end. The planned south-east tower above the organ chamber was never built, which means that the building is less dominant in the streetscape than the nearby United Reformed church with its tower and short spire, which is of 1873 by George Bidlake.

The whitewashed interior is spacious with a wide nave, divided from the aisles by arcades with slender round columns and pointed arches with chamfers in an early Decorated style. The tall chancel arch is without capitals giving a more Perpendicular style appearance. It is spanned by a wooden openwork screen with tracery also in the Perpendicular style, but with separate openings for the pulpit and lectern. The windows contain some stained glass by Charles Eamer Kempe, but a great treasure is the glass in five other windows by Archibald Davies of the Bromsgrove Guild. Installed between 1930 and 1934 they show scenes from the life of Christ, of which the Resurrection in the west window is particularly fine. The latter was given in 1934 by Sir Charles Marston, proprietor of the Villiers Cycle Components Company, to commemorate his family.

TIPTON   ST. JOHN THE EVANGELIST, UPPER CHURCH LANE

The ancient settlement of Tibbington lay around St. John's church to the north-east of the present town centre of Tipton. The earliest documentary references seem to be from the thirteenth century and there was a medieval moated site, probably that of the manor house, towards Ocker Hill.

By the eighteenth century the village had moved to the south-east, towards Horseley Heath, and a new church of St. Martin (the previous dedication of this historic parish church) was erected there in 1797 on Lower Church Lane. The old parish church had been decaying and surrounded by industry, and by 1763 there were plans to rebuild it. However, delays in raising funds, albeit partially offset by a grant from Queen Anne's Bounty, meant that when rebuilding went ahead in 1793, a new site was chosen, and this church became ruinous. There was then a dispute over the mining rights to the church site and surrounding glebe lands, but in 1798 the materials from the church excluding the monuments were sold. A few headstones of the seventeenth and eighteenth centuries survive around the edge of the present churchyard. Most of the outside walls and tower of the old church survived any demolition, though the south wall was destroyed in a storm in 1820.

In 1849 the rector, William Wilday, proposed a new building for a Sunday school in which services could also be held for a renewed population at the old village. A new parish of St. John was created in 1854, following completion of this present building in 1850 to the design of Thomas Henry Wyatt and David Brandon. The remaining outer walls of the nave and chancel were replaced, though the tower was retained. The ground level had risen by over six feet through the dumping of industrial spoil, so foundations to a depth of nine feet had to be constructed. The tower is therefore also shorter by six feet than it was originally. This is particularly evident inside, where the line of the blocked tall rounded arch from the tower into the nave is visible immediately above the present west doorway into the nave, and a blocked south window is now at ground level. The tower itself is plain with trefoil-headed double lancet bell openings and battlements. Suggestions that it is of Anglo-Saxon date are erroneous as it is largely a rebuilding of the seventeenth century using earlier masonry. This is recorded on the inscription to the sundial with a small Classical pediment on the south side, which states that 'this steeple was built Anno Domini 1683 John Nightingale William Clare Church

Tipton, St. John the Evangelist from the south-east

Wardens'. The architecture of the rebuilt body of the church is much inclined towards its intended mission type use. The nave and chancel, with a single span low pitched roof, are of five bays in blue bricks with double lancets with iron lattice glazing. These bays are divided by shallow red brick piers. There is also an unusual gabled south porch. The east wall has a widely spaced stepped triple lancet window.

The south side was much rebuilt in the 1920s following a collapse as a result of mining subsidence which had led to the church being closed once again in 1913. A new mission church of St. Joseph was erected nearby, and this served the parish during the First World War. St. John's church later reopened with substantial buttressing added to the south side. In 1928 the plain rendered organ chamber was added to the north and a sacristy to the west by local architect Frederick Beck. In the 1980s a parish room was built to the north of the church.

The interior of the building is plainly decorated, though it was furnished to suit a Catholic style of worship during the twentieth century. The stained glass in the east window was installed in 1903 by Evans and Co. of Smethwick in memory of Susannah Tozer, wife of the second incumbent, Samuel Tozer, who is himself commemorated by the font cover of 1904.

TIPTON   ST. MARTIN, LOWER CHURCH LANE

The second church in Tipton was erected between 1795 and 1797 by J. Keyte, and was renovated as a house between 2002 and 2006 after years of dereliction. It has a large rectangular nave with white stucco walls, the sides of which are ornamented with five large round-headed arches surrounding the windows. There are pedimented doorways to the west end with round windows above and to the sides to light the staircases for the galleries. In the 1960s, following subsidence damage, the round tower at the west end was rebuilt by Charles Gray to a plain design and lower in height than the original. It was given its glass dome during the recent conversion. At the east end a new square chancel with a sympathetic round-headed window was erected at the same time as the tower to replace the chancel of 1874-6 by A.P. Brevitt. The interior has been altered to make it suitable for residential accommodation, but originally there were galleries on the north, south and west sides with iron supporting columns. Some stained glass with floral designs remains in the windows. The restoration of the church is most welcome in a part of the town where many other historic buildings have recently been lost, including the Victorian police station and Black Countryman public house.

Tipton, St. Martin from the south-west

TIPTON   ST. MATTHEW, DUDLEY ROAD

The nineteenth-century settlement at Tipton grew up to the west of what had been known as Tipton Green. In 1644 this was the scene of an indecisive skirmish, the so-called Battle of Tipton Green, between Royalist and Parliamentarian troops, as the latter under Lord Denbigh prepared to lay siege to Dudley Castle. From the beginning of the eighteenth century, industrial development of the area was rapid as a result of ironworking and the extraction of limestone and coal. Coneygree Colliery to the south was the location of the first steam-powered engine to be installed by Thomas Newcomen in 1712. Manufacture of heavy iron goods continued throughout the nineteenth century at large factories such as the Horsley Works and Barrow and Hall, but these industries have all but disappeared during the twentieth century.

St. Matthew's church was erected to serve the expanding town between 1876 and 1881 to designs by John Hall Gibbons, and executed by the Cheltenham firm of Davies and Middleton. The large brick building remains relatively unaltered, and has an aisled nave with clerestorey, two storey west porch, chancel with five-sided apse, north vestry and large south-eastern tower with tall pinnacles. The church is in the Early English style with lancet windows throughout, and set above the central west doorway is a tympanum with a carved figure of St. Matthew.

The arcades of six bays have pointed arches on round piers, and the capitals have foliage carving. The chancel arch is of similar design. There are fine timber roofs, with iron supports to that in the nave. The base of the tower also serves as the organ chamber. The east windows have twentieth-century stained glass showing Christ surrounded by the four Evangelists.

TIPTON   ST. PAUL, OWEN STREET

The heart of Tipton today is Owen Street, which developed in the early nineteenth century between two branches of the Birmingham Canal. There were thirteen miles of canal within the boundaries of the borough, which led to it being referred to as the 'Venice of the Midlands'. Even today the canal junction in Tipton is a significant landmark. With the emergence of the railways, the borough of Tipton remained an important transport centre, with seven passenger railway stations and six goods depots.

St. Paul's church was built in 1837-8 as a chapel of ease to St. Martin and reflects the move of population in Tipton at the time. The architect was Robert Ebbels and the brick church is of the Commissioners' type with a short chancel and large nave and porches, together with a west tower which is embellished with battlements and short pinnacles. The long lancet windows are in the Early English style, and the building is similar to Ebbels' other churches such as St. James, Handsworth.

The interior has galleries to the north, south and west as designed by Ebbels. The new parish of St. Paul was created in 1843, but since the closure of St. Martin's church this has become the parish church and is properly known as St. Paul and St. Martin.

TIVIDALE   ST. MICHAEL, TIVIDALE ROAD

A new parish of Tividale was created out of parts of Tipton and Rowley Regis in 1878. The place name appears to be a corruption of Anglo-Saxon words for 'deer gate', possibly a reference to the edge of the royal manor of Rowley. Industrialisation along the canal, including the establishment of the steel mill at Brades, took place here from the 1760s, followed by the first deep mine in the 1790s. Coalmining and ironworking continued throughout the nineteenth century. Today the area is largely residential between Dudley to the west and Oldbury to the east. The Hindu Balaji Temple on Dudley Road which opened in 2006 is the largest of its kind in Europe

The parish was closely allied to the High Church movement from its foundation. St. Michael's church was erected on Dudley Road in 1874 to the designs of John Middleton of Davies and Middleton. It was a large brick building with an aisled nave, chancel, with organ chamber and vestry. The north-west pinnacled tower was a prominent landmark, but the church was demolished in 1985 because of structural problems. The replacement low brick church was constructed in 1996. It has a wide interior, which is light and whitewashed. The chancel is divided from the main worship space by a low semi-circular arch. The square east window has modern stained glass showing the Crucifixion.

TIVIDALE   HOLY CROSS, ASHLEIGH ROAD

The church was erected together with a hall in 1966 and serves the southern part of the parish of St. Michael.

UPPER GORNAL   ST. PETER, KENT STREET

High above the communities of Lower Gornal and Gornal Wood, Upper Gornal is situated on the ridge between Sedgley and Dudley with magnificent views to the west. Indeed the name Gornal means the mill on the ridge and nearby survives the round tower of Ruiton Windmill, which was erected in 1830. Part of the parish of Sedgley, the area was industrialised heavily by the early nineteenth century, though today it is largely residential. The 'Pig on the Wall' public house along the street from the church recalls the notion that domestic pigs, an important food source, were treated as part of the household in the Black Country, and a local story that one family even let their pig stand on the wall to watch the band pass by.

The church of local stone, darkened by weathering, was built to the designs of Robert Ebbels in 1840-1 at a cost of over £2,000. The foundation stone was laid by William Ward, Viscount Dudley in 1838. It is different in appearance from Ebbels' other churches in the area such as St. Paul, Tipton. There is no tower to this Commissioners' type church and it has mainly lancet windows in the Early English style. At the east end the characteristic short chancel was extended in 1854 and given a three-light east window with cusping to the tops of the lancets. The west end is more prominent, flanked by porches and with turrets now reduced to parapet level on each side of the Perpendicular style west window, in the manner of King's College Chapel, Cambridge. The west front has a similarly powerful effect on the streetscape to that of 1837 at Holy Trinity, Tewkesbury in Gloucestershire and is comparable to St. Luke, Cradley Heath.

The original interior arrangement was of box pews and a large central pulpit in front of the communion table at the east end, with galleries to the north, south and west sides. All of these were subsequently removed. A new altar was provided for the chancel and new furnishings were installed in the first half of the twentieth century with parclose screens to each side of the chancel arch.

WALL HEATH

ASCENSION, DUDLEY ROAD

Wall Heath is a mainly suburban residential area between Kingswinford and Himley on the very edge of the conurbation and close to the present boundary between the borough of Dudley and Staffordshire. Open countryside extends to the west with views towards Highgate Common. To the north, the seventeenth-century Holbeche House, home of the Roman Catholic Stephen Lyttleton, was the scene of the capture of Robert Catesby, Thomas and Robert Wintour after the failure of the Gunpowder Plot in 1605.

The church stands by the main crossroads in the village centre. It originated as a mission church in the parish of St. Mary, Kingswinford, and was founded by the Bagot family of Summerhill. William Bagot of Wall Heath House laid the foundation stone in 1892. The church consists of a nave and chancel with south-west porch and west belfry with spirelet. It is a very pretty building in an Arts and Crafts Perpendicular style, with square-headed windows and a timber-framed west gable which has a further upper window, giving it the appearance of a small Cheshire church. The timber framing is an indicator of the timber roof construction to be found inside to both nave and chancel, which are divided by a simple pointed arch. The interior is otherwise whitewashed with simple modern furnishings, although the original

Wall Heath from the west

small font and panelled pulpit remain. Most of the windows contain clear glass which makes the interior very light, but there is fine early twentieth-century stained glass in the east window which depicts the Ascension, and late twentieth-century glass in the central west window showing the Baptism of Christ.

The town of Walsall is at the centre of the large borough. Although it is a place of Anglo-Saxon origin, it appears now largely as an urban area of the nineteenth and twentieth centuries. The place name means 'the vale of the Welsh', and probably refers to a surviving British community here in Anglo-Saxon times, as with the names Walcot and Walton. There has been a market here since the first charter was granted in the thirteenth century. Through the fourteenth and fifteenth centuries the manor was held by the Earls of Warwick, when it prospered with the growing exploitation of its natural resources of coal, iron ore and limestone. Indeed the famous Arboretum is on the site of a limestone quarry. From the sixteenth century Walsall became noted for the production of metal goods primarily related to horses, such as stirrups, bits, spurs and buckles. This led to a growth in leatherworking, and particularly saddlery by the nineteenth century. Numerous factory buildings associated with this trade still exist today. Regeneration of the declining town in the twentieth century was assisted by the erection of the new Art Gallery to promote the borough's fine collection of paintings, especially the Garman Ryan Collection.

St. Matthew's church dominates the town centre from the hill to the south. It has a powerful presence, but is separated from the town by the steep ascent at the end of the High Street. This was the heart of the medieval town, but the area of small cobbled streets and lanes by the church has largely been cleared. There was a church on this site by the beginning of the thirteenth century when it came into the patronage of Halesowen Abbey. It was known as All Saints until the eighteenth century. Medieval work mainly from the fifteenth century is readily evident in the sandstone of the chancel, but the general appearance of the building today is the result of the rebuilding in 1820-21 by Francis Goodwin. West of the chancel, the long nave has side aisles which in turn have short outer aisles which appear like transepts, whilst the tower is in the south-west corner. The western parts are faced in dressed Bath stone. The spire was rebuilt in the seventeenth century, heightened in 1777, and further rebuilt in 1951.

The Perpendicular chancel was erected after 1462 but much restored between 1877 and 1880 by Ewan Christian, when the organ chamber and vestries were also added. However, it still retains the character of the east end of a prosperous late medieval Midland town church with its large Perpendicular windows. An original window survives blocked inside on the north wall, and the remainder were remodelled by Christian in a similar

Walsall, St. Matthew showing evidence of the steep ascent from the town to the west end (lower), and a detail of the window tracery in the south transept (top)

Walsall, St. Matthew — the Perpendicular chancel

Walsall, St. Matthew — the nave ceiling

form. An unusual feature is the passageway beneath the east end, which is very similar to the processional way beneath the chancel at Walpole St. Peter, Norfolk, where the church has similarly been extended to the eastern boundary of the churchyard. To the west of this passage below the body of the chancel is a vaulted crypt which appears to be of the fourteenth to fifteenth centuries. To the west of this, an inner crypt has in the east wall what seems to be a blocked Norman doorway and two Early English lancet windows, suggesting that this marks the line of the east wall of the earlier chancel. These crypts probably served as vestries as both can be accessed by narrow stairs from the chancel.

The nave and aisles follow the medieval plan. Large side aisles represent the building work of the fifteenth century, when the nave was reconstructed with a clerestorey. The outer chapel to the north was dedicated to St. Clement and was erected by 1468 by the merchant Guild of St. John, whilst that to the south was dedicated to St. Catherine and was probably built before 1475 by the craft guilds of the town. All this was incorporated in Goodwin's rebuilding, when much of the medieval stonework was encased and the large Perpendicular style side windows with their fine cast iron tracery were erected. This tracery was identical to that at Goodwin's fine Christ Church, West Bromwich, which is now lost. There is a Gothic porch at the west end, which replaced a Classical style Georgian addition, and new porches were added to the transepts on the north and south sides.

The nave ceiling is from Goodwin's reconstruction of the medieval clerestorey and roof. It is very pretty, of plaster and flat but with fan vaulting and bosses to the sides and central pendants. Below there are Perpendicular style arcades with cast iron columns and side galleries. Goodwin's rebuilding was not just

Walsall, St. Matthew — two of the misericords

on account of the poor state of the fabric by 1820, but the doubling of the size of the population of Walsall during the late eighteenth and early nineteenth centuries also made the provision of greater seating space very necessary. The chancel arch was rebuilt by Christian in 1877, when two small Perpendicular windows were placed in the gable above. The chancel has a timber roof in contrast to the nave. Here Christian also restored the fifteenth-century piscina, the lectern and remains of the sedilia. The octagonal font in the south aisle is also Perpendicular, and is carved with angels holding coats of arms, which include those of Beauchamp and Stafford, as well as the instruments of the Passion (see illustration on p.13). The lead lining is dated 1712. A rood screen was recorded in 1463, though the present screen by Bateman of Birmingham is of 1915. The chancel has a fine set of fifteenth-century stalls. Between the poppy heads and moulded arm rests are eighteen misericords, the best to survive in the old county of Staffordshire. Amongst the carvings of foliage, beasts and grotesque masks, there are two centaurs and a pelican in her piety, along with representations of a man holding a club and another carrying a sack. Perhaps the most unusual is the man playing a stringed instrument with a bow whilst seated on a dragon. The organ was built in 1773 by Samuel Green of London, but much rebuilt in 1952-3. The box pews and high three decker pulpit of Goodwin's rebuilt nave were replaced in 1879. The north chapel was refurnished as a war memorial in 1920 and other furnishings have been introduced since the 1970s.

The stained glass in the west window is of about 1850 after the destruction of the previous glass in a gas explosion in 1847, whilst the east window by Burlison and Grylls commemorates Sister Dora, who died in 1878 (see illustration on p.140). Sister Dora, or Dorothy Wyndlow Pattison, worked as a nurse in Walsall during the smallpox epidemics here in 1868 and 1869, having joined the Sisterhood of the Good Samaritans in 1864. She actively campaigned for a hospital in the town which opened just before her death, and she is also commemorated by a statue at 'The Bridge' in the town.

Walsall, St. Matthew — the lychgate

The worn effigy in the south aisle to a member of the Hillary family was long believed to be that of Sir Roger Hillary of Bescot who died in about 1400, but as the costume is of a fashion about fifty years earlier this is unlikely. There are many memorial tablets in the church.

A chiming clock is recorded in the tower in 1468 but the present clock dates from 1865. Ten of the thirteen bells were recast in 1929, though the earliest dates from 1553. The church is one of just thirty-five in the country to have over twelve bells. The present memorial lychgate is a fine timber structure of 1927, and the churchyard contains a variety of grave memorials, while the First World War memorial is an outdoor pulpit situated on the steps down the hill towards the town. The area to the south of the church was rebuilt as St. Matthew's Close in 1950 and includes a memorial garden and pavilion by Sir Geoffrey Jellicoe. The square of housing terminates in a church hall and office to the east end.

WALSALL   ST. ANDREW, BIRCHILLS STREET, BIRCHILLS

Birchills is an area of mainly Victorian terraced houses to the north-west of the town centre and is bisected by the Wyrley and Essington Canal at Walsall Locks. The name is derived from the Anglo-Saxon word *bryce* meaning 'enclosure', and is not connected with birch trees.

St. Andrew's church started as a mission in 1855 from nearby St. Peter's church, and services were held in the school in Hollyhedge Lane. Land for a new church was given by the Earl of Bradford and construction commenced in 1884. Funds were short and work on the building, which cost almost £4,000, was often delayed so that the church was not opened until 1887, with St. Andrew becoming a separate parish the following year. Designed by John Edward Knight Cutts and John Priston Cutts, St. Andrew's church bears several similarities to their church at Hasbury, near Halesowen. It is built in red brick with stone dressings in the Early English style with characteristic lancet windows, and is a tall, aisled building with clerestorey and steeply pitched roofs. The wooden bellcote with spirelet is placed at the division between nave and chancel. A western baptistery has porches to the sides in a similar manner to St. Augustine, Dudley. The chancel has a chapel to the north and organ chamber to the south.

The interior is dominated by the Early English style arcades with their round columns and pointed arches. The use of whitewash to parts of the walls around the arches and in the aisles is an effective contrast to the exposed brickwork elsewhere in the church. There is a wealth of early twentieth-century stained glass, with figures of saints in most of the lancet windows, reflecting the High Church tradition which became firmly established here under the vicar Ronald Wynn Griffith between 1890 and 1927. There are early twentieth-century furnishings in the Lady Chapel, as well as shrines and Stations of the Cross. The reredos commemorates those lost in the First World War, whilst the Crucifix and prayer desk of Sister Dora (for whom see under St. Matthew, above) are particular treasures.

The church hall was completed in 1902, whilst the former vicarage was built in 1916 in the Queen Anne style and is similar to that at St. Peter, Spring Hill in Birmingham. The large Crucifix at the east end is a First World War memorial.

WALSALL   ST. GEORGE, PERSEHOUSE STREET

This church was founded as a mission from St. Matthew's church in 1873 on land which was given by the second Lord Hatherton close to the location of the Arboretum, the establishment of which was perhaps his most philanthropic gesture to the borough of Walsall. The parish was created out of St. Matthew in 1878, but united with St. Paul in 1964 when this church was demolished. It was designed in the Early English style by Stafford architect Robert Griffiths and completed in 1875, though a side chapel was added in 1911. The planned tower and spire were never erected. There was an aisled nave and a chancel with a vestry and organ chamber. The church was built in limestone with sandstone dressings, whilst the interior was predominantly faced in brick.

WALSALL   ST. LUKE, SELBORNE STREET, CHUCKERY

Dominated by the nearby tower blocks, this mission church was founded in 1879 from St. Matthew's church to replace a previous mission of 1871 in Bott Lane. St. Luke's church serves an area on the east side of St. Matthew's parish which developed in the nineteenth century on the church fields from which the name Chuckery is derived. It is a long building of nave and narthex in red and blue brick with stone dressings designed by H.E. Lavender, extended with the addition of a chancel in 1934, all under a single roof in a simple late Perpendicular style. The light whitewashed interior was reordered in the 1990s to provide a community hall and facilities which are divided from the worship space by an imposing glazed screen.

WALSALL   ST. MARK, BUTTS ROAD

St. Mark's church was erected as a mission chapel in 1871 within the parish of St. Michael, Rushall on the north-east side of Walsall. It was consecrated in 1925, but closed in 1973 and demolished the following year. The church was designed by Robert Griffiths who was also architect of nearby St. George's church. It was a brick building in the Early English style, and had an unaisled nave with bellcote and chancel with an organ chamber. The west vestry was added in 1949. A sixteenth-century wooden Flemish reredos from St. Mary, Wolverhampton was installed here in 1948 — it was transferred to St. Paul's church when St. Mark's closed.

WALSALL   ST. MARTIN, SUTTON ROAD

The church was established on the corner of Daffodil Road as a mission from St. Matthew's church to serve the growing housing estates on the east side of Walsall. The brick building was designed by Shipley and Foster of Walsall in 1960, and has a striking, tall hipped roof.

WALSALL   ST. MARY AND ALL SAINTS, DALE STREET, PALFREY

The district of Palfrey, named after Palfrey House, developed in the nineteenth century to the south of Caldmore, and St. Mary's church was established as a mission church in the parish of St. Michael in 1893, becoming a separate parish in 1902. The church was erected to designs of John Edward Knight Cutts, John Priston Cutts and Edward Turner. It is a large red brick building in the Perpendicular style with an aisled nave and clerestorey, north and south porches and bellcote. To the east is the chancel with north and south chapels, organ chamber and vestry. The influence of the Arts and Crafts movement in the design is very evident. The church was closed in 1997 and the parish divided between St. Michael, Caldmore and St. Gabriel, Fullbrook. Since 2002 the church has been the Greek Orthodox Church of the Nativity of the Mother of God. The colourful mosaics on the exterior at the west end include an icon of the Virgin and Child. The foundation stone of the adjacent vicarage was laid by the Earl of Lauderdale in 1909.

WALSALL ST. MICHAEL AND ALL ANGELS, BATH ROAD, CALDMORE

A mission to the Caldmore area from St. Matthew's church opened in 1866 and the parish was created in 1872. The red sandstone church with limestone dressings of 1870-1 was built in the Early English style to designs by James Read Veall and Henry Lovett and lies on a sloping site. It has an apsidal chancel and nave, though the north aisle was not added until 1878 and the south aisle in 1880. Some of the windows are lancets whilst others have plate tracery, and there is a rose window at the west end. The planned north tower with imposing broach spire was never built. The vicar, J.F. Laing, added the apsidal south chapel between 1880 and 1884, followed by the north chapel and vestry in the 1920s in memory of his sister, Elizabeth, who had been responsible for the construction of the vicarage in 1913. The west porch of 1870 is of two storeys with the vestry above.

Inside, the nave arcades have round columns with carved foliage to the capitals and pointed arches; above these pairs of clerestorey lancets are divided internally by shafts with smaller carved foliage capitals. The wide chancel arch has carved capitals and further banded shafts to the sides. The font and pulpit are Victorian with carved decoration. There is an elaborate reredos with statues of saints in the apse behind the high altar. The church has been of the High Church tradition since the nineteenth century.

The church was seriously damaged by fire in 1964 and the roofs date from the subsequent reconstruction which was completed by 1967.

WALSALL   ST. PAUL, ST. PAUL'S STREET

A chapel in Queen Mary Grammar School dedicated to St. Paul had been founded in 1797, and in 1826 the first church of St. Paul was built to the designs of Francis Goodwin, architect for the rebuilding of St. Matthew's church. It was Classical in appearance and of brick like his church of St. Leonard, Bilston, and comprised a nave and west tower to which a larger chancel was added in 1852. In 1875 a parish was established to serve the Wisemore area in the parishes of St. Matthew and St. Peter and in 1892-3 the church was replaced by the present sandstone structure designed by John Loughborough Pearson, though the planned tower and spire were never

Walsall, St. Paul now provides a centre with shops and a café

erected over the south porch. It is in the Decorated style and has an aisled nave with clerestorey, north and south porches, transepts and apsidal chancel. The south chapel is also apsidal and there is an organ chamber on the north side of the chancel.

The interior has been transformed by the conversion of the church in 1995 to form 'The Crossing at St. Paul's'. The centre with shops and café takes its name from the cruciform shape of the Victorian church. The arcades of five bays of which the eastern arches open into the transepts, along with the chancel arch and those to the organ chamber and side chapel are all Decorated in style. There are fine timber roof structures. There was oak panelling to the chancel with carved choir stalls and an elaborately carved stone font. There are several good stained glass windows and the pulpit was erected as a memorial to the pupils of Queen Mary Grammar School. Some of the earlier furnishings remain in the side chapel, but the principal worship space is now at roof level in the nave.

Sister Dora was a member of the congregation of St. Paul's chapel. Her work for the sick of the town is commemorated in the nearby statue and a stained glass window at St. Matthew's church.

WALSALL   ST. PETER, STAFFORD STREET

St. Peter was erected to serve the north-western area of the parish of St. Matthew between 1839 and 1841. The site was the gift of Lord Hatherton, Member of Parliament for Staffordshire and keen promoter of railways. The light brown brick Commissioners' type church was designed by local architect Isaac Highway working with Stourbridge architect Thomas Smith, and has a tower at the east end facing Stafford Street, for the church is unusually orientated with the chancel at the west end. The tower has lancet bell openings, battlements and pinnacles, with a main doorway as well as side porches. There is a wide nave typical of this type of church, with lancet windows, a low pitched roof and parapets. The chancel was lengthened in 1910 using red brick but in a similar style and has a triple lancet end window. The vestry and organ chamber are to the sides.

Inside, the gallery at the tower end supported by cast iron columns remains as one of the few original features to the attractive interior, which was largely refurnished in the early twentieth century. The side galleries have been removed and box pews replaced. In the chancel there is a fine alabaster reredos with statues of Christ, St. Peter and St. Chad. This, together with the panelling and choir stalls, was the gift of C.E. McCreery, vicar here in the early twentieth century. There is also a stone sedilia. The carved wooden pulpit was installed in 1904 as a memorial to Job and Eliza Wheway, and the screen erected in 1907 to commemorate members of the Gnosill family. Much of the stained glass dates from the mid twentieth century. Amongst the memorial tablets can be found those to the second vicar, Charles Dunn, who died in 1863, and his son who died eleven years previously.

WALSALL   ST. STEPHEN, RYECROFT

A mission church was founded here in 1890 from St. Michael, Rushall to serve the area between Rushall and St. Peter, Stafford Street. The church became a chapel of ease to St. Mark, Butts Road from 1920, but had closed by 1946.

WALSALL WOOD   ST. JOHN, HIGH STREET

Walsall Wood from the south-west

Close to Brownhills, Walsall Wood straddles the busy Walsall to Lichfield road. This was the southern end of Cannock Chase which developed in the late nineteenth century as a result of coalmining and brickmaking. Indeed Vigo, the southern part of Walsall Wood, is named after the large Vigo brickworks. Near Shireoaks Country Park are the earthworks of a prehistoric hillfort.

St. John's church lies on the north side of the main road at the village centre. There was a mission church here from St. Matthew, Walsall by the 1820s before which services were held in a schoolroom. The church is a brick building of 1837 originally designed by Isaac Highway, two years before he began work on St. Peter, Walsall. Only the plain blue brick west tower with lancet bell openings in the Early English style and west wall of the nave survive. In 1886 the body of the church, which had just nave and chancel under one roof, was rebuilt in red brick with a south aisle and new short chancel, and then the north aisle and vestries were added by H.E. Lavender in 1895, all using the same Early English style. A large Scandinavian style timber and glazed entrance with steep roofs was added to the south-west corner in 1987, with a western extension to house community facilities

The interior is whitewashed and light. The nave arcades have cast iron columns with thin, pointed arches. The style is more 1830s than 1880s or 1890s. The chancel arch is complementary Early English. The simple wooden furnishings all date from the recent renovation and reordering, whilst the stained glass in the east window shows the Crucifixion as a memorial to Edward Lazenby who died in 1908. Glass in a further window is a memorial to John Coleridge Patteson, first Bishop of Melanesia, who was closely associated with the work of Bishop Selwyn of Lichfield whilst he was in Auckland, New Zealand. Patteson was killed on a mission when visiting the island of Nukapu in 1871 and is commemorated as a martyr. His portrait is in the glass.

WARLEY WOODS

ST. HILDA, ABBEY ROAD

Warley Woods, St. Hilda from the south-east

Warley is a district without a centre, yet it gave its name to a county borough including Smethwick, Oldbury and Rowley Regis. Warley Abbey was a substantial Gothic house of 1819, which was built on the site of a Grange that belonged to Halesowen Abbey, and so named by Hubert Galton who erected it on the family estate. Landscaped in the eighteenth century by Humphrey Repton, the park at Warley Woods still forms an attractive undulating open space in which Warley Abbey survived until 1957. Nearby, St. Hilda's church was founded as a mission church from Christ Church, Quinton in 1906. The first building was erected in Rathbone Road. With the increasing housing development in the area after the First World War the need for a new church was quickly established, though the present St. Hilda's church was not consecrated until 1940 on a new site along Abbey Road. The building in Rathbone Road is now used by the Plymouth Brethren.

The last church to be designed by Edwin Francis Reynolds, it is orientated north to south, and built of red brown brick in the Byzantine style. The wide nave leads to an apsidal northern chancel with small round-headed windows. At the south end of the nave is an oblong open belfry with hipped roof. Reynolds was a Birmingham architect who continued the Arts and Crafts tradition and was often inspired by early Christian architecture. Together with St. Germain, Edgbaston and St. Mary, Pype Hayes in Birmingham, this church reflects a following of the principles of William Richard Lethaby in producing finely composed, high quality buildings. A new porch with wide entrance was added beneath the belfry in 1995.

The whitewashed brick interior is simply furnished. It has a barrel-vaulted roof in the manner of a Roman public building, with the small windows opening above the line of the spring of the vault. There is a fine view into the apse around the altar which stands in a raised sanctuary area. A gallery at the back of the nave houses the organ of 1962 by Rushworth and Dreaper.

WARLEY WOODS

ST. KATHERINE, GEORGE ROAD, BRISTNALL FIELDS

The side chapel dedicated to St. Katherine in St. Hilda, Warley Woods recalls the simple iron mission church in George Road, which closed in 1961. This had been founded in 1898 to serve part of Quinton parish and was typical of its date, with a louvred belfry and short spire at the west end of the nave. The dedication recalls a chapel known to have existed at nearby Brand Hall in 1308. Today the most prominent church in this part of the town is the large Italianate Roman Catholic church of Our Lady and St. Hubert, built in 1935 on land given by Major Hubert Galton of the prominent family of ironmasters.

WEDNESBURY   ST. BARTHOLOMEW, CHURCH HILL

Wednesbury takes its name from the Anglo-Saxon god, Woden. The area around the top of Church Hill is the site of an Iron Age hillfort, which is the earliest evidence of settlement here. It may be that there was a temple to Woden within the fort during the pagan Anglo-Saxon period of the fifth and sixth centuries, but the element 'bury' is more likely to refer to the continued occupation of the prehistoric earthwork than to the story that a fort was constructed by Ethelfreda, a Mercian princess and daughter of King Alfred. With clearance of many other early buildings from around the hilltop, the site once again has an air of openness with expansive views across the Black Country towards Dudley in the south and Walsall in the north. The medieval manor house was to the north-east of the church, but the town centre developed to the south beyond High Bullen, and had a market which was granted a charter in 1709. Telford's London to Holyhead road was the focus of further development from the 1820s, and fine civic buildings including an Art Gallery were erected after the town became a municipal borough in 1886, though the centre has been in decline during more recent years. Earthenware pottery known as Wedgbury Ware was made here from the seventeenth century. Iron, coal and limestone were all mined and worked here, but the town specialised in the manufacture of tubes, including

Wednesbury, St. Bartholomew from the south

gun barrels, from the eighteenth century, followed by gas mains and vehicle shafts from the nineteenth. Although the Patent Shaft Works closed in 1980, some small ironworks are still in existence, and Wednesbury today is surrounded by business and retail parks.

Visible from miles around, the blackened sandstone St. Bartholomew's church and the neighbouring brick Roman Catholic church of St. Mary of 1873 by Gilbert Blount with its green copper spire, make a memorable picture on the top of the hill. The large church consists of a west tower with spire, aisled nave with clerestorey and porch, transepts and chancel with apse, side chapels and vestry. It is likely that there was a significant Anglo-Saxon church here but no evidence can be seen. The earliest identified masonry seems to be the west tower arch of the fourteenth century, though the north wall

Wednesbury, St. Bartholomew, the lectern

113

Wednesbury, St. Bartholomew, the east end

*Wednesbury, St. Bartholomew,
the altar and reredos*

of the north aisle contains what may be a reset and blocked round-headed twelfth-century arch, as well as a Perpendicular window. The church was much rebuilt in the sixteenth century by the town guild and a chapel dedicated to the Virgin was founded. A seven-sided apse was added to the east end similar to that at St. Michael, Coventry, one of the most prosperous churches in the West Midlands which was also much supported by craft guilds. The medieval patrons of Wednesbury were Halesowen Abbey.

The tower contains further medieval masonry whilst the spire was rebuilt in 1757 and 1854. The nave and north transept were rebuilt in 1827 by George Lindley Dickinson, encasing much medieval fabric. There are three-light Perpendicular style windows with transoms. The church was restored between 1873 and 1879 by George Bidlake and Thomas Henry Fleeming, and in 1890 the east end including the apse and the south transept was rebuilt by Basil Champneys, broadly following the design of the medieval building and all in the Perpendicular style.

The beautiful interior is striking and unexpected. The box pews and galleries of the light Perpendicular style nave were replaced later in the nineteenth century and the east end is highly ornamented, giving a great sense of the medieval church. The wall painting of Christ in Majesty over

Wednesbury, St. Bartholomew, the window at the west end of the south aisle showing the destruction of the temple of Woden and its replacement with a church

the chancel arch is by Godfrey Gray, a Cambridge artist and stained glass designer (see also rear cover). The paintings on the chancel walls are executed on canvas and mounted. The screens in the chancel arch are by Bridgeman of Lichfield, as are the fine alabaster communion rails and reredos with statues of St. Chad and the five saints to whom the churches of Wednesbury were dedicated. The sanctuary pavement is fine mosaic work and the altar elaborately painted. The screens to the side chapel and the organ chamber are by Bateman and Bateman. Some earlier fittings also survive. The wooden fourteenth-century lectern, carved with an extraordinary fighting cock, is a most unusual survival. The fine wooden pulpit is dated 1611 and has panels ornamented with both arabesque designs and blank arches. The painting showing the Descent from the Cross, now at the west end, is a former altarpiece of 1698 by Jean Jouvenet. It had subsequently been overpainted, and was acquired in 1883 by a local man called Perks who removed the later paint by hand and presented the uncovered image to the church in 1888. The font dates from 1856, when it was presented by the then vicar, Isaac Clarkson. The nineteenth-century organ is from the demolished Christ Church, West Bromwich.

Wednesbury, St. Bartholomew,
the pulpit

One of the great glories of the church is the set of fifteen stained glass windows by Charles Eamer Kempe and his successor, Walter Tower of C.E. Kempe and Co. Ltd. They range in date from 1890 to 1927, and many bear Kempe's customary wheatsheaf mark. Most of the north aisle windows show Old Testament characters whilst most of those in the south are of saints. The chancel windows depict scenes from the life of Christ, together with images of Abraham and King David. The window at the west end of the south aisle, showing the destruction of the temple of Woden and its replacement with a church, dates from 1904.

There is a fine collection of memorials. The largest, moved in 1885 from the chancel to the west end of the south aisle, is the effigy of Richard Parkes who died in 1618. He is shown next to that of his wife, Dorothy, who died in 1628. They are in contemporary costume and she is dressed as a widow. The chest is decorated with strapwork. In the chancel is a small tablet with the kneeling figures of Thomas Parkes, of the same family, who died in 1602 with his wife, Eleanor, above their six children. Three memorial tablets by Peter Hollins of Birmingham include a bust of Isaac Clarkson who died in 1860. The fine wooden panelling is a series of memorials including to those who died in the First World War, while a piece in the north aisle records John Ashley Kilvert, a survivor of the Charge of the Light Brigade in the Crimea in 1854, who was mayor in 1905. The earliest bell in the tower is dated 1614.

WEDNESBURY   ST. ANDREW, DARLASTON ROAD, KINGS HILL

A chapel of ease to St. Bartholomew's church dedicated to St. Andrew started as a mission in 1851 to the area between Wednesbury and Darlaston. The church, dedicated in 1894, is a plain small brick building with a nave and chancel with lancet windows to the east and west. There are also lancet windows beneath double gables to the sides in the Early English style, but slender square-headed lights to the rest of the sides and to the porches by the western narthex. There is a small octagonal turret to the west end, and a central louvred turret with spirelet.

WEDNESBURY   ST. JAMES, ST. JAMES STREET

St. James' church stands close to the site of Russell's Tube Works in Dudley Street, now part of the ring road. Cornelius Whitehouse developed the butt-welded tube here in the 1820s, the manufacture of which led Wednesbury to be known as 'Tube Town' by the end of the century.

The parish was created in 1844. The church was built in 1847 in light brown sandstone to designs by William Horton. It is a Commissioners' type church, and had a small apsidal chancel at the east end of a large nave, with Early English style lancet windows throughout. The tower was never completed and is finished with a pyramidal cap. However, the chancel was extended in 1857 by William Darby Griffin and John Weller, whilst a large apse was added in 1865 as memorial to the wife of the rector, Richard Twigg. In 1888 vestries and a new chapel were designed by S. Horton for the north side of the chancel as a memorial to Lt. Col. John Nock Bagnall of the Staffordshire Rifle Volunteers, whose family owned the Leabrook Ironworks. This considerable enlargement of the east end represents the adoption here of High Church practice in the second half of the nineteenth century. Richard Twigg was involved in Catholic evangelism in London and brought this to Wednesbury, as a result becoming known as the 'Apostle of the Black Country'. Curates were sent into nearby parishes such as Tividale and Willenhall.

Wednesbury, St. James from the south

The whitewashed interior has been recently refurbished. It is striking in its contrast between the Commissioners' nave and the Gothic Revival chancel in the Decorated style, with its clerestorey and heavily chamfered arcade to the side aisle. The result is similar to that at Oldswinford. The nave was originally fitted with box pews and central pulpit in the Protestant style of the day. The west gallery remains with cast iron supports and a central projection. The font is of the nineteenth century and pulpit of the early twentieth century. The three stalls were brought from St. Bartholomew's church. The wrought iron screen to the side chapel was erected in 1912. These and other more simple modern furnishings are complemented by the black and white stone floor. The church contains many statues of saints, several of which are nineteenth-century memorials. There is a memorial brass in the form of a cross to the wife of the first rector, William Cole, who died in 1856, in whose memory the carved eagle lectern was also given. There is also a memorial to the charismatic Richard Twigg, who died in 1879.

The clock was installed in the tower in 1894 to commemorate the fiftieth anniversary of the parish's foundation. The rectory was built in 1849, whilst the schools across the street date from 1860.

WEDNESBURY   ST. JOHN, LOWER HIGH STREET

The site of St. John's church is opposite the Quaker Meeting House which was founded in 1680 (and rebuilt after construction of the railway cutting caused it to be demolished in 1862), and next to the Congregational Church of 1848. The church was opened in 1846 and consisted of a chancel, aisled nave with clerestorey and north-west tower with tall broach spire. It was designed by Samuel Whitfield Daukes and John Hamilton of Gloucester and was in the Early English style with lancet windows. The parish was merged with that of St. James and the church was demolished in 1985, at a great loss to the Wednesbury skyline. A tall limestone cross, a memorial to the Trow family, survives in the graveyard.

WEDNESFIELD

ST. THOMAS, HIGH STREET

A small village until the nineteenth century, Wednesfield has Anglo-Saxon origins and the name refers to the Anglo-Saxon god, Woden, (as it does at neighbouring Wednesbury). Wednesfield is reputedly the site of a victory by the Anglo-Saxons led by King Edward the Elder of Wessex over the Danes in 910. The site of the battle is described in the *Anglo-Saxon Chronicle* as near Tettenhall, but is perhaps linked to Wednesfield because of the readily identifiable Anglo-Saxon place name. Now on the outer eastern fringe of Wolverhampton, industry developed here following the opening of the Wyrley and Essington Link Canal. There was a variety of small scale metal working, including

Wednesfield, St. Thomas from the south-east

the manufacture of keys, but the town became more noted for the making of animal traps. Sidebotham's trap factory is now reconstructed at the Black Country Living Museum. Housing developments from the 1950s, including some high rise flats, are served by a rebuilt shopping area in the town centre, all of which overshadow the remaining attractive terrace of nineteenth-century cottages and shops to the west of the church in Church Street.

The church was first built in 1751 as a chapel of ease to St. Peter, Wolverhampton. A chancel was added in 1842-3 by Thomas Henry Wyatt and David Brandon. However the church was gutted by fire in 1902 and had to be extensively rebuilt by Frederick Beck in the following year. Today it is an elegant red brick Classical style building. It has a slender west tower with balustrades to the top and acorn finials to the corners rather than pinnacles. At the base is a pedimented west doorway with a round window above, and round-headed bell openings in the upper stage. The nave has square windows to the lower level with both rectangular and round-headed windows above. The nave parapet has some balustrading. The chancel is taller and built in a more orange brick with side windows with rounded pediments over abutting side vestries with square windows. At the east end is a lower semi-circular apse with large round-headed windows.

The interior is largely painted in a pink wash and has barrel-vaulted ceilings to the nave and aisles. The coved ceiling to the apse is decorated with thin plaster ribs. The wide round-headed chancel arch is spanned by a dark wooden rood beam, and has double pilasters to the sides. These are Doric below and Ionic above. The side galleries are supported by Doric columns with Ionic columns above to complement the chancel arch. All the main elements are dark coloured, though the columns supporting the galleries are in a bright shade of pink. In the apse can be found a Classical style reredos and communion rail. The tall pulpit stands by the chancel arch and has open Classical style arches to the sides, and rests on five columns. Access is by an elegant stair with bannister. There is an octagonal font with a cover in the form of a cupola. Several memorial tablets include some encaustic tiles. The stained glass in the nave windows includes two windows of 1949 and 1950 by Archibald Davies of the Bromsgrove Guild, whilst in 1971 two further windows were installed by Bronwen Gordon, a tutor of stained glass at Wolverhampton Polytechnic.

The small triangular churchyard forms an attractive green oasis to the shopping street with its mature trees, and contains some good nineteenth-century memorials, particularly that of the 1840s to John, Ann and Jane Bate with an urn on a tall plinth.

WEDNESFIELD   ST. ALBAN, GRIFFITHS DRIVE, ASHMORE PARK

In 1965 a new church was built to serve the housing estates of Ashmore Park to the north-east of Wednesfield. The church was designed by Norman Cachmaille-Day, architect of distinguished churches such as St. Mary, Twyford in London and Epiphany, Gipton in Leeds, but executed by the Rev. A.S.B. Hill after Cachmaille-Day's retirement in 1965. The church is orientated north to south with a low saddleback tower at the north end. It is constructed in yellow brick with a low pitched roof (see illustration on p.11). Opposite on the green is preserved the earthwork of a medieval moat which surrounded buildings on the estates of St. Peter's church, Wolverhampton. The purpose of the site in medieval times is unclear.

WEDNESFIELD   ST. CHAD, STUBBY LANE

This church was built in 1957 on the corner of Lichfield Road and Stubby Lane to serve the housing developments to the north-east of the town centre. It is a plain building in contemporary style which also serves as a community centre.

WEDNESFIELD   ST. GREGORY THE GREAT, BLACKHALVE LANE

Erected in 1965 to serve the growing housing estates to the north-west of Wednesfield, St. Gregory's church was designed by Clifford Tee and Gale of Edgbaston. The imposing entrance facade is in red brick and glass with low gables to the side walls behind. The interior is simple, light and contemporary. Towards the road is a plain, thin campanile which stands to less than the height of the church.

WEST BROMWICH   ALL SAINTS, ALL SAINTS WAY

Until the nineteenth century West Bromwich was a parish of scattered settlements on the high heathlands to the west of the Sandwell Valley. The medieval settlement was centred on All Saints, the ancient parish church, and the Manor House. Remarkably, both still exist about one mile to the north of the present town centre in what is now a mainly twentieth-century residential area. The medieval manor was held by the Devereux and Marnham families. The timber-framed house, which was probably erected for William de Marnham in the fourteenth century, is now a public house in Hall Green Road. It was rescued from dereliction in the late 1950s, and with its medieval hall, solar and chapel and Tudor gatehouse is one of the best preserved small moated manor houses in the Midlands. About a mile to the east of the church is the cottage in Newton Road which was the home from 1746 of Francis Asbury, who became the first Bishop of the American Methodist Church in 1784. He preached throughout the eastern United States until his death in 1818, and is often referred to as the John Wesley of America. As a child Asbury attended All Saints' church, and his childhood home is now a museum.

The red sandstone church retains its Decorated tower of about 1400, with characteristic west window and bell openings. There is an octagonal stair turret on the north side and the top is crowned with battlements and pinnacles. On the south side is a sundial. The medieval church was replaced in 1872 to the designs of Somers Clarke by a new nave with north porch, south aisle together with a chancel, south chapel and north organ chamber, all in the early Decorated style. This was built under the patronage of the Earl of Dartmouth of Sandwell Hall, along with Frederick and Mary Willet, and her father, John Nock Bagnall of Wednesbury. The south aisle stands on the site of the medieval nave, and the east wall of the reconstructed medieval south chapel has a reset, worn plaque dated 1691. There is early Decorated style tracery to the windows.

Inside most features are the work of Somers Clarke. The chamfered pointed arches to the arcades and the chancel arch are in the Early English style. The shafts to the chancel arch are echoed in the internal shafts to the east window. However, the octagonal font is Perpendicular with carved shields in quatrefoils to the sides. The medieval chest is a 'dug out' from one tree trunk. A fragment of a Norman column is preserved under the tower, indicating that the previous church dated at least to the twelfth century. It is recorded that from about 1230 the church (then dedicated to St. Clement, a dedication retained until 1801) became a possession of Sandwell Priory. The western part of the church has now been partitioned to create space for community facilities.

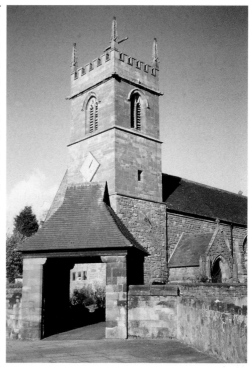

*West Bromwich, All Saints
from the south-west*

The stained glass in the north and south windows of the chancel are of 1872-3 by James Powell and Sons to the designs of H.E. Wooldridge. There is a good collection of memorial tablets, particularly from the early nineteenth century. However there are two earlier effigies. When the medieval church was undergoing alteration in the eighteenth century, they were placed together on one chest. The male figure is probably Field Whorwood who died in 1658, whilst the female is believed to be Anne Whorwood who died in 1599, both of Sandwell Hall. The Whorwood Chapel stands to the south of the medieval nave but was extensively reconstructed and converted to a vestry during the nineteenth-century rebuilding.

The large churchyard is adjacent to the open countryside of Sandwell Valley Park on the east side. It contains a variety of grave memorials of which the earliest are seventeenth century. The lychgate by the tower is a memorial of 1876 to churchwarden Thomas Jesson, whose family had long been associated with the iron industry in West Bromwich.

WEST BROMWICH   CHRIST CHURCH, HIGH STREET

The destruction of Christ Church has robbed West Bromwich of one of its most important town centre buildings. The graveyard, with its avenues of lime trees leading to the site of the church, forms a garden area opposite the former Victorian Town Hall and Edwardian Library at the heart of the town. A short distance to the south, the sixteenth-century timber-framed Oak House with its curious lantern is an unexpected survival amongst the Victorian terraces. After centuries of occupation by the Turton family, the house was bought in 1894 by Reuben Farley who presented it to the town as a museum. The main street grew up along the line of Thomas Telford's London to Holyhead road. Further development of the sparse heathlands was rapid and the population expanded from just under 6,000 to about 65,000 during the nineteenth century. There was extensive coalmining and ironworking from which the principal products were bedsteads, flat irons, stoves and grates. Interesting twentieth-century personalities include film star Madeleine Carroll, who grew up in Herbert Street on the east side of the town centre. The town is well known for the football club West Bromwich Albion who play at the Hawthorns on the boundary with Birmingham.

The Earl of Dartmouth laid the foundation stone of Christ Church in 1821. This was the first new church to be built in West Bromwich amidst growing concern from the church authorities about the lack of provision of church buildings in such a fast expanding settlement. Faced in sandstone from Tixall which became smoke blackened, it was designed by Francis Goodwin and finally completed in 1829 in an imposing Gothic design. It was very similar to his contemporary church of St. George, Kidderminster, and had a west tower of 114 feet in height with long bell openings and tall pinnacles. An elaborate portal led to the large, high nave with Perpendicular style windows with iron tracery, similar to that installed by Goodwin at St. Matthew, Walsall. Beyond was a short chancel. In 1858 the church was restored by Ewan Christian following damage by mining subsidence, and there was a further restoration for the same reason in 1876.

The original furnishings were much altered by the early twentieth century with the replacement of the large three decker pulpit and the box pews being reduced in height. There were three galleries, with the first organ on the west gallery. In 1878 a new organ was installed on the north side of the chancel, and this is now in St. Bartholomew, Wednesbury. The church was closed in 1978, gutted by fire in 1979 and completely demolished during the following year.

WEST BROMWICH ST. ANDREW, DUDLEY STREET, CARTERS GREEN

West Bromwich, St. Francis from the south-east

The church was begun in 1925, but not completed until 1940, to serve the housing estates at Swan Village. It replaced a plain brick mission chapel by Somers Clarke of 1867 in Old Meeting Street. The present church was designed by Wood and Kendrick, and has an aisled nave and chancel with clerestorey. The building is of red brick and in the Perpendicular style, but it is orientated east to west. At the east end is a lower baptistery and there are turrets to frame the east front, with a porch to the side. Inside the walls are whitewashed, which highlights the stone arcades with round columns and pointed arches. It has been recently reordered and is attractively laid out. The low stone screen at the entrance to the chancel has been retained, as has the altar with reredos of painted panels with figures of Christ and four saints. Today it serves as a joint Anglican and Methodist church.

WEST BROMWICH ASCENSION, WALSALL ROAD, STONE CROSS

A mission church from St. Francis was built in 1938 but closed in 1958 and demolished. The building had been extended by Scott and Clark in 1951.

WEST BROMWICH   **ST. FRANCIS OF ASSISI, FREEMAN ROAD,**
FRIAR PARK

Friar Park, once in the parish of All Saints, was made part of the parish of St. Paul, Wood Green in 1875. With the widespread housing developments of the twentieth century it was established as a parish with plans for a new church by 1937. St. Francis was completed in 1941 to the designs of William Alexander Harvey and Herbert Wicks and is a most memorable building, like their church of St. Francis, Bournville in Birmingham of some ten years earlier. It is a basilica, in an Italian Romanesque style, and has a long aisled nave with clerestorey and porches towards the west end. The carvings on the porch entrances are of Christ surrounded by saints and angels. The tower is at the east end, over the chancel, with an apse beyond. The vestry and organ chamber form a south transept just to the west of the tower and there is a chapel on the north side of the north aisle. The windows and openings are all round headed. The roofs are mainly of pantiles, whilst the tower has a curving capped roof supporting a gilded figure of Christ.

Inside there are plastered walls and round-headed arches on octagonal piers to the arcades. The choir has galleries, and there is a sedilia and screen in the chancel, on which are placed kneeling figures with a Crucifix above. The roofs are finely painted. The furnishings and woodwork are contemporary, including the pews and choir stalls, whilst the stone font has prominent mouldings. The chapel in the south aisle was furnished as a First World War memorial. Some of the furnishing work was undertaken by Italian prisoners of war.

WEST BROMWICH   **ST. JAMES, HILL TOP**

The Earl of Dartmouth and James Bagnall were the main subscribers to the building of a new church as a chapel of ease to All Saints in the north-western part of West Bromwich. Work began in 1842 and St. James' church opened two years later. The site had been the gift of Joseph Hateley, a member of a prominent West Bromwich family of landowners. The brick building was designed in the Perpendicular style by Robert Ebbels with a large nave and west front with twin pinnacles, and was similar to his church at Upper Gornal. A tower was added to the south-west corner in 1890, unbalancing the symmetry of the building. The furnishings were largely replaced in 1892, when the box pews were removed, and the side galleries removed in 1904.

The church was demolished in 1989. It was replaced by the present brick church and community building in 1995, which forms a landmark on the main road from West Bromwich to Wednesbury.

WEST BROMWICH   **ST. MARK, DUKE STREET**

An iron mission church was opened here from Christ Church in 1892. It was replaced by a brick church in 1904, which closed in 1933 and has subsequently been demolished.

WEST BROMWICH   **ST. MARY MAGDALENE,**
BEACON VIEW ROAD, CHARLEMONT FARM

A new church was erected on the Charlemont Farm Estate in 1966. It is a small, simple, square, brick building with sloping roof, somewhat overshadowed by the neighbouring tower blocks. The interior has exposed brick walls and is laid out in a traditional manner with contemporary furnishings.

WEST BROMWICH   **ST. MICHAEL AND ALL ANGELS, BULL LANE**

This church of 1881 was designed by Wood and Kendrick with a nave and baptistery, a chancel and vestries. The site was given by Henry Jesson, the curate at St. Andrew, in which parish this was a chapel of ease. The church was closed in 1953 and demolished in the 1970s.

WEST BROMWICH   **ST. PAUL, BAGNALL STREET, GOLDS HILL**

Golds Hill is a hidden area between Hill Top and Great Bridge on the far western side of West Bromwich, close to the Tame Valley Canal. The church originated as a mission at the Golds Hill Ironworks of James Bagnall and was a chapel of ease to St. James, Hill Top. In 1887 a separate parish was created from the western part of St. James. The brick church was built in 1881-2 and has a nave and chancel with bellcote above the chancel arch. Many of the furnishings were brought from a mission chapel founded by Bagnalls for their workforce in Bilston.

WEST BROMWICH   **ST. PHILIP, BEECHES ROAD**

This church was built in 1897-8 to the designs of West Bromwich architects Wood and Kendrick on land close to Dartmouth Park given by the Earl of Dartmouth. It replaced a plain church of 1892 which then became a hall. This in turn had replaced in 1874 an earlier mission church established from Christ Church. The brick church is in the Early English style with an aisled nave of 1898, to which a chancel, Lady Chapel and vestries were added in 1913.

WEST BROMWICH   **GOOD SHEPHERD AND ST. JOHN THE EVANGELIST, LYTTLETON STREET**

A new church to replace the earlier churches of the Good Shepherd and St. John was erected on a new site in 1967-8 to the designs of John Taylor from the Birmingham practice of John Madin, whose Central Library in Birmingham has been the subject of great controversy throughout its forty-year history. The blue brick building combines church and community facilities.

A mission chapel of the Good Shepherd had opened in Ault Street in 1880 and was replaced by a second chapel in 1902 in Spon Lane. A church was then built in 1908-9 to the designs of Wood and Kendrick on the adjacent site with endowments from the Chance family, and a separate parish was established in 1910 from parts of St. John and Holy Trinity parishes. The church was an attractive Arts and Crafts style building and had an aisled nave with clerestorey with porches and south-east bell turret, and a chancel with vestry and organ chamber. It was in the Perpendicular style with some attractive details such as the battlements and spirelet to the turret. This church was demolished when the new church was erected in Lyttleton Street in 1968.

The site of the earlier church of St. John in Sams Lane was given by W.H. Dawes of the Bromford Ironworks and was founded as a chapel of ease to Christ Church in 1876-8. It was designed by West Bromwich architect Elliot Etwall, and was a brick building in the Early English style. It was first built with a chancel and nave with a south aisle, to which a north aisle was added in 1892. Transepts, vestry and organ chamber were further added in 1903 to complete the original design. The church closed in 1960 and was demolished in 1963.

WEST BROMWICH

HOLY TRINITY, TRINITY STREET

*West Bromwich, Holy Trinity
from the west*

Amongst the Victorian terraced housing to the east of the ring road, Holy Trinity church was built in 1840-1 to serve the south-eastern part of the developing town as a chapel of ease to Christ Church, and became a separate parish in 1842. The site of the church, vicarage and school was given by George Silvester. William Chance, of the family which owned the nearby glassworks in Smethwick, was amongst the subscribers to the new building.

The Commissioners' type church is pleasantly situated in a small churchyard within a square of streets. It is a red brick building and was designed by Samuel Whitfield Daukes of Gloucester in the Early English style. The west tower has a plain parapet and short pinnacles with lancet bell openings. The large nave with low pitched roof has lancet windows, and at the east end there is a short chancel with a north porch. Further porches were added at the west end in the 1870s.

The attractive interior is light and spacious. The chancel was restored after a fire in 1861, at which time the organ was moved from the east end to the west gallery. It was returned to the chancel in 1902 when the east end was again refurnished. The three galleries remain, but the box pews were replaced in 1884 and the nave has recently been further reordered.

The Georgian style vicarage to the east was built in 1844.

WILLENHALL

ST. GILES, WALSALL STREET

A village of Anglo-Saxon origin, Willenhall developed from the sixteenth century as a centre of the manufacture of locks. Initially these were of wood, but with the development of ironworking by the nineteenth century, specialist companies grew up, of which perhaps Parkes' and Yale are the best known. In common with other industries in Black Country towns, many small firms producing handmade locks operated from individual premises leaving a heritage of small industrial buildings. Many of these have subsequently been removed during redevelopment, but at least one locksmiths works, Hodson's, is preserved as a museum in New Road. A number of eighteenth- and early nineteenth-century buildings also survive in the town centre, such as the Georgian Dale House in Bilston Street. The many recorded instances of men with 'hump backs' which resulted from hours of filing intricate metalwork also indicate that conditions in the town were notoriously hard. There is a memorial in Doctor's Piece Gardens recording the burial ground used in the 1849 cholera outbreak when the churchyard was unable to accommodate the bodies of the 292 people who died in less than fifty days.

Until 1840 Willenhall was in the parish of St. Peter, Wolverhampton, though there has been a church on this site since the Middle Ages. As at

Willenhall, St. Giles from the south-west

Rowley Regis the dedication to St. Giles, popular in the Middle Ages, is perhaps an indication of its early history. The present church is the third on the site and was built in 1866-7 by William Darby Griffin. It is an imposing brown sandstone building with a west tower, nave with large side aisles and chancel. The south chapel and transept were added in 1895. The style is Early English to Decorated with different designs to the geometrical tracery of the windows throughout the aisles, transepts and chancel. Around the traceried bell openings, gabled hoods to the sides of the tower create an unusual effect at the top stage, whilst the parapet above is stepped to the centre rather than battlemented. The pinnacles have been removed. The present tower replaced its medieval sandstone predecessor in 1866. The earlier tower, heightened in 1788, had lower stages which were perhaps fourteenth century. The Georgian top stage had Gothic bell openings and a simple parapet with pinnacles around a pyramidal roof. The medieval nave and chancel may have been timber framed, but were replaced by a brick structure in 1750.

The nave arcades have columns with four shafts supporting capitals carved with foliage and pointed arches. The eastern bays are wider at the entrances to the transepts whilst the narrow bays at the west end are related to a gallery which is now lost. The fine timber roof is in the fourteenth-century style. The chancel arch and arcade to the south chapel are Early English in style, and a further arch leads to the organ chamber on the north side. The organ by Norman and Beard was dedicated in 1898. The furnishings are mainly of the refurbishments of 1911 and 1927, but the chapel in the south transept was opened in 1991, perpetuating the memory of the demolished mission church of St. Matthias. The east window has fine glass of 1867, when it was installed by Ralph Dickenson Gough, whilst that in the Lady Chapel is a memorial to John and Mary Carver of 1933.

There are numerous memorial tablets including some of the early nineteenth century from the previous church. One records the sudden death of William Hall in a railway carriage on the way to Birmingham in 1855, and his burial in a vault by the pew he occupied for fifty years. William Moreton, the vicar in the early years of the nineteenth century, was apparently addicted to the popular local sport of cock fighting, and kept a cockpit at the vicarage.

WILLENHALL   ST. ANNE, ANN STREET, SPRING BANK

Spring Bank is an area of terraced housing to the north-east of St. Giles' church which developed during the later nineteenth century. St. Anne's church was founded as a mission in 1858 but became a parish church in 1861. The church was erected in 1856-8 by Henry Jeavons, an amateur architect, as a memorial to his wife. Although it is all in the Decorated style, it has the appearance of a church which has evolved over centuries rather than being designed as one piece, with a variety of gables and a disproportionately large aisle under a separate steeply pitched roof to the north of the nave. There are a chancel, north porch and a slender, short west tower which is open at the base to form a processional route. The vestry and organ chamber were added in 1904.

The furnishings were largely installed during the early twentieth century, and include an alabaster font of 1907 as a memorial to Dennis Minors, and a stone altar in 1909 in memory of the then vicar William Ward. The Lady Chapel was furnished as a First World War memorial.

This extraordinary building is now in a poor state of repair and surrounded to the north and east by industrial units.

Willenhall, St. Anne from the south-east

WILLENHALL   ST. MATTHIAS, SHEPWELL GREEN

A mission church in St. Giles' parish was opened on this road to the east of the town in 1907. It was demolished in 1988, and is commemorated in a chapel created in St. Giles' church.

WILLENHALL   ST. STEPHEN THE MARTYR, WOLVERHAMPTON STREET

The west end of the town developed in the early nineteenth century, and by the 1840s St. Stephen's church was planned to serve a growing population in this part of St. Giles' parish, close to the Portobello Lock Works of Josiah Parkes founded in 1840. The church was erected in 1853-4 to the designs of William Darby Griffin and consisted of an aisled nave with porch and chancel with side chapels and vestry. A mission chapel was built in Portobello in 1890.

However, by 1978 the building had become unsafe and was demolished. The new church was designed by Harold Goldstraw and Christopher Yorath of Wood, Goldstraw and Yorath of Stoke-on-Trent. Completed in 1979, it is of brick with sloping roofs and long narrow windows. The roof at the east end projects south to form a wedge, creating the effect of a short tower. The church hall is immediately to the west and opens into the church itself.

The furnishings are mainly contemporary but the statues of St. Stephen, St. Peter, St. Chad and St. James were preserved from the pulpit of the old church, along with the choir stalls, altar and Crucifix with statues of the Virgin and St. John from the rood beam.

WOLLASTON   ST. JAMES, BRIDGNORTH ROAD

At the north end of the ancient parish of Oldswinford, Wollaston is a settlement of Anglo-Saxon origin which became enveloped by the expansion of Stourbridge from the eighteenth century. The manor house, Wollaston Hall, was home to the Foley family during the seventeenth century, when they made their fortune developing the iron industry in the area. The house was demolished in the late 1920s, though it was the earlier sale of the estate by the Foleys in the mid nineteenth century which prompted the development of the village with mainly late Victorian housing. Wollaston became a separate parish from Amblecote in 1861.

Wollaston from the north-west

The Foster family who owned the steam engine manufacturing business lived at nearby Stourton Castle from 1833. The entrepreneurial James Foster died in 1853, and his heir William Orme Foster financed the building of Wollaston church, and subsequently the school in 1859-60 and vicarage in 1861. The church and former school survive, but the vicarage in Vicarage Road was demolished in 1965. The architect of this group of buildings was George Bidlake of Wolverhampton, who used Staffordshire blue bricks with limestone dressings to link the three together. The church has a north-west tower, nave with aisles under one roof, north and south porches and transepts, and chancel. The tower is elaborate, with the west doorway and its portal forming part of the west front. The bell openings are pairs of traceried lancets under triangular hoodmoulds, above which the arcaded parapet runs between the large corner pinnacles. The windows are Early English to Decorated in style. The nave is lit by a series of gabled dormer windows which form unusual clerestories to either side.

The interior is remarkably plain with whitewashed walls and Early English style arcades. There is some good nineteenth- and twentieth-century stained glass. The church benefited further from the generosity of Foster, as it was heated by pipes running directly from the family ironworks from the time it opened.

The gatepiers and railings to the churchyard are also by Bidlake and in matching materials to church and school. The school is to the north and is in the Early English style with a pretty bellcote with spirelet. The parish hall to the east has been designed to complement the older buildings on this significant site.

WOLLESCOTE   ST. ANDREW, OAKFIELD ROAD

Wollescote is to the south-east of The Lye and together they constituted an urban district in the nineteenth century before being absorbed into Stourbridge. There was a hamlet on this part of the remote heathlands of Lye Waste from the Anglo-Saxon period within the parish of Oldswinford. Part of the area became industrialised by the nineteenth century around Oldnall Colliery, and then largely residential in the twentieth with estates sprawling to the south of the principal landmark, Wollescote Hall. This fine seventeenth-century house was home to the Milward family until 1848. After several subsequent changes of ownership it was purchased in 1930 by the philanthropic Ernest Stevens and presented to the district council, and remains in institutional use. The large park stretches north down the hill to the cemetery.

St. Andrew's church is a simple building erected on the housing estate in 1939 to replace a mission chapel at nearby Belmont, which had been founded in 1878 from Christ Church, The Lye.

WOLVERHAMPTON   ST. PETER, LICH GATE, QUEEN'S SQUARE

Wolverhampton received city status only in 2000, but its roots go back much further. The first known reference to Hampton is in a charter of 895, and then in 994 a Mercian noblewoman, Wulfrun, granted land to a monastery here. A church was probably already in existence on this hilltop site by this time, and this further endowment elevated its status. It was dedicated to St. Mary but this had changed to St. Peter by the twelfth century. Wulfrun's name was added to Hampton, which later evolved to Wolverhampton.

The town grew up around the church, and its prosperity during the early Middle Ages was due to the wool trade. At least a couple of sixteenth-century timber-framed houses survive from this period. Despite the later decline of the wool trade, prosperity continued as the town became an important market by the seventeenth century, and then industrialisation began in the eighteenth century. Unlike many Black Country towns there was a diverse range of industry here, and so it was less affected by economic recession. Ironworking was particularly important, and this led to the production of rolling stock for the railways, with bicycles and motor vehicles being manufactured from the nineteenth century. Smaller scale work included lock making, and the town also became famous along with Bilston for its Japanned ware. By 1850 the arrival of the railways enabled swift development, and the town expanded towards the outlying villages of Tettenhall to the west, Penn to the south, and Bushbury to the north, as well the growing urban sprawl of the Black Country to the east. There was much redevelopment of the town centre in the twentieth century, particularly in the building of the Mander and Wulfrun Shopping Centres, but the area around St. Peter retains several historic buildings along with the modern Civic Centre.

On a green by the south door to the church stands a ninth-century cross, the most important Anglo-Saxon monument in the Black Country. It is a circular sandstone pillar standing some five metres high and carved with geometric and foliage designs. It may be the shaft of a preaching cross, and can be compared to the bases of similar date discovered at Penn and Bushbury. By the time of the Norman Conquest the church appears to have been a royal chapel with a college of priests. It was given by William I to his chaplain, Samson, and then after being held by three bishops returned to royal control under Henry II. Like St. Michael, Tettenhall, this was one of several collegiate churches in Lichfield diocese to remain royal free chapels through the medieval period, possibly to reduce the power of the bishops over such a large area. The other royal free chapels in the diocese were St. Mary, Bridgnorth; St. Mary, Shrewsbury; St. Lawrence, Gnosall; St. Michael, Penkridge; St. Mary, Stafford and St. Editha, Tamworth, but St. Peter's outlasted these because William Dudley, who was Dean here in the 1460s, was also Dean of St. George, Windsor, and the two deaneries were combined by Edward IV. At the reformation, the college at St. Peter's was briefly dissolved but reinstated by Mary I. It was then closed during the Commonwealth, but after the Restoration continued as a royal peculiar jointly with Windsor until being abolished in 1848.

Wolverhampton, St. Peter
— the Anglo-Saxon cross

The dark red sandstone church rises behind the cross, and although much restored in the nineteenth century it remains the most impressive medieval church in the region. It is cruciform in plan with a central tower, aisled nave with south porch and north vestries, transepts and chancel. The earliest surviving part is the crossing beneath the tower, which is thirteenth century with four Early English pointed arches with chamfers, as well as moulded capitals and bases. Much of the south transept is probably early fourteenth century and has an elaborate east window of five lights with geometrical tracery. The nave is late fifteenth century and has a fine Perpendicular clerestorey with transoms to the square-headed windows. Panelled battlements and pinnacles surround the low pitched roof, and it is similar to the nave of St. Mary, Kidderminster. The south transept was remodelled at this time and has a similar clerestorey to the nave above the larger Perpendicular window on the south wall. The north transept was built as a chapel dedicated to St. Catherine and St. Nicholas at the end of the fifteenth century and has large, almost round-headed windows with large central mullions to the north and east. The date of these is uncertain and they look like post-medieval alterations. Both transepts have battlements and low pitched roofs. The tower rises three stages above the crossing and is a magnificent piece of late Perpendicular architecture. It has panelling to each face, though less to the north, and single two light openings to the middle stage with pairs of similar openings to the upper stage. All the openings have hoodmoulds with crockets. The battlements are panelled and there are crockets to the tall pinnacles. There is also a slight projection for a staircase in the north-east corner. The medieval chancel was rebuilt from ruins in 1682-4, but the present long, Decorated style chancel with a three-sided apse at the east end

was built in 1867 to designs by Ewan Christian during his restoration of the church between 1852 and 1865. Christian renewed much of the exterior stonework and most of the windows to the aisles and west front. Extra light has been provided by the dormer windows concealed behind the battlements to the aisles. The two storey porch was also rebuilt, though much medieval masonry remains in the lower storey.

The interior is impressive and has walls of exposed sandstone throughout. The nave has Perpendicular arcades with octagonal piers on moulded bases rising to deeply chamfered arches above moulded capitals with carving at the spandrels. The roof of the north transept is also Perpendicular with carved bosses. The chancel roof has hammerbeams and has been fashioned at the east end to accommodate the curve of the apse, where it was strikingly coloured in 1968. The nave roof was also painted and gilded in 1970.

The earliest medieval fitting is the fine fourteenth-century piscina in the south transept. The Perpendicular stone pulpit at the east end of the south arcade is a rare survival. It has traces of medieval paint to the traceried panels with carved foliage above and below. Access is by the original staircase which wraps around the pier, complete with panelled wall and bannister with a large carved stone crouching lion for a terminal. The Swinnerton coat of arms appears on the staircase which may indicate the family of the donor. There are Perpendicular image niches by the east window of the north transept, whilst the wooden parclose screens to the south transept are also fifteenth century. The medieval stalls with misericords, now in the transepts and in the chancel, were brought here from Lilleshall Priory in Shropshire in 1546 after the Dissolution. They have carved animals and grotesques to the arm rests. The octagonal font is Perpendicular and has figures in niches around the stem with stylised designs including a sun and a bell to the sides of the bowl which bears the date 1660. Could this represent its restoration after

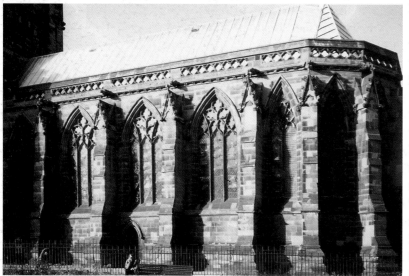

Wolverhampton, St. Peter, from the south
— the tower (top) and the chancel (lower)

the Commonwealth? The organ by Father Henry Willis of 1860 is at the east end of the nave above the tower arch, where the medieval rood loft was located until its removal in 1572. The west gallery with its turned balusters was erected in 1610 by the London Merchant Taylors Company for the use of pupils of the town's grammar school. There is an altar table now in the south transept which was controversially consecrated in 1635 by Archbishop Laud. The wall paintings east of the tower arch, showing Moses and Elijah, are all that survive of the scheme executed in the new chancel in 1865. The nineteenth-century painting under the tower is of two pupils from St. Peter's Bluecoat School, which was located near the church from 1695 until its closure in the 1930s. The metalwork cross with a crown above the altar at the crossing was made in 1990 by members of staff of St. Peter's Collegiate School. The north transept was refurnished as a Second World War memorial in 1948, and the statues of saints in the reredos were carved by members of the Bromsgrove Guild. The woodwork to the inner south porch of 1932 by Celestino Pancheri, previously of the Guild, was a memorial to Sir Charles Mander of Wightwick. In 2007 a new nave altar and choir stalls were installed and the entrance to the church was enhanced with glazed doors.

There is much good nineteenth- and twentieth-century stained glass. The south transept east window showing a Tree of Jesse was installed in 1919 as a First World War memorial. The seven windows in the apse have glass showing scenes from the life of Christ by O'Connor of London. The panels of sixteenth- and seventeenth-century Flemish and German glass in the side windows of the chancel were brought from St. Mary, Stafford Street in 1948. Most show further scenes from the life of Christ, but there are also German coats of arms including a double-headed eagle, and a figure of St. Jerome. The west window was installed in 1854 to designs by William Wailes to commemorate the Battle of Waterloo and depicts Moses, Joshua, Gideon and King David. Three south aisle windows date from the 1890s and are by Charles Eamer Kempe. The window at the west end of the south aisle showing historical figures associated with this church, including Wulfrun, was installed in 1947. The window showing the needy poor in the north aisle is a memorial to Sarah Brevitt who died in 1912 and is by Archibald Davies of the Bromsgrove Guild (see rear cover), as is that of the Holy Grail to Archibald Fisher Smith who was killed at Ypres in 1917. In 1921 Davies installed the South Staffordshire Regiment Memorial window at the west end of the north aisle.

There are numerous memorials inside the church. The alabaster chest tomb and effigies of John Leveson, a wealthy merchant and sheriff who died in 1575, and his wife Joyce in the south transept is the earliest to survive. The work is attributed to Robert Royley of Burton-on-Trent, and the statuettes to the sides are of Leveson's children and their spouses. In the north transept is a large memorial also attributed to Robert Royley to Thomas Lane of Bentley, who died in 1585, and his wife Catherine. At his feet there is a small dog. Their children, including two who died as infants, are shown on the side, with the Lane coat of arms and those of Trentham, her family. The large Classical memorial to the west is to Colonel John Lane who died in 1667 and who had assisted Charles

Wolverhampton, St. Peter, the pulpit
(see also the illustration on p.12)

129

II to escape to France after the Battle of Worcester in 1651. At the base are carved a crown and an oak tree commemorating this event. This monument has been attributed to Jasper Latham. Sarah, the wife of another John Lane, is commemorated by a tablet on the east wall. She was the last of the family to be buried here — in a silver-plated copper coffin in 1784. The tall bronze figure with reclining cherubs in the south transept is the remaining part of a large memorial to Vice Admiral Sir Richard Leveson who died in 1605. It is of about 1635 by Hubert Le Sueur, court sculptor to Charles I (see illustration on p.17). Leveson had taken part in both the defence against the Spanish Armada in 1588 and the expedition to Cadiz of 1596. The monument was destroyed during the Commonwealth but these parts were saved by the family from being melted down, and were returned to the church in 1714. There is a tablet in the north transept to Richard Fryer who died in 1846. He was a local banker who became the first Member of Parliament for Wolverhampton after the Reform Act of 1832. The Boer War memorial of 1902 is an interesting piece of Jacobean revival.

The only medieval bell to have survived is the sanctus bell, whilst the peal of ten bells was recast in 1911. The seventeenth-century weathercock from the tower is now preserved in the north transept. The churchyard railings and gates were made by the Bromsgrove Guild. To the south-east of the church is

Wolverhampton, St. Peter — the statue of Wulfrun by Charles Wheeler, installed in 1922

a curious stone of uncertain date, with a hole through which bargains are believed to have been guaranteed by a handshake. The war memorial cenotaph to the west of the church is of 1922, whilst the statue of Wulfrun by Charles Wheeler was installed in 1974. To the north-west is Giffard House which was built in the 1720s as a mass house by the recusant Catholic Giffard family of nearby Chillington Hall. Behind this lies the Roman Catholic church of St. Peter and St. Paul erected in 1825, one of the earliest post-Reformation Catholic churches in the Midlands and only visible from the street once the surrounding buildings were demolished. The seventeenth-century Deanery House, which stood to the north of the church, was demolished in 1921. The buildings of the University of Wolverhampton now occupy the site.

WOLVERHAMPTON   ALL SAINTS, ALL SAINTS ROAD

In 1865 a mission church for the expanding population of the southern part of the parish of St. John was opened in Steelhouse Lane by the vicar, Henry Hampton. The present church was built in 1877-9 to designs by T. Smith and G.F. Roper. The chancel, vestries, organ chamber and north chapel were added in 1892-3 by Frederick Beck. The reredos is by Sir Charles Nicholson, with paintings to the sides by A.K. Nicholson.

WOLVERHAMPTON

ST. ANDREW, ST. ANDREW'S CLOSE, WHITMORE REANS

Wolverhampton, St. Andrew, seen from the north-west

Whitmore Reans is an area of Victorian terraced housing on New Hampton Road beyond West Park and the church lies in a green space close to the centre of the community. It originally consisted of a nave and short chancel built in 1869-70 by William Lowder, to which a longer chancel, organ chamber, vestries and side chapel were added in 1893 by Frederick Beck. However, the church was destroyed by fire in 1964 and just Beck's lychgate and vicarage survive on New Hampton Road, whilst the foundation stones from the previous church are set in the wall by the car park.

The present church was built in 1965-7 to the designs of Richard Twentyman of Twentyman and Percy and is a solid, brick building. It is without windows to the east and south where it was intended that a major road was to be built, though this never happened. The hall and community facilities to the west are linked to the church by a glazed lobby. The large, square body of the church has a hexagonal chapel attached to the north side by another glazed link. The bell hangs on a brick frame to the east.

Inside, there is a single space with the altar by the east wall next to a dated stone from the old church. The furnishings are by Twentyman in a contemporary style. To the side, the organ loft remains empty. The west window was designed by John Piper and made by Patrick Reyntiens in 1966 and is a representation of the Sea of Galilee, with vibrant blue colouring. The Lady Chapel has furnishings rescued from the old church, and there are two small panels of stained glass.

WOLVERHAMPTON

ST. BARNABAS, WEDNESFIELD ROAD

This church of 1892-3 by Thomas Henry Fleeming is of brick and in the Early English style. It was erected to serve the growing population of the Springfield area, but was closed in 1964 and now serves as the New Testament Church of God.

WOLVERHAMPTON

ST. CHAD, OWEN ROAD

This church was built as a chapel of ease to the south-west of the town in the parish of St. Paul in 1907-8 by Frederick Beck. It is of brick and terracotta in a mixed Gothic but mainly Perpendicular style, and is similar to St. Stephen's church in the Springfield area of the town. At the east end is an apsidal chancel with organ chamber, whilst the nave has a small apsidal baptistery at the west end with bellcote above, and to the south are substantial vestries in the same style.

WOLVERHAMPTON CHRIST CHURCH, WATERLOO ROAD

Originally built in 1867 by Edward Banks and extended with aisles by George Bidlake in 1869, this was a large church faced in red sandstone in the Early English to Decorated styles, but unfinished as the tower was never built. In 1903 the fine chancel was decorated with paintings in 1903 by J. Edie Read and Wyndham Hughes. An Arts and Crafts type panel by the chancel arch was a memorial to Edward Glover. The church was closed in 1967 and demolished.

WOLVERHAMPTON ST. GEORGE, ST. GEORGE'S PARADE

This Commissioners' type church was erected in 1828-30 to serve the growing industrial area to the south-east of the town centre. It is to designs by James Morgan, a partner of John Nash, famous for his designs of Regent's Park and Regent Street in London. The church is in the Classical style with a symmetrical west front with central doorway in a portal with Tuscan columns, and side doorways to the aisles. The square tower rises above with round and rectangular openings and is crowned by a balustrade and spire. The body of the church has a large nave with short chancel. The east window is Venetian in style whilst the side windows are round headed to the upper stage and segmental below. There are several parallels to the earlier St. John's church, which is just a short distance to the west. This church was closed in the 1960s and converted to form the entrance area of a large supermarket. The exterior is little altered on the south and east sides, but has a hooded entrance canopy to the west and is obscured by the new building to the north.

  The church interior was gutted, though the columns to the galleries appear to be boxed within the supermarket café. The burials in the graveyard were removed to Bushbury.

Wolverhampton, St. George, seen from the south

WOLVERHAMPTON ST. JAMES, ST. JAMES STREET, HORSELEY FIELDS

In 1843 a new church was provided for the Horseley Fields area to the east of the town centre in the parish of St. Peter. St. James' church had an aisled nave and chancel with a west tower and was built in the Early English style. It was closed in 1955 and demolished during the following year.

WOLVERHAMPTON   ST. JOHN-IN-THE-SQUARE, ST. JOHN'S SQUARE

The expansion of Wolverhampton in the eighteenth century included the creation of George Street, St. John's Square and Church Street as new residential areas. Today George Street has been restored to something of its former splendour. Although the layout of Church Street and St. John's Square survive, the houses have long since been demolished albeit that new buildings are designed to reflect the scale of their Georgian predecessors. The south side of the square, however, has been lost to the ring road. St. John's church survives in the centre of the square in its large rectangular churchyard surrounded by a low brick wall and with fine eighteenth-century gatepiers, though the wrought iron gates date from 1907. The church was erected between 1756-9 probably by Wolverhampton architect Roger Eykyn, though Thomas Pritchard has also been named. It is in the style of the London churches by James Gibbs, and is similar to Eykyn's church of St. Paul in the Jewelry Quarter, Birmingham. On the gallery stairs is a benefaction board recording donors to the building fund for the church, including ironmaster Benjamin Molineux and Japanner Thomas Wightwick. The fourth Earl of Stamford and Warrington who had estates at Envillle was principal patron. The church was a chapel of ease to St. Peter's church until a separate parish was created in 1847.

The exterior has a wealth of Classical detailing and is faced with sandstone though this dates to 1960 when the church had to be entirely refaced by Anthony Chatwin as a result of pollution damage to the original stone. Much of the funding for this work was provided by the Hayward Trust, founded by Charles Hayward who had developed the sidecar for the Sunbeam motorcycle. At the west end the square tower has round-headed bell openings beneath an octagonal third stage, with blind round-headed openings, which stands on a round base with a cornice. The tall spire has round lucarnes. The symmetrical west front has a central round-headed entrance with rusticated Doric columns to the sides under a pediment. The windows to either side and on the north and south walls are in two stages with round heads above and segmental heads below. The Venetian style east window to the chancel is blind, and there are doorways to the east wall and the west ends of the side walls.

Wolverhampton, St. John-in-the-Square, the west front

The interior has vaulted ceilings above arcades with Doric columns. The chancel arch is rounded and there is a further vaulted ceiling to the chancel, which also has Georgian style panelling and a reredos dating from 1899. The late eighteenth-century painting of the Descent from the Cross is by local artist Joseph Barney. It is behind the altar of 1929. The galleries survive on three sides of the nave and the gilded royal arms of George II are on the west gallery. These are believed to have been made by William Ellam who also produced the gilded commandment boards. The fine late seventeenth-century organ by Renatus Harris was made for Temple Church, London, but removed because of a dispute. It was taken instead to Christ Church Cathedral, Dublin, but was later removed by a Wolverhampton organ builder, probably John Byfield. In 1762 it was installed in St. John's church.

The marble font with inlaid decoration was installed in 1866 and the wrought iron communion rail and tall wooden pulpit on marble columns date from the refurbishment of the interior by John Drayton Wyatt in 1869-70. The screens to the side chapels include a First World War memorial. The furnishings made by the vicar Joseph Hartill in the 1950s for the north chapel were moved to the main part of the church when this chapel was converted to a vestry. The south chapel has some fittings from the demolished church of St. Paul, and is known as St. Paul's chapel. Further reordering has continued through the twentieth century including the provision of kitchen and toilet facilities in the former western vestries.

There is stained glass of the nineteenth century in several of the windows, including work by Ward and Hughes of 1882-4 and George Joseph Baguley of 1893. The two Evans memorial windows on the north side are of 1910 and 1912 by Florence and Robert Camm. The glass commemorating William Garfield, who was killed in the Boer War, was designed by Samuel Evans of Smethwick in 1901. In two of the north windows the glass is by Archibald Davies of the Bromsgrove Guild — that in memory of Florence Allen is of 1912, whilst that to John, Sarah and George Higham is of 1918. Both show scenes from the life of Christ.

There are numerous late eighteenth- and early nineteenth-century memorial tablets on the walls, whilst a tablet in the south chapel to Alfred Edward Sephton commemorates his posthumous award of the Victoria Cross. He was killed in action off Crete in 1941. There are further good memorials of the eighteenth and nineteenth centuries in the churchyard, including one to Henry Evans, a stonemason who was killed in a fall from the tower during its construction in 1760. He was the first person to be buried in the churchyard. The bell in the tower is older than the church and dates from 1706. It was acquired from St. Martin-in-the-Bull Ring, Birmingham.

WOLVERHAMPTON   ST. JUDE, TETTENHALL ROAD

Tettenhall Road developed in the second half of the nineteenth century as one of Wolverhampton's most prestigious residential areas. The church was built in 1867-9 to designs by George Bidlake. It has a large aisled nave and chancel with organ chamber and vestry. The south-west tower and spire with flying buttresses and traceried parapet was added later in the nineteenth century by Thomas Henry Fleeming. The body of the church is in the Early English style with geometrical tracery to the windows.

The spacious interior has arcades with pointed arches on thin polished granite columns with carved foliage capitals, and transept and chancel arches in similar style. There several Victorian fittings. Fifteen rows of pews still retain the doors with which they were fitted and are very late examples of box pews. There are commandment boards in the chancel. The fine lectern with angels is of brass, and the font has carved arcading. The stained glass in the east window is of 1869, whilst that in the west is a memorial to Mary Davis who died in 1886. The former vicarage next door is of 1897 by local architect William Johnson Harrison Weller.

WOLVERHAMPTON   ST. LUKE, UPPER VILLIERS STREET

This is an extraordinary church of 1860-1 by George Thomas Robinson of Leamington. It is polychrome, not unlike a church by William Butterfield, using red, yellow and blue brick. There is plate tracery to the

Wolverhampton, St. Luke, from the south-east, with a detail of the brickwork of the tower

side windows, whilst those in the clerestorey have curved sides to triangular openings which are filled with roundels. The apsidal chancel has gables over the windows and the organ chamber is also gabled. On the north side is a chapel. There is a west narthex with iron shafts to the entrance and a carving of the Journey to Emmaus in the tympanum. The large tower has a south-eastern stair turret with spirelet. The doorway also has iron shafts and a carving of St. Luke above. The second stage of the tower has lancet openings whilst the upper stages are octagonal with a short spire with gabled lucarnes to the base.

Inside, there are cast iron columns to the nave with trumpet scallop capitals; the extensive use of iron is a surprise at this date, when it was considered less suitable for use in Gothic churches and more for industrial or institutional buildings. The arches inside continue the polychrome work from outside. There is a wide arch to the chancel and further short arcades to the chapel and organ chamber, which have screens where they open to the chancel. The altar has arcading whilst the reredos is carved with the Last Supper. Other nineteenth-century fittings include the pulpit, choir stalls, and font. The reredos in the side chapel is a First World War memorial, and the stained glass in the window is of 1913. The chancel has nineteenth-century stained glass.

The walls to the churchyard are contemporary with the church and have quatrefoil openings. The nearby Pond Lane Mission was founded from St. Luke in 1896 and is still in use today.

WOLVERHAMPTON   ST. MARK, CHAPEL ASH

This Commissioners' type church was built to serve the prosperous suburb immediately to the west of the town centre. To the north, the beautiful Victorian West Park was laid out in 1881 on the site of the racecourse. The church was built in 1848-9 to designs by Charles Wyatt Orford of Birmingham. The west tower with broach spire has clock faces beneath gables to each side, and forms an important landmark at the foot of Darlington Street when viewed from Queen's Square in the city centre. The church is in the Early English style with lancet windows and has an aisled nave with porches, and an apsidal chancel with vestry and organ chamber as low transepts. The nave arcades have alternating thin quatrefoil and octagonal piers.

The church was closed in 1978, when the parish was united with that of St. Chad, and was converted to offices in 1990. Although the interior features are preserved, the furnishings have been dispersed, the organ being moved to the Grammar School.

WOLVERHAMPTON   ST. MARY, STAFFORD STREET

Funded by Theodosia Hinckes of Tettenhall, this church was erected in 1840. She collected Flemish glass on her continental travels. This was installed in the church, but removed to St. Peter's church when the church was closed in 1948. The church has since been demolished. The reredos was taken to St. Mark's church and then St. Paul, Walsall.

WOLVERHAMPTON   ST. MATTHEW, EAST PARK WAY

Work on the layout of East Park began in 1892 after the site was given to the town by Alfred Hickman to provide an open space amongst the growing industrial sites in the eastern suburbs of Wolverhampton. It was never as fine as West Park but still preserves its entrance lodges and clock tower. St. Matthew's church is on the approach to East Park from Willenhall Road. The original church was built in 1849 by Edward Banks and had an aisled nave with porches and chancel. The church was rebuilt in 1969 as a brick cruciform building with low pitched roofs.

WOLVERHAMPTON   ST. PAUL, ST. PAUL STREET

St. Paul's church was built in the Early English style in 1836 at the expense of the first incumbent, William Dalton. It had a chancel and nave with west porch and tower. The church itself was demolished in 1960 to make way for the Penn Road Island on the ring road but the church hall remains, now used by another denomination. It is off Jeddo Street by the former Sunbeamland cycle factory. Some of the furnishings from this church are now in St. John's church.

WOLVERHAMPTON   ST. STEPHEN, HILTON STREET, SPRINGFIELD

Springfield is an industrial area close to the canal and railway to the east of the city centre. One of the key buildings is Mitchell and Butler's brewery of 1873 which includes a fine cast iron entrance canopy of 1880, though the main buildings were destroyed by fire in 2004. Close to the brewery, this church was built in

1907-9 to the designs of Frederick Beck in an Arts and Crafts style using brick with terracotta dressings. The nave and chancel are under one roof, but there are side aisles and a western narthex. The apsidal side chapel and baptistry on the north side both have battlements. The vestries are south of the chancel. There is an unusual design to the Perpendicular style windows in the clerestorey, which are surrounded by arches which reach above the octagonal piers in the arcades. They are visible externally and the motif is repeated with the window on the east wall. There is a small belfry with spirelet above the chancel.

WOLVERHAMPTON   HOLY TRINITY, CHURCH STREET, HEATH TOWN

Holy Trinity stands on the edge of Heath Town Park in the eastern suburbs of Wolverhampton. The park was laid out as a First World War memorial in 1920, with the sculpture of a bronze soldier by G.A. Walker as the centrepiece. The inscribed panels in the lychgate at the entrance to the churchyard of 1920 are also First and Second World War memorials, and the path between forms an avenue. The red brick Tudor style almshouses at the side of the churchyard were erected for industrialist Henry Rogers in 1850. Rogers was also a donor towards the cost of the church, the site itself being given by local landowner John Moor Paget.

The church was built in 1850-2 to the designs of Edward Banks and has a large aisled nave with clerestorey and chancel with organ chamber. The south-west tower has an impressive broach spire and Decorated style lucarnes. The windows and other features are all fine work in the Decorated style.

Inside, the nave arcades and chancel arch have quatrefoil piers and pointed arches. There is a reredos with arcading, stone pulpit and octagonal font. The chancel screen was installed in 1902. There are several memorial tablets including some ceramic plaques. Some of the windows contain nineteenth- and early twentieth-century stained glass, including a fine depiction of the Annunciation of 1922 in the chancel, which is in the style of William Morris.

WOOD GREEN   ST. PAUL, WOOD GREEN ROAD

St. Paul's church is easily seen from near junction 9 on the M6 on the approach to Wednesbury. To the south is a mainly Victorian residential area around Brunswick Park and the cemetery, whilst to the north and east is the site of Wednesbury Forge which was powered by the River Tame. The Elwell family owned this from the sixteenth century and the forge developed a speciality in the manufacture of edge tools, such as small axes and saws, before becoming Bescot Drop Forgings by the twentieth century. The site is now redeveloped as a business park.

The Elwell family were also responsible for building the church though the architect is apparently unrecorded. Constructed in 1874 in the Early English to Decorated styles, it is of brown sandstone with chancel, nave with west porch and clerestories above both the north aisle and south aisle which has a separate pitched roof. The new parish was created out of parts of Wednesbury and West Bromwich in the following year. In 1887 the tower and broach spire were added to the north side of the chancel, whilst a vestry was built in place of the north porch in 1922.

Inside, the arcades have pointed arches on round columns with moulded capitals.The chancel arch of similar style rests on similarly styled corbels and shafts. There are sedilia and a piscina in the chancel. Most of the older furnishings date from the end of the nineteenth or start of the twentieth centuries, including the font of 1888 and wrought iron screen. The reredos was installed by Bridgeman of Lichfield in 1903 as a memorial to Alfred Elwell. The stained glass in the west window was presented by Job Edwards, proprietor of Eagle Tube Works, in memory of the popular Bishop Selwyn of Lichfield and following his death in 1878. The glass in the east window is a memorial to Edwin Richards who died in 1880. Richards, who lived at 'The Limes' in the parish and was the owner of the Portway axle works, was a great collector of works of art. These were bequeathed to the town in 1885 by his widow, who also provided considerable funding towards the establishment of the Art Gallery in 1891. Glass in other windows commemorate parishioners largely involved in the town's industry, while the window of 1919 in the north aisle is a First World War memorial.

The lychgate at the entrance to the churchyard was erected in 1926 as a memorial to another Edwin Richards.

WOOD GREEN   ST. LUKE, ALMA STREET, MESTY CROFT

The streets to the east of Brunswick Park make up the Mesty Croft area of Wood Green. A mission of St. Paul's church was established in 1879 in a school building belonging to the Elwell family. This was rebuilt as a simple brick church in 1894 which was demolished and replaced in 1973 by the present church and hall, a low red brick building with attractive sloping roofs.

WORDSLEY   HOLY TRINITY, HIGH STREET

The glass industry in the Wordsley part of Kingswinford was given a boost with the completion of the Stourbridge Canal from 1776. Today, the cone at the Redhouse Glassworks of Stuart Crystal next to the canal is one of the most obvious reminders of this industrial heritage, and the Redhouse Works is one of the most complete remaining glass factories. Most of these cones have disappeared but they would have been a feature of the landscape of this area in the same way that the conical brick kilns dominated the Potteries. Wordsley stands towards the northern end of the 'Crystal Mile' between Amblecote and Kingswinford.

Holy Trinity lies just to the north of Redhouse Works on the brow of a hill, with some good Georgian and early Victorian cottages and houses close by in the High Street. In 1826 the decision was taken to build a new parish church here in the growing part of Kingswinford parish, and that St. Mary's, the old church, would become a chapel of ease. The foundation stone was laid by John Hodgetts Foley MP, and funds raised locally were complemented by a grant of £3,000 from the Church Commission. The architect was Lewis Vulliamy, designer of several London churches including All Saints in Ennismore Gardens. Work was completed in 1831, and the church became the parish church until the role reverted to St. Mary's church in 1846.

The aisled nave with clerestorey and low pitched roofs and the west tower with battlements and pinnacles are still as they

Wordsley from the south-west

Wordsley graveyard

would have originally appeared. It is a Commissioners' type church with grand architecture in the Perpendicular style, though the aisle windows incline more towards the Decorated and the long bell openings to the tower have much in common with other contemporary Commissioners' churches. The short chancel was replaced in 1883. The incumbents through the later nineteenth and early twentieth centuries were influenced by the High Church movement, and reordering of the new east end had been undertaken by J.B. Davis of Dudley in 1878 to provide an altar with pulpit and lectern to the sides to replace the original central three-decker pulpit.

There are fine Perpendicular style arcades with galleries to the aisles. The extension of the east end in 1883 allowed for a more traditional arrangement with altar and choir stalls. The marble reredos, designed by Julius Alfred Chatwin of Birmingham and carved by Bridgeman of Lichfield, features the Adoration of the Magi surrounded by statues of saints. It was presented by Mary Webb of the seed merchant family, who is commemorated in the east window at Oldswinford. The organ of 1910 is by Connacher of Huddersfield. In 1914 the box pews were replaced with the present pews. The Lady Chapel furnishings date from 1931, along with the lectern and altar rails, whilst in 1932 the pulpit was installed. All these fine furnishings were designed by George Hammer and Company of London. There is good nineteenth- and twentieth-century glass and a fine early twentieth-century enamel memorial plaque which is believed to be the work of the Birmingham School artist Sidney Meteyard.

The vast churchyard is typical of the Black Country. Amongst the memorials are one to Stanley Carder, seven-year-old son of Frederick Carder who established the Steuben glassworks in New York. Frederick made the terracotta panels himself. The memorial to John Northwood, who developed acid etching as a glass decorating technique, includes a miniature stone replica of the first-century Roman glass Portland Vase (now in the British Museum), the cameos of which he sought successfully to replicate. The parish also includes the community churches of St. Mary and St. Francis and that of St. Clare which meet in local schools.

Walsall, St. Matthew — the Sister Dora Memorial Window

Glossary

ABACUS - a flat slab on top of a capital, often decorated with carving.

AISLE - side extensions to the nave of the church (also sometimes used to refer to the walkways between the pews).

ALIEN PRIORY - an English priory under the direct control of a continental monastery.

APSE - a semi circular or polygonal projection from the main church building.

ASHLAR - dressed blocks of stone.

AUMBRY - a rectangular medieval recess by the altar, which would once have been a secure storage space for sacred objects. It is rare to find them with their original doors.

BALLFLOWER - a carved decorative projection in the form of a bud usually found on Decorated architecture.

BARREL VAULT - see VAULT

BAY - a vertical section of a building.

BELLCOTE - a small arched structure in which a bell is hung.

BELL OPENING - an opening in the tower, through which the sound of the bells could escape.

BILLET - a rectangular or cylindrical motif.

BOX PEW - an enclosed pew installed in a church between the seventeenth and nineteenth centuries. They were numbered and were rented by those who could afford them.

CANOPY OF HONOUR - a large canopy above an altar or rood.

CAPITAL - at the top of a pier, the capital forms a flat bed from which the arches spring. The carved decoration of a capital is likely to be a good indication of the date of the arch.

CARTOUCHE - part of the decoration to a Classical monument, taking the form of an unrolled scroll, on which the inscription is found.

CHANCEL - the east end of the church.

CHANTRY CHAPEL - a medieval chapel where mass was celebrated and prayers offered for the soul of the deceased benefactor.

CHOIR - the part of a large church where the choir gathers to sing.

CLERESTOREY - an upper storey to the nave or chancel usually of a large church, which had windows to give extra light.

COLLEGIATE CHURCH - a church endowed for a 'college' or group of clergy.

COMMANDMENT BOARD - a large board with the text of the Ten Commandments, usually eighteenth or nineteenth century.

COMMISSIONERS' CHURCH - a church erected with funding from the £1 million allocated for church building by Parliament in 1818 and overseen by Lords Commissioners of the Treasury. Designed economically with large naves to accommodate large numbers of people, such churches set a trend for a type of church design during the first half of the nineteenth century.

COMMUNION RAIL - a rail to protect the communion table or altar, first used in the seventeenth century.

COMMUNION TABLE - a table which replaced the altar in church from the seventeenth century.

CORBEL - a projecting stone support.

CORBEL TABLE - a line of corbels.

CORNICE - a surround to a ceiling.

CROCKET - a carved decorative projection, sometimes leaf-shaped, to be found on pinnacles and canopies in Gothic architecture.

CUSP - a small point between two curves in later medieval architectural features.

DECORATED - the Gothic architectural style of the period from the late thirteenth to the late fourteenth centuries.

EARLY ENGLISH - the Gothic architectural style of the period from the end of the twelfth to the late thirteenth centuries.

EASTER SEPULCHRE - a large medieval recess to the north of the altar, where the Sacrament was kept between Maundy Thursday and Easter Sunday.

FAN VAULT - see VAULT.

GARGOYLE - a projecting stone feature to a parapet, usually containing a water spout, and often carved with grotesque beasts.

HATCHMENT - a panel, usually diamond shaped, on which were painted the coat of arms of a deceased person, and which was left in the church after being carried in the funeral procession.

LADY CHAPEL - a chapel in a large church, with an altar dedicated to the Virgin.

LEDGER - a large flat grave memorial slab, with an inscription.

LIERNE - a short intersecting rib in a later medieval vault (see also Vault).

LOZENGE - a diamond-shaped motif.

LUCARNE - an opening in a spire.

LYCHGATE - a gateway, often with a roof, at the entrance to the churchyard. The name is derived from the Anglo-Saxon word lich which means corpse — the lich gate marks the entrance place for a funeral procession to the churchyard.

MANDORLA - an oval-shaped panel in a painting or sculpture.

MASS DIAL - a sundial set out to give the times at which mass should be celebrated.

MEMENTO MORI - reminder of the inevitability of death.

MERLON - the projecting part of a battlement.

MISERICORD - a wooden seat for a cleric, which is hinged and usually kept vertical as it has a platform on which the occupant could rest when standing. The underside of this platform is sometimes elaborately carved.

NAVE - the main, western part of the church used by the congregation.

NORMAN - the Romanesque architectural style of the Norman period from the mid eleventh to the late twelfth centuries.

OGEE - an S-shaped curve in Gothic architecture.

PARCLOSE SCREEN - a screen to separate a chapel from the rest of the church.

PERPENDICULAR - the Gothic architectural style of the period from the late fourteenth to the mid sixteenth centuries.

PISCINA - a small stone basin in the chancel, with a drain, where the priest could rinse the communion vessels after a service.

PLATE TRACERY - Early English style tracery with openings cut through stone.

PRIEST'S DOORWAY - the small doorway for the priest in the side of the chancel.

QUATREFOIL - a carved decorative feature in the shape of four leaves.

REBUS - a pictorial way of depicting a pun on a name, such as a small barrel for Lyttleton.

REREDOS - a solid panelled stone screen behind the altar.

RETICULATION - window tracery with ogee curves linked to give a latticed effect.

RIB - a raised band of stone or wood, which strengthens a vault or ceiling.

ROMANESQUE - the architectural style of the Anglo-Saxon and Norman period in England, from the seventh to the twelfth centuries.

ROOD - Crucifix, from an Anglo-Saxon word meaning cross.

ROOD BEAM - the beam to which the Rood was affixed.

ROOD LOFT - a gallery above the rood screen, often used by musicians and accessed by the staircase.

ROOD SCREEN - a screen dividing the nave from the chancel in a medieval church, which carried a Crucifix or Rood before the Reformation.

ROYAL PECULIAR - a church exempt from the jurisdiction of the diocesan bishop, but subject to the authority of the monarch.

SACRISTY - a room next to the chancel in which valuables and the church plate were stored.

SADDLEBACK ROOF - a gabled roof to a tower.

SANCTUS BELL - a small bell rung at the start of the 'Sanctus' during mass.

SEDILIA - stone seats in the chancel for the sacred ministers.

SHAFT - the upright part of a pier, above the base and below the capital.

SPANDREL - the area of stonework between the arches of an arcade.

STOUP - a medieval stone vessel, which was placed near the doorway to the church, to hold holy water for the use of worshippers to make the sign of the cross.

STRAPWORK - decoration of the sixteenth and seventeenth centuries which had the appearance of intertwining straps.

STRING COURSE - a line of projecting horizontal stonework on a Norman wall.

TESTER - a flat canopy above a pulpit, usually seventeenth- or eighteenth-century, to help to project the preacher's voice.

THREE-DECKER PULPIT - a pulpit, usually seventeenth- or eighteenth-century, with accompanying desks for the clerk and minister, arranged in a stepped formation.

TIERCERON - an intermediate rib in a later medieval vault.

TOWER PORCH - a tower which incorporates a porch in the base.

TRACERY - the open stonework or woodwork in the upper part of a window or opening.

TRANSEPTS - side chapels, often placed to the sides of a central tower, with roofs at right angles to the roofs of the main body of the church.

TRANSOM - a horizontal stone bar in a window.

TREFOIL - a carved decorative feature in the shape of three leaves.

TRIFORIUM - an arched passage in the wall of a large church, above the arcade but below the clerestorey.

TRIPTYCH - three folded panels, painted with religious or family and heraldic illustrations.

TRUMPET SCALLOP - a carved form of decoration, usually found on Norman capitals.

TYMPANUM - either the stone above the lintel and below the arch of a doorway, particularly of the Norman period, or the area of wall, often timber-framed, above the rood screen dividing the nave and the chancel.

VAULT / VAULTING - medieval stone ceilings were constructed as vaults, which become more elaborate as the centuries progressed. Simple Norman tunnel shaped vaults are called Barrel Vaults, whereas more elaborate Decorated vaults had several stone ribs with tiercerons, liernes and carved bosses. These were known as Lierne Vaults. The most elaborate Perpendicular Vaults were Fan Vaults with many more ribs and a cone-shaped effect to the side sections.

VESTRY - the room in which vestments are kept, and where the clergy prepare for a service.

VOUSSOIR - a small wedge-shaped piece of stone in the curved upper part of an arch.

WAGON ROOF - a timber roof constructed in a similar curved manner to the interior of a covered wagon.

WATERLEAF - a carved stylised leaf design of the thirteenth century.

Bibliography

Abbreviation used

TWAS *Transactions of the Worcestershire Archaeological Society*

Addleshaw, G. & Etchells, F. *The Archaeological Setting of Anglican Worship*, 1948

Albutt, R. *The Stained Glass Windows of A.J.Davies of the Bromsgrove Guild Worcestershire*, 2005

Allen, J.S. *Old St. Martin's Church, Tipton - A Short History*, 1971

Allen, W. *Black Country*, 1946

Archer, M. *An Introduction to English Stained Glass*, 1985

Atterbury, P. & Wainwright, C. (ed.) *Pugin, a Gothic Passion*, 1994

Barker, P. & Pagett, T. 'Romanesque Carving from St. John the Baptist Church, Hagley and Dudley Priory', *TWAS*, Third Series, XI, 1988, pp.27-34

Barnes, G. *Frederick Preedy*, 1984

Barrett, H. & Phillips, J. *Suburban Style*, 1987

Betjeman, J. *Collins Guide to English Parish Churches* (The North), 1968

Bettey, J.H. *Church and Parish, A Guide for Local Historians*, 1987

Beulah, K. *Church Tiles of the Nineteenth Century*, 1987

Binney, M. & Burman, P. *Change and Decay, The Future of our Churches*, 1977

Buck, B. *St. Michael's Parish Church, Brierley Hill*, 2003

Blythe, R. *Divine Landscapes*, 1986

Bott, I.M. *Wednesbury in old Photographs*, 1994

Bottomley, F. *The Church Explorer's Guide*, 1978

Burritt, E. *Walks in the Black Country*, 1868 (rep 1976)

Chamberlin, R. *The English Parish Church*, 1993

Chandler, G. & Hannah, I.C. *Dudley*, 1949

Chitham, E. *Rowley Regis a History*, 2006

Clarke, B.F.L. *The Building of the Eighteenth Century Church*, 1963
Church Builders of the Nineteenth Century, 1938

Clifton-Taylor, A. *English Parish Churches as Works of Art*, 1974

Coldstream, N. *The Decorated Style, Architecture and Ornament 1240-1360*, 1994

Cooper, D.H. *Kingswinford Parish Church at Wordsley*, 1933

Cox, J.C. & Ford, C.B. *Parish Churches*, 1934

Crossley, F.H. *English Church Monuments, AD 1150-1550*, 1921

Cunnington, P. *How old is that Church?*, 1990

Davies, M.R. *The Knight Effigy in St. Matthew's Church*, Walsall, 1991

Dickens, G.C.B. & McClatchey, D. (ed.) *Diocese of Worcester, 1300 Years: The People of Worcestershire and their Church*, 1980

Dirsztay, P. *Church Furnishings*, 1978

Dixon, R. & Muthesius, S. *Victorian Architecture*, 1978

Douglas, A. & Moore, D. *Memories of the Black Country*, 1985

Downing, M. 'Medieval Military Effigies up to 1500 remaining in Worcestershire', *TWAS*, Third Series XVIII, 2002, pp.133-210

Duffy E. *The Stripping of the Altars, Traditional Religion in England 1400-1580*, 1992

Eames, E. *English Medieval Tiles*, 1985

Ekwall, E. *The Concise Dictionary of English Place Names*, 1960

Farmer, D.H. *The Oxford Dictionary of Saints*, 1978

Fisher, M. *Pugin-Land*, 2002

    Hardman of Birmingham - Goldsmith and Glasspainter, 2008

Foster, A. *Birmingham, The Pevsner Architectural Guide*, 2005

Frampton, K. *Modern Architecture, A Critical History*, 1992

Friar S. *A Companion to the English Parish Church*, 1996

Grice, F. 'Two Victorian Sculptors—James and William Forsyth', *TWAS*, Third Series XI, 1984, pp.101-106

Hackwood, F.W. *Oldbury and Round About*, 1915 (rep 2002)

    A History of West Bromwich, 1895 (rep 2001)

Hall-Matthews, J.C.B. & Shield, I. *The Collegiate Church of St. Peter, Wolverhampton*, 1993

Harries, J. *Discovering Churches*, 1979

Harris, J. & Lever, J. *Illustrated Glossary of Architecture, 950-1830*, 1966

Harvey, D. & Richardson, E. *Hidden Gems of the Black Country*, 2007

Harvey J. *The Perpendicular Style*, 1978

Harvey, J. *English Medieval Architects*, 1987

Hickman, P. *St. John's Church, Wolverhampton*, 2005

Hill, R. *God's Architect - Pugin and the Building of Romantic Britain*, 2007

Houghton, F.T.S. *Worcestershire: The Little Guide* (revised by Matley Moore), 1952

Howell P. & Sutton I. *The Faber Guide to Victorian Churches*, 1989

Hunt, J. *A History of Halesowen*, 2004

Inett, D. *A Brief History of All Saints Church, Sedgley 1829-2004*, 2004

Jeffery, P. *The Collegiate Churches of England and Wales*, 2004

Jenkins, S. *England's Thousand Best Churches*, 1999

Johnson, M. *Our English Church Heritage from the Beginning to 1662*, 1987

Jones, G. *Saints in the Landscape*, 2007

Kerr, M. & N. *Anglo-Saxon Architecture*, 1983

Knowles D. *The Religious Orders in England* (vols. 1-3), 1979

Lang, J. *Anglo-Saxon Sculpture*, 1988

Leatherbarrow, J.S. *Worcestershire* (1974)

Lee, L., Seddon, G. & Stephens, F. *Stained Glass*, 1989

Lees-Milne, J. *Worcestershire, A Shell Guide*, 1964

Leonard, J. *Staffordshire Parish Churches*, 1995

Livingstone, E. *Concise Oxford Dictionary of the Christian Church*, 1977

Maude, T. *Guided by a Stone-Mason*, 1997

Mayr-Harting, H. *The Coming of Christianity to Anglo-Saxon England*, 1972

McGregor-Smith, J. *John Cotton, The Life of a Midlands Architect 1844-1934*, 2002

Mee, A. *Staffordshire*, 1937

    Worcestershire, 1938

Meech, J. *Curiosities of the West Midlands*, 1993

Midmer, R. *English Medieval Monasteries 1066-1540*, 1979

Miller, G. *The Parishes of the Diocese of Worcester*, vol II, 1890

Molyneux, N.A.D. 'A late Thirteenth Century Building at Halesowen', *TWAS*, Third Series IX, pp.45-54

Morris, R. *Cathedrals and Abbeys of England and Wales*, 1979

    Churches in the Landscape, 1989

Osbourne, J. *Stained Glass in England*, 1981

Palmer, R. *The Folklore of the Black Country*, 2007

Parkes, G. *Old Pedmore and the Rebuilding of its Church*, 1982

Parsons, H. *The Black Country*, 1986

Peacock, R. *St. Mary's Church, Oldswinford, Stourbridge - A Victorian Church*, 2003

Perry, A. *Lady Wulfrun's Hampton*, 1993
> *Wool Town Church*, 2000

Perry, N. *A History of Stourbridge*, 2001
> *The Story of St. Mary's Church and the Parish of Oldswinford*, 1999

Pevsner, N. *The Buildings of England, Worcestershire*, 1968
> *The Buildings of England, Staffordshire*, 1974

Pevsner, N. & Brooks, A. *The Buildings of England, Worcestershire*, 2007

Pevsner, N. & Newman, J. *The Buildings of England, Shropshire*, 2006

Pevsner, N. & Wedgwood, A. *The Buildings of England, Warwickshire*, 1966

Platt, C. *The Parish Churches of Medieval England*, 1981

Porter, S. *Destruction of the English Civil Wars*, 1997

Raven, M. *Black Country Towns and Villages*, 1991

Raven, M. *A Guide to Staffordshire*, 1988

Rodwell, W. *The Archaeology of the English Church*, 1981

Rowlands, M.B. *The West Midlands from AD 1000*, 1987

Rouse, E.C. *Discovering Wall Paintings*, 1980

Salter, M. *The Old Parish Churches of Staffordshire and the West Midlands County*, 1996

Service, A. *Edwardian Architecture*, 1977

Shield, S. *The Light Shines Through, The Stained Glass Windows of St. Peter's Collegiate Church, Wolverhampton*, 1997

Shepherd, A.P. & Roper, J.S. *The Story of St. Thomas, Dudley*, 1979

Symondson, A. & Bucknall, S. *Sir Ninian Comper*, 2006

Taylor, D. *Images in Wood; The Medieval Misericord Carvings of St. Matthew's Church, Walsall*

Taylor, R. *How to Read a Church*, 2004

Thomas, C. *Christianity in Roman Britain to A.D. 500*, 1985

Thorold, H. *Staffordshire, A Shell Guide*, 1978

Thurlby, M. 'A Note on the former Barrel Vault in the Choir of St. John the Baptist, Halesowen', *TWAS*, Third Series, IX, 1984, pp.37-44.
> *The Herefordshire School of Romanesque Sculpture*, 1999

Tilley, R. *St. Edmund's Church, Dudley*, 1983

Victoria County History, *The History of the County of Stafford*, I-XVII 1959-

Vodden, D.F. *Bloxwich*, 1997
> *The Black Country Living Museum, 25 Years*, 2000
> *The Parish Church of St. Matthew, Walsall*, 1995

Watt, Q. (ed.) *The Bromsgrove Guild*, 1999

Whiffen, M. *Stuart and Georgian Churches*, 1947

White, W. *History, Gazetteer and Directory of Staffordshire*, 1851

Williams, N. *Black Country Chapels*, 2004
> *More Black Country Chapels*, 2006
> *Black Country Chapels, A Third Selection*, 2008

Willetts, C. *The Ancient Parish Church of St. Bartholomew, Wednesbury*, 1988

Willis, Bund J. (ed.) *The History of the County of Worcestershire*, I-IV, 1906-26

Websites

www.a2a.org.uk (Access to Archives)
www.achurchnearyou.com
www.birmingham.anglican.org (Diocese of Birmingham)
www.blackcountrysociety.co.uk

www.churchplansonline.org (The Archive of the Incorporated Church Building Society)
www.cofe-worcester.org.uk (Diocese of Worcester)
www.cradleylinks.co.uk
www.crsbi.ac.uk (Corpus of Romanesque Sculpture in Britain and Ireland)
www.ecclsoc.org (Ecclesiological Society)
www.genuki.org.uk (Genealogy in the U.K. and Ireland)
www.imagesofengland.org.uk (English Heritage listed buildings photographs)
www.lichfield.anglican.org (Diocese of Lichfield)
www.localhistory.scit.wolv.ac.uk (Wolverhampton's listed buildings)
www.pmsa.org.uk (Public Monuments and Sculpture Association)
www.revolutionaryplayers.org.uk
www.sedgleylocalhistory.org.uk
www.sedgleymanor.com
www.the-staffordshire-encyclopaedia.co.uk
www.walsall.gov.uk/index/leisure_and_culture/localhistorycentre.htm
www.wolverhamptonhistory.org.uk

Index